THE CHANGE WE CHOOSE

Also by Gordon Brown MP

Where There's Greed: Margaret Thatcher and the Betrayal of Britain's Future (co-author)

John Smith: Life and Soul of the Party (editor)

Values, Visions and Voices: An Anthology (editor)

Maxton: A Biography

Speeches 1997–2006

Moving Britain Forward: Selected Speeches 1997–2006

Courage: Eight Portraits

Britain's Everyday Heroes

Wartime Courage: Stories of Extraordinary Courage by Ordinary People in World War Two

Being British: The Search for the Values That Bind the Nation (co-editor)

THE
CHANGE
WE CHOOSE

Speeches 2007–2009

GORDON BROWN

MAINSTREAM
PUBLISHING

EDINBURGH AND LONDON

All royalties are being donated to the Jennifer Brown Research Laboratory within the University of Edinburgh's Research Institute for Medical Cell Biology

First published in Great Britain in 2010 by
MAINSTREAM PUBLISHING COMPANY
(EDINBURGH) LTD
7 Albany Street
Edinburgh EH1 3UG

ISBN 9781845966324

A catalogue record for this book is available
from the British Library

Typeset in Caslon and Requiem

Printed in Great Britain by
CPI Mackays of Chatham Ltd, Chatham, ME5 8TD

1 3 5 7 9 10 8 6 4 2

ACKNOWLEDGEMENTS

Gordon Brown has been unstinting in his support for this anthology, and without his support and agreement to quote from his speeches there would be no book.

We are very grateful to Amartya Sen, Joseph Stiglitz, the estate of the late Edward M. Kennedy, Ian Luder, Kofi Annan, Nick Anstee, Kevin Rudd, Alan Greenspan, Shimon Peres, Mohamed ElBaradei, Barack Obama, José Luis Rodríguez Zapatero, Nicolas Sarkozy, Angela Merkel, Ara Darzi and Sarah Brown for agreeing to contribute introductions or allowing us to reprint existing material.

Bill Campbell and all the staff at Mainstream Publishing have managed the publication process with great skill and have been a pleasure to work with.

CONTENTS

INTRODUCTION

'I would like to mention the positive things achieved by the UK government in general and by Gordon Brown's leadership in particular. One is the recognition of the need for the global world community to get together – in the crisis period he was arguing for the G20 to meet and which he organised in April 2009, and it was, in a sense, a turning point. We needed global understanding of the crisis and a joint determination to deal with it.

'Secondly, you need not only global cooperation but also economic strength, not just at home but everywhere – to have a lot of sick economies doesn't help. One of the problems we faced was the huge burden of debt in the developing countries, which leads to stricken economies. This was something Gordon Brown was aware of, and it was he that got agreement on debt relief at the G8 in Gleneagles in 2005.

'Thirdly, Gordon Brown was rightly sceptical of the deregulation initiatives of the 1990s. He was aware of the fact that the success of market economies is dependent on there being good state institutions as well and that the banks' incentive system for their employees was wrong and needed to be changed.

'Gordon Brown showed leadership in emphasising the need for global cooperation, the need for financial reform and in recognising that the global threat is a mutually interdependent affair.'

Amartya Sen, Nobel Prize for Economics 1998
Transcript from filmed interview, September 2009

'Had it not been for the actions that have been undertaken, the global economic crisis would have been much worse and the situation today would have been much worse.

'Gordon Brown's response to the global economic crisis exhibited real leadership not only in the substance but also in moving the world into a new global framework which he planned and which has proven to be an important framework in getting the whole world together to deal with what is the most significant economic crisis of the last 75 years.

'I think Gordon Brown really deserves very high marks for the way in which he responded to this crisis. There are alternative economic approaches – fortunately the UK has been lucky to have somebody who has been able to sort out these various arguments and come out with the right perspective.

'One of the distinctive elements of Gordon Brown's approach to these problems is that, although he has been working hard on the global financial crisis, he has not lost sight of the bigger picture.'

Joseph Stiglitz, Nobel Prize for Economics 2001
Transcript from filmed interview, September 2009

On Wednesday, 27 June 2007, Gordon Brown accepted the invitation of Her Majesty the Queen to form a government. On the steps of 10 Downing Street he said:

This will be a new government with new priorities, and I have been privileged to have been granted the great opportunity to serve my country, and at all times I will be strong in purpose, steadfast in will, resolute in action in the service of what matters to the British people, meeting the concerns and aspirations of our whole country.

I grew up in the town that I now represent in Parliament. I went to the local school. I wouldn't be standing here without the opportunities that I received there, and I want the best of chances for everyone. That is my mission – that if we can fulfil the potential and realise the talents of all our people then I am absolutely sure that Britain can be the great global success story of this century.

As I have travelled round the country and as I have listened, I have learned from the British people, and as Prime Minister I will continue to listen and learn from the British people. I have heard the need for change – change in our NHS, change in our schools, change with affordable housing, change to build trust in government, change to protect and extend the British way of life.

And this need for change cannot be met by the old politics. So I will reach out beyond narrow party interests, I will build a government that uses all the talents, I will invite men and women of goodwill to contribute their energies in a new spirit of public service to make our nation what it can be. And I am convinced that there is no weakness in Britain today that cannot be overcome by the strengths of the British people.

On this day, I remember words that have stayed with me since my childhood and which matter a great deal to me today – my school motto: 'I will try my utmost.' This is my promise to all of the people of Britain, and now let the work of change begin.

This book examines the key speeches made by Gordon Brown during the first two and a half years of his premiership. It reflects how the values and beliefs that have defined his political career have shaped his response to what have been arguably some of the greatest challenges to have faced a new prime minister in our entire peacetime history.

From a terrorist attack in Glasgow, within only three days of his coming to office, wars in Iraq and Afghanistan and the growing prospect of a climate catastrophe to a global financial crisis that threatened the economic security of entire nations, many of the issues facing Gordon Brown as Prime Minister have required an unprecedented degree of international cooperation. Much of this cooperation has been driven by necessity. As he said to the United Nations in 2009, we face 'a clear choice – to fail separately or to succeed together'. And yet, from this cooperation, Gordon Brown has argued that there is an immense opportunity for multilateral progress, and the vision he has set out for a global society – based on his long-standing values of fairness, responsibility and opportunity for all – is a defining theme of his premiership.

The speeches that relate to this vision of a global society are collected in Part I of this book. As the Prime Minister argued in his address to the Lord Mayor's Banquet in 2008, 'we are taking the first tentative steps towards what I will call a global society . . . what is at stake now is not just the success and legitimacy of our global economy but ultimately the prosperity and security of nations and communities in every corner of the world'.

In Part II of the book are collected speeches by the Prime Minister that explore how that new global society might address the five great challenges to threaten civilisation in the modern age – the need to stabilise and reshape the modern economy, the problem of climate change, the threat to security from global terrorism, the need for faster progress to meet the Millennium Development Goals and the challenges of nuclear proliferation. In each case, as the Prime Minister argues, global problems can be met only by global solutions.

In Part III are speeches that address the nature of the relationship between Britain, Europe and America and the role of this special relationship in meeting the five challenges that threaten the prospect of a truly global society. With the momentum of a new American president and the strength of the personal relationships between the Prime Minister and his international counterparts, the Prime Minister gives new impetus to the process of international consensus-building and sets out the opportunity for a new era in the relationship between these two long-standing allies. As he said in his address to the US Congress in March 2009, 'you now have the most pro-American European leadership in living memory. It is a leadership that wants to cooperate more closely together in order to cooperate more closely with you. There is no old Europe, no new Europe, there is only your friend Europe.

'So once again I say we should seize this moment, because never before have I seen a world willing to come together so much, never before has that been more needed and never before have the benefits of cooperation been so far-reaching.'

Part IV brings together speeches on domestic issues, including on constitutional reform – the subject of Gordon Brown's first Commons Statement as Prime Minister, in July 2007, and an issue that became increasingly high-profile with the widespread loss of trust following an unprecedented parliamentary expenses scandal in the summer of 2009. Part IV also includes speeches on fighting the recession, on liberty and citizenship and on the Prime Minister's vision for the transformation needed in our public services in Britain. Even though many of these issues are predominantly domestic in their focus, Gordon Brown has always addressed them in the context of the ever more globalised world in which Britain must now compete and succeed. And right from the outset, in his first speech on the steps of 10 Downing Street, the Prime Minister recognised that Britain's success would be more dependent than ever before on its global position.

In Part V are two party conference speeches in which Gordon Brown sets out the tasks ahead for the Labour Party and for the government he leads.

The speeches in this book trace what will be seen by historians as an extraordinary time in British and international peacetime history. We can learn a lot about his premiership by looking at the Prime Minister's penetrating and insightful speeches in this period, as he sets out his thinking on domestic and foreign policy and responds to the events that have shaped his period in office. We also learn much about Gordon Brown, the man, from the insights of those who have kindly agreed to contribute introductions and from the person who knows him best of all – his wife, Sarah, who introduced his party conference speeches.

PART I

TOWARDS A GLOBAL SOCIETY

In a number of speeches given over the period of his premiership, starting well before the financial crisis struck, the Prime Minister identifies and argues for a new global society. His starting point is that, 'History is not destiny. It is the sum total of the choices of each generation – the record of the vision of those who imagined and could see a better future and believed they could touch the stars.' And he goes on to suggest that the twenty-first century can be 'the first progressive century, in which we created the first truly global society'.

Gordon Brown argues that in a global society, 'where people can communicate, lobby, petition and express and organise their views freely across continents', it will be in all our best interests to cooperate and build alliances 'on the enduring and humane values we share in common' – values that emphasise the dignity and liberty of the individual, the indispensability of justice within and between nations and our responsibilities as citizens.

He goes on to propose that this should not mean a new version of the old balance of power arrangements based on 'opposing powers bargaining for their own narrow advantage'. Nor should it mean countries abandoning their national interests. Instead, he calls for a new version of the Kennedy doctrine of interdependence – nations pursuing their national interests by invoking broader global alliances, grounded in shared global goals and globally agreed rules and institutions.

I

A New World Order

Introduction by the late Edward M. Kennedy

'All of us are very proud of the remarkable ties of history and heritage that bind the United States and Great Britain. Our ties are strong, deep and enduring, and in these troubled times they surely offer the best hope for a better and more peaceful planet in the years ahead. That warm relationship is based on profound mutual respect and a genuine commitment to the fundamental principles and ideals we share. Our common goal is to advance the cause of freedom and the basic human rights of all peoples everywhere. Our mutual vision of the world is a future of lasting peace and prosperity in which all people have the opportunity they deserve to fulfil their dreams.

'Prime Minister Brown's remarkable ability to advance the causes that our nation cares so deeply about as well reflects his extraordinary leadership and vision for a better world. He refuses to back down from tough, complicated issues, and he refuses to abandon people who suffer from great hardship and oppression. He understands the reality and severity of the threat of global inequality. In his heart and soul, he believes we have the knowledge, the ability and the technology to end poverty in today's world, if we have the moral and political will to do so. He has never hesitated to act on these beliefs, and it's made him a world leader in reducing poverty. At the G8 Summit of major industrialised countries in 2005, he negotiated a landmark commitment to seek the eradication of poverty for the world's poorest countries. By next year, Great Britain will become the largest donor to the World Bank's lending programme for those countries.

'On all of these issues and many others, the Prime Minister has fought with great boldness, passion and dedication, and his commitment is making a large difference in the lives of millions of peoples throughout the world. He often states that the guidance of his parents and the words of Dr Martin Luther King were among his highest sources of inspiration. As Dr King said, "Everyone can be great because everyone can serve." These were words that Gordon Brown learned in his youth, and he honoured and heeded them all his life.

'He's one of the finest public servants I know, and I'm honoured to call him my friend. He's a leader of great principle, integrity and courage. He knows how to confront the difficult challenges before us in today's demanding and ever-changing world. It's a very special honour to welcome him to my brother's library and to introduce him now – Prime Minister Gordon Brown.'

In this fine speech, given at the Kennedy Presidential Library and Museum in Boston, the Prime Minister puts forward a bold and ambitious programme to combat the challenges that all countries and nations now face – the efforts to rebuild the global economy, climate change and the environment, terrorism and global poverty – pointing out that none of them can be solved without us finding new ways of working more closely together.

Paying tribute to President Kennedy's vision of an interdependent world, he says, 'Yet no one in 1962 could have foreseen the sheer scale of the new global challenges that our growing interdependence brings . . . Challenges that all point in one direction – to the urgent necessity for global cooperation.' And in a call to action, Gordon Brown argues, 'To recognise this is important. But simply to acknowledge that there are no "Britain-only" or "Europe-only" or "America-only" solutions to the global threats and challenges we face – or to say we are all internationalists now – will change nothing in itself. Instead, we must go much further, acknowledging that our common self-interest as nation states can be realised only by practical cooperation, that "responsible sovereignty" means the acceptance of clear obligations as well as the assertion of rights.'

The Prime Minister's solution starts from the premise that people do not cooperate only out of need; there is a shared moral sense that we are responsible each to the other – country to country as much as person to person. And he goes on to argue that for the first time in human history we have the opportunity to come together around a global covenant, to reframe the international architecture and build the truly global society.

His vision is for 'a new World Bank; a new International Monetary Fund; a reformed and renewed United Nations, mandated and resourced, that is greater than the sum of its parts; strong regional organisations, from the European Union to the African Union, able to bring to a troubled world the humanitarian aid, peacekeeping and the support for stability and reconstruction that has been absent for too long – all built around a new global society founded on revitalised international rules and institutions and grounded in the great values we share in common'.

KENNEDY MEMORIAL LECTURE

Kennedy Presidential Library and Museum, Boston, 18 April 2008

It is a great privilege to be here in Massachusetts, in Boston, and to be present with such distinguished guests in this library where history comes alive and values endure.

And a privilege, too, to be introduced by Senator Kennedy – and I cannot speak too highly of the legislative record of Senator Kennedy – who has served in the Senate for almost a quarter of the Republic's life, earned his place as one of the greatest senators in more than two centuries. And for its record of public service the Kennedy family is respected and renowned not just in this continent but in every continent of the world.

In the years since John F. Kennedy's presidency, man has walked on the surface of the moon, directly as a result of his commitment made on 25 May 1961; the Berlin Wall that he so famously denounced has been reduced to rubble – the cold war ended – freeing Eastern Europe and making Europe whole again; and Nelson Mandela has walked free and apartheid, which John Kennedy denounced as 'repugnant', has been swept away. Great events – once the vision of one man, now landmarks in the history of the world.

And although he was president for less than three years, I believe that much of the progress of this half-century has been testament to the scope of John Kennedy's dream, the worth of the ideals he lived for, the breadth of hope he inspired in us and, most of all, amid all the wit, style, elegance and statesmanship that adorned the Kennedy presidency, his summons to service – one that never fails to inspire people to see farther and reach higher, a call which still reverberates around the world and always will.

And his influence for good is so powerful that, as Pericles said in ancient times, even when he has left this world his influence 'abides everywhere . . . woven into the stuff of other men's lives'.

And although it is perhaps risky for a British prime minister to come to speak in Boston shortly before Patriots' Day, I am pleased that over the past half-century the special relationship between America and Britain, which John Kennedy prized, remains strong and enduring – so firmly rooted in our common history, our shared values and in the hearts and minds of our people that no power on earth can drive us apart.

Nothing in President Kennedy's enduring legacy has greater importance now, at the beginning of the twenty-first century, than his words on your Independence Day in 1962, when he proposed a new and global declaration of interdependence.

'Today Americans must learn to think inter-continentally,' he said. 'Acting on our own, by ourselves, we cannot establish justice throughout the world; we cannot ensure its domestic tranquillity or provide for its common defence or promote its general welfare or secure the blessings of liberty to ourselves and our posterity. But joined with other free nations we can do all this and more.'

So if the 1776 Declaration of Independence stated a self-evident truth – that we are all created equal – JFK's Declaration of Interdependence in 1962 added another self-evident truth: that we are all of us, all of us throughout the world, in this together. Each of us our brother's keeper, each of us, to quote Martin Luther King, part of an 'inescapable web of mutuality'.

Yet no one in 1962 could have foreseen the sheer scale of the new global challenges that our growing interdependence brings, their scale, their diversity and the speed with which they have emerged – the globalisation of the economy; the threat of climate change; the long struggle against international terrorism; the need to protect millions from violence and conflict and to face up to the international consequences of poverty and inequality. Challenges that all point in one direction – to the urgent necessity for global cooperation. For none of them, from economy to environment, can be solved without us finding new ways of working more closely together.

To recognise this is important. But simply to acknowledge that there are no 'Britain-only' or 'Europe-only' or 'America-only' solutions to the global threats and challenges we face, or to say we are all internationalists now, will change nothing in itself.

Instead, we must go much further, acknowledging that our common self-interest as nation states can be realised only by practical cooperation, that 'responsible sovereignty' means the acceptance of clear obligations as well as the assertion of rights.

And my argument today is simple. Global problems require global solutions; the greatest of global challenges demands of us the boldest of global reforms; the most urgent of tests demand the broadest of global cooperation; and to address the worst evils of terrorism, poverty, environmental decay, disease and instability, we urgently need to step out of the mindset of competing interests and instead find common interests, summoning up the best instincts and efforts of humanity in a cooperative endeavour to build new international rules and institutions for the new global era.

Let me sketch out the challenges we face, the new directions I favour and the solutions I propose.

The first, and perhaps because of the credit crunch the most immediate, challenge is economic globalisation itself. And does not the recent sharp and still unresolved credit crunch, which has affected the whole world, now demonstrate that, with global flows of capital already replacing the old national flows and global sourcing of goods and services replacing the old local sourcing, national systems of supervision and economic management are simply inadequate to cope with the huge cross-continental flows of capital in this interdependent world?

But is not the issue even bigger than that? That we are seeing in the scale, scope and speed of globalisation the biggest restructuring of economic life since the industrial revolution? Already Asia is manufacturing more than Europe and soon America; China alone is producing half the world's clothes and half the world's electronics. And we are only at the beginning of this shifting balance of power, as every day more and more of the four billion Asian people are entering the world's industrial economy.

And the reality is that we are all affected now by what happens in Asia or Latin America or Africa. And if we do not work across countries and continents to create a globalisation that is inclusive for all, then not only will the poorest of the world, who lose out, react to being excluded, but people in our own countries will feel, as many do today, victims not beneficiaries of the process of change – losers and not winners – and protectionist sentiment will gain ground.

I am optimistic about the benefits of interdependence and certain that globalisation need not be a zero-sum game that says if China or India benefits, America or Europe loses. Why? Because over the next 25 years we will see the world economy doubling in size, creating a billion new professional or skilled jobs worldwide, offering opportunity for any who have the creativity, ingenuity, skills and talent to benefit – a time of huge opportunity, even if it is also a time of change and risk.

And in the spirit of John Kennedy, who summoned us to think of how we can make our interdependence work for the benefit of all, I believe a new global deal is possible. In the industrial countries, like ours, a guarantee that even if we cannot keep people in their last job, we can ensure people will be able to obtain the next job – through investment in skills and income support wherever necessary; and in the poorest countries, a new deal that in return for opening up to trade, freeing regimes from corruption and a commitment to economic growth, we support the development of education, infrastructure and health care.

And the benefits will flow most widely and more effectively if, instead of trying to pursue beggar-my-neighbour policies or erecting national barriers to shelter people from change, we cooperate across frontiers to maximise the opportunities. But to do this we have no choice now – and this is my main argument – but to consider and agree new global rules and create new global institutions, so that not some but all can benefit from change.

And how do we face up to the second great global challenge, that of climate change, which is already creating the first climate change droughts, the first climate change evacuations, the first climate change refugees?

It is this challenge that starkly defines the most basic truth of our human condition – that if, as far ahead as we can foresee, there is no other planet for us and our children, we must cooperate to make our stewardship of this earth work.

So it will not be enough to discuss purely national initiatives or even to quarrel over the burden of sharing emission reductions while global warming continues unchecked. Because global problems cannot be solved without global solutions, we need to join together in recognising that cooperation in an interdependent world means a single framework for global and national targets and, for the first time, a truly global carbon market.

A third force of globalisation is the sobering reality that has already struck home in both Britain and America – that we are exposed, unpredictably but directly, to the risk of violence and instability originating in failed and rogue states around the world. Once we feared rival nations becoming too strong; now the worst threats come from states that are too weak. And we know that the richest citizen in the richest country can be directly affected by what happens to the poorest citizen in the poorest country.

So, today, no country can say that failed or failing states are someone else's problem. They are a problem for us all. Instability in one country affects stability in all countries; an injustice anywhere is now a threat to justice everywhere. And that is how we must respond. Not walking away as we did in Rwanda, at the cost of hundreds of thousands of lives, but by engaging as hard-headed internationalists – through diplomatic, economic and, yes, when necessary, military action – to prevent crimes against humanity when states can no longer do so.

Linked to failed and failing states is the spread of international terrorism in the form of loosely affiliated global networks that threaten us and other nations across oceans and continents, and let me praise President Bush for leading the world in our determination to root out terrorism and our common commitment that there be no safe haven for terrorists.

Where once we imagined that nuclear or biological weapons were a state monopoly, now there is the prospect of hidden unofficial arsenals in the hands of terrorists. And to counter such threats effectively we must work together across national borders.

We will, at all times, be steadfast and resolute against terrorism at home and abroad, using all our resources – military, security, policing, intelligence – to expose and defeat terrorists. And vitally in this struggle we must mobilise the power of ideas, of shared values and of hopes that can win over hearts and minds.

Just as importantly, we must recognise that our enemy, as George Marshall put it in a great speech in Boston 60 years ago, will never be just one country but 'hunger, poverty, desperation and chaos'. And while today many millions live well, we have 2.5 billion neighbours who subsist on less than $2 a day – a fact that demonstrates what Winston Churchill once called 'the gaping sorrows of the left-out millions'.

And ours is already a world where no 'us', however rich or influential, can pull up the drawbridge in an attempt to gain protection from a 'them'. New contagious diseases can advance swiftly from the national to the global with all the speed of international air travel. And as global transport networks and global communications erode or abolish traditional frontiers, national crime all too readily becomes international crime.

So, global neighbours are closer than ever before – and we to them. And the critical question is this: how we plan and act together across continents to tackle disease, crime, mass migration and mass poverty.

And we must recognise, too, that our interdependence in the economy, environment, security, poverty, disease and crime is now underpinned by the truly revolutionary impact of advancing technology, whereby a device on a desk or in the palm of our hand puts us in contact with anyone, anywhere, anytime. It is a revolution that is rewiring, multiplying and accelerating social, economic and political connections within and between our nations – to their total and irreversible transformation. A revolution which, potentially, transforms democratic life and means the world can never be the same again.

A few years ago, in regime after regime, sentries could stand over fax machines as governments sought to deny information to their peoples. Today, as we have seen in Burma, pictures of repression sent across the Internet can alert the whole world and, as we saw in the Philippines, one million people exchanging text messages on mobile phones brought down a country's leader – what was called the first 'coup de text'.

So the dawn of the digital age is enabling people to become the authors of change rather than its subjects, the agents of history rather than its victims. And within a decade or two, it will create a virtual world of individuals speaking instantly across once virtually impassable distances, communities springing up across the Internet, a rising sense of global consciousness of millions of global citizens in the making.

To adapt an aphorism of President Kennedy, the new frontier is that there is no frontier – no frontier for the Internet, for the mobile phone, for e-mails, for the cyber-world; no frontier for the capacity of individuals to influence, inform or even infuriate each other. And because times are new we must, in Robert Kennedy's words, think anew. We must, as he said, leave behind yesterday and embrace tomorrow.

So, while in President Kennedy's time foreign relations were founded almost exclusively on the relative power of governments, today we must recognise the relevance to foreign policy of what we see before our eyes – that everywhere around us people are forming global associations, global connections and global communities; that all over the world, from culture to education to social action, individuals are harnessing people power to transcend states, for good and sometimes for ill. And they are compelling institutions and authorities to follow their example, with regulators, environmental and development agencies, militaries, law enforcement and judges all having to cooperate directly across frontiers.

As greater people power drives forward the creation of this new world order, foreign policy has increasingly to be explained daily to a questioning public, who will increasingly also demand to know the basis on which we act.

And if in the eighteenth and nineteenth centuries nation states looked to the concept of the balance of power for their security, and in the latter half of the twentieth briefly put their faith in the concept of mutually assured destruction, we, amid the emerging complexities of the twenty-first century, must recognise afresh the power of John Kennedy's Declaration of Interdependence and must firmly root our international system in the values we hold in common, shaping more than a new world order, creating instead a truly global society. A global society no longer just based on the power of states delineated by borders but on the aspirations of people that transcend borders; a global society no longer founded just on balancing competing interests but on building institutions that foster mutual interests because they are grounded in common values.

Indeed, I would go further. In democracies such as ours – and now in a global society where people can communicate, lobby, petition and express and organise their views freely across continents – acting upon our interdependence demands that we found our cooperation and build alliances upon those enduring and humane values we share in common – values that emphasise at all times the dignity and liberty of the individual, the indispensability of justice within and between nations and our responsibilities as citizens of both our own nation and of the world.

Throughout history, we have too often allowed ourselves to believe that the foreigner was at best a stranger and at worst an enemy – that across national borders our ethical values could be as different as our cuisine or fashion or language. In fact, the more we discover about each other, the more we find how often we subscribe to similar ideals – regardless of geography, history or identity.

For through each of our diverse heritages there runs a single, powerful moral sense – one that is reflected and replicated throughout the world's great religions and also in the moral philosophy of those who adhere to none – that shows we are not moral strangers but there is a moral sense common to us all.

When Christians say, 'Do to others what you would have them do to you'; when Muslims say, 'No one of you is a believer until he desires for his brother that which he desires for himself'; when Jews say, 'What is hateful to you, do not to your fellow man'; when Hindus say, 'This is the sum of duty: do naught unto others which would cause pain if done to you'; when Sikhs say, 'Treat others as you would be treated yourself'; when Buddhists say, 'Hurt not others in ways that you yourself would find hurtful', they reflect a common truth dear to billions of adherents of those and other religions that is true also of all the great secular thinkers – that we not only cooperate out of need, but there is a human need to cooperate. And that cooperation is built on the desire for liberty and the call to justice – respect for the dignity of every individual and our sense of what is equitable and fair.

Call it as Lincoln did 'the better angels of our nature'; call it as Winstanley did 'the light in man'; call it 'our moral sentiment' as Adam Smith did; call it 'conscience'; call it 'the moral sense'. It is on the basis of our common humanity and common values that even people thousands of miles apart can share the pain of others and believe in something bigger than themselves. And it is for our generation to bring to life these shared values – which already have the capacity to unite people across the world – in proposals to create the architecture of a global society.

Acting upon our interdependence does not mean a new version of the old balance of power arrangements based on opposing powers bargaining for their own narrow advantage. But nor does it mean abandoning national interests. Instead, the very fact of interdependence requires nations to work out new ways of working founded on the recognition that they can best pursue their national interests by invoking broader global alliances – and that these global alliances must be grounded in shared global goals and globally agreed rules and institutions.

There have been four great moments in the modern age when statesmen have come together to reorder the world. In 1648, in the Westphalia Treaty that followed Europe's catastrophic Thirty Years War; in 1815, at the Congress of Vienna after the Napoleonic wars; and twice in the last century – disastrously in 1919 at Versailles and, most significantly, in the late 1940s, when, in a world wracked by total war, new global arrangements were agreed.

At that time – and in a breathtaking leap forward into a new world order – American visionaries helped form the United Nations, the World Bank, the International Monetary Fund. And they put in place a policy of unprecedented generosity, the Marshall Plan, which transferred one per cent of America's national income each year for four years to the war-ravaged economies of Europe and saved the free world.

Such was the impact of what they did for their day and age that Dean Acheson spoke of being 'present at the creation'. And in a new era, when the challenges of 2008 are different from those of 1945, we must summon inspiration from the vision, humanity and leadership shown by those reformers to guide our actions today.

And this is no longer an academic debate that can wait because change is too difficult to implement or because we must consider at length what is to be done – with a view to doing nothing. This is urgent. And the challenge is far-reaching.

The great Bostonian Emerson not only summed it up when he said, 'What lies behind us and what lies before us are tiny matters compared to what lies within us,' but also warned us of the radical consequences that follow: 'Do not go where the path may lead; go instead where there is no path and leave a trail.'

Those who build the present only in the image of the past will, in the words of Winston Churchill, 'miss out entirely on the opportunities of the future'. And when he warned of countries facing change who were too timid – that they were 'resolved to be irresolute, adamant for drift, solid for fluidity, all-powerful to be impotent' – it is a powerful reminder of the need to act now.

First, a global society must embody and enact our obligations to each other not just within borders but across borders. So I am proposing, today, reforms that will enable our international and regional institutions to do what they failed to do in the Rwandan genocide 15 years ago and are even now still failing to achieve amidst the tragedy of Darfur – to prevent conflict, to stabilise and then to reconstruct failing and failed states and, specifically, to shield men, women and children who are being threatened by genocide, ethnic cleansing, war crimes or crimes against humanity. And so the United Nations must become a consistent defender of the interests of the world's people – not simply those of states.

And this means new actions to prevent and respond to the breakdown of states and societies by helping vulnerable nations develop the capacity to uphold the rule of law – by encouraging civil society, training police and security forces; more systematic use of earlier Security Council action, including targeted sanctions and, as a last resort, the threat, and if necessary the use, of military force; new resources in the form of a UN crisis recovery fund, to ensure proper financing for stabilisation and reconstruction in countries emerging from conflict; and new encouragement for regional organisations, from the African Union to the European Union, to mount peace, stability and reconstruction efforts.

In 1960, President Kennedy called for an American peace corps, harnessing the idealism Americans felt in the face of deprivation and underdevelopment. Today, in the same spirit, we should create a new kind of global peace and reconstruction corps – an international stand-by capacity of trained civilian experts ready to go anywhere at any time to help rebuild states.

Second, I favour strengthening the role of international institutions in ensuring a unified global response to terrorism through asset freezes, travel bans, proscriptions, raising international legal standards and unflagging resistance to extremist ideologies – measures led by President Bush, as we discussed yesterday. But, as he and I agree, terrorism will ultimately be defeated only when it is isolated and abandoned.

So I propose a new cultural effort on the scale of the cultural cold war in the '40s, '50s and '60s: an initiative that involves foundations, charities, faith groups, elders and young people, and engages TV, radio, the Internet and all forms of multimedia communication across all cultures, faiths and tongues, to make the case for democracy and respect for human rights – how these offer the best future for us all and how, in the face of these arguments, violent extremism is both unnecessary and wrong.

We will support interfaith dialogue in every part of the world. And with people power in a global society already advancing democracy widely across the world – from 20 per cent of nations being democratic in the early 1970s to 60 per cent today – we must encourage the development of the daily accountability, transparency and responsiveness, and the civil societies which are at the heart of true democracies.

Third, a global society demands new global agreements and strengthened global institutions to protect and safeguard essential global resources.

So, by the end of next year, we must secure a new global climate change agreement with the UN at its centre, with binding targets for all developed countries, including America and Britain. I want to see at least a halving of global emissions by 2050. And we need new incentives for developing and emerging economies – helping them slow their growth in emissions through new flows of finance and technology.

A global agreement is more than a set of targets; it must include an international carbon market as the surest and most efficient way to achieve our aims, eventually generating up to $100 billion a year to fund 'green' development.

And while we strengthen the World Bank's focus on poverty reduction, I have a radical proposal to make the World Bank a bank for development and the environment – transferring billions in loans and grants to encourage the poorest countries to adopt alternative sources of energy and, in doing so, ensuring that its development programmes provide an integrated approach to both poverty eradication and global warming.

We require a similar global coordination of effort on food, where we face the worst food shortages for decades, and on disease and global pandemics where, led by the World Health Organisation, the priority is to improve early warning, increase the stocks of global vaccine supplies and develop a more coordinated global response. We need now to ensure there are clear responsibilities and decision-making procedures at every level. And Britain will bring together all interested parties to agree the new international action that is now essential to prevent pandemics and the spread of ill health.

Globalisation can work if it is an inclusive globalisation, and protectionism can be avoided only by means of open economies, free trade and flexibility, accompanied by policies for fairness and justice – policies that include investment in education and other social goods in the industrialised countries and a new deal for the poorest countries.

And my proposal here is that we set new global rules for a new twenty-first-century global economic system with a global trade deal that benefits rich and poor countries alike; new international financial architecture and economic institutions that end the mismatch between global capital flows and only the national supervision of them – with the IMF an early-warning system for the global economy, focused on crisis prevention rather than just crisis resolution; and a new deal, as bold as the Marshall Plan of the 1940s, between rich and poor under which developing countries open up to trade, address corruption and pursue policies for economic development and developed countries agree to make available new resources, so that we can say of this generation: the preventable diseases of TB, polio and malaria are eradicated and, for the first time in our history, every child enjoys education.

And let me just explain why it is so important. When I visited Abuja, in Nigeria, I found that side by side with a dilapidated school that we did not support enough was a madrasa, where al-Qaeda-inspired extremists were enticing children into their school offering free high-standard schooling. So our offer of education for all is not just an education and economic policy for the developing world; it is a defence and security policy for the developed world.

So a new World Bank; a new International Monetary Fund; a reformed and renewed United Nations, mandated and resourced, that is greater than the sum of its parts; strong regional organisations, from the European Union to the African Union, able to bring to a troubled world the humanitarian aid, peacekeeping and the support for stability and reconstruction that has been absent for too long – all built around a new global society founded on revitalised international rules and institutions and grounded in the great values we share in common.

And during the year to come, I want this debate about change to become a global dialogue about renewal, as we embark upon a task perhaps more ambitious than even the Bretton Woods Conference in 1944.

Already, the Commonwealth of 53 nations has agreed to convene a task force on these issues, the first meeting in London in June. Reform and renewal should feature on the G8 and EU agendas. I welcome Harvard University's interest in taking forward work on the proposals. I suggest next year a series of international conferences and meetings to agree how to transform these ideas into real change. And we must engage business, NGOs, faith groups and individuals from all nations and continents in these debates.

American leadership is and will be indispensable. And now is an opportunity for a historic effort in cooperation; a new dawn in collaborative action between America and Europe – a new commitment from Europe that I believe all European leaders can work with America to forge stronger transatlantic links. For I sense common ground between our two great continents in the urgent need for renewal and reform.

And I also sense that this is the moment to bring in China, India, South Africa, Mexico, Brazil and other emerging countries to the heart of this debate – offering a greater role with the G8, to offer them more say in the IMF and World Bank and to reform the security council of the United Nations.

Today, as we face these new global challenges, the tantalising possibilities of a world where, as John Kennedy put it, the strong are just, the weak secure and the peace preserved are matched only by the terrifying risks of us failing to seize this moment.

For the first time in human history, we have the opportunity to come together around a global covenant, to reframe the international architecture and build the truly global society. So today my call is not just to the public purpose of this generation but to the idealism of this and the next generation.

History is not destiny. It is the sum total of the choices of each generation – the record of the vision of those who imagined and could see a better future and believed they could touch the stars.

And if the nineteenth century became known as the century of industrialisation and the twentieth century became defined as the century of world wars, the twenty-first century can be the first progressive century in which we created the first truly global society.

Forty years ago this year, amidst tragedy and grief, America lost two towering visionaries – Martin Luther King in April and Robert Kennedy in June.

Both of them refused to accept that the way things are is the way things must be and the way things must stay. Both of them were men of conscience and courage who turned history in the direction of our best hopes. Both of them believed in essential truths that I am celebrating today – that peace and prosperity are indivisible, that prosperity to be sustained has to be shared – and both of them believed, too, that the greatest of social changes are built on the strongest of ethical foundations.

And when today cynics dismiss as an impossible dream or naïve idealism proposals to create the institutions of a truly global society, let us remind them that people used to think black civil rights a distant dream, the end of the cold war an impossible hope, the ending of apartheid in our generation the work of dreamers, debt relief for the poorest countries an unrealisable idea.

It is fitting that this library, standing at the edge of the sea, is shaped like a great sail. For those it memorialises, to paraphrase Robert Kennedy, truly did send forth 'ripples of hope' that continue to move across history as a mighty wave. And so let us have confidence we can discover anew in ourselves the values we share in common, let us have confidence we can act upon John Kennedy's Declaration of Interdependence and let us have confidence we can create a global covenant across nations to make peace and prosperity real in our generation.

2

Working for a Secure International Order

Introduction by Ian Luder

'It is a special pleasure, Prime Minister, to welcome you and Mrs Brown back to Guildhall for your second Lord Mayor's Banquet, accompanied by a number of your senior ministers, and we all appreciate the time and effort which you have taken to attend. At this time of financial crisis and impending economic recession, it is all too easy to forget our history. The City has built its world position because it has been able to attract large numbers of very highly skilled people who know that, irrespective of gender, race or creed, they can create successful careers and enjoy a good quality of life here.

'Prime Minister, since this banquet a year ago, and especially in the past two months, the financial services industry worldwide has been hit by a storm of an intensity not experienced since the beginning of the First World War. My immediate predecessors warned of the dangers of "complacency" and that "we must not crow". Prophetic words indeed. And I do not make light of this. To lose one's livelihood, one's house, one's savings and to see years of investments and pension plummet in a matter of days is truly devastating. But, equally, it is important that we don't gravitate to the other end of the spectrum and talk ourselves into a greater crisis or recession.

'The recent actions of your government, dramatic as they have been, were essential. Of course, not everyone agrees with every action taken. But without direct intervention it would not have been possible to start the process to try to restore vital stability and avoid a much deeper fall in the real economy. Other governments across Europe, in the US and elsewhere are following your lead, and whilst this is not a quick remedy, it is wholly appropriate that we congratulate you now for what you have done.

'The lessons of what has happened must be understood, so that they can help shape sensible remedies and changes and avoid the same thing happening again.'

The speech by the Prime Minister to the Lord Mayor's Banquet in the Guildhall each November is, by convention, devoted to foreign affairs. It gives the Prime Minister a chance to reflect on UK policy in this area and to range widely over the issues.

In this speech, the financial crisis is the dominant theme. As the then Lord Mayor Ian Luder suggests and the Prime Minister confirms, since it began the crisis has dominated the agenda. The consequence is that most of the Prime Minister's efforts have had to be centred on the protection of the British economy, British jobs and firms and British living standards. However, the Prime Minister also makes the point that the livelihoods of British families and businesses are shaped in an ever more interdependent world, so we can see this year as one where 'we not only came to recognise our deep and irreversible interdependence, each nation with other nations, but acted upon it. Nations agreeing not just on high aspirations but on practical actions; governments ready to act collectively and quickly to take radical, indeed previously unthinkable, measures to avert global meltdown; discovering a common purpose amid the necessity of dealing with the financial crisis – a common approach forged first to deal with the financial crisis but one that will, I believe, enable us to respond positively also to climate change, conflict and poverty. And in doing so to build the confidence in the future that is key to bringing back confidence today.'

The Prime Minister's central argument on this occasion is that since this is a global downturn it requires a global solution: 'As was the case with the bank stabilisation plan, the benefits of any individual country's fiscal actions will be all the greater if this is part of a concerted and fairly distributed international response to maintain global demand. There is now a growing international consensus that, especially for those countries with low debt, like the UK, maintaining essential public investment is the right and sensible approach, while allowing a temporary and affordable increase in borrowing to support economic growth.'

Gordon Brown recalls how 75 years ago, at a time of recession, nations met in London in a World Economic Conference and because the talks broke up in failure, the world entered a long decade of protectionism and retrenchment. Looking forward to the forthcoming meetings in Washington, the Prime Minister confirms that the British government will work with its G20 partners to establish consensus and 'begin to build a new Bretton Woods with a reformed, modern IMF that offers, by its surveillance of every economy, an early-warning system and a crisis-prevention mechanism for the whole world'. And he also argues that the alliance between Britain and America, and more broadly between Europe and America, can and must provide leadership in this period to lead and broaden the global effort to build a stronger, secure and more equitable international order.

He goes on to suggest that 'if we do so, 2008 will be remembered not just for a financial crash that engulfed the world but for the decisiveness and optimism with which the world faced the storm, endured it and prevailed. And remembered, too, for how in doing so we discovered and refashioned the global power of nations working together.'

SPEECH TO THE LORD MAYOR'S BANQUET
Guildhall, London, 10 November 2008

These last weeks and months will be studied by generations to come. Historians will look back and say this was no ordinary time but a defining moment – an unprecedented period of global change, a time when one chapter ended and another began for nations, for continents, for the whole world.

To us falls the challenge of leading Britain through the first financial crisis of this new global age and, as reflected in the huge volatility in the price of commodities, its first resources crisis too.

But these crises reflect underlying and unprecedented transformations in our world – the rise of Asia and the shift of global manufacturing power; growing resource pressures, from oil to food; the undeniable reality of climate change; and new political instabilities and conflicts. All accompanied by the growing gap between rich and poor countries and, of course, by the impact of new technology and the rise of the Internet giving millions of people, for the first time, the ability to communicate, do business and organise across frontiers.

The range, complexity and impact of these forces underline just how much we are taking the first tentative steps towards what I will call a *global society*. And that what is at stake now is not just the success and legitimacy of our global economy but ultimately the prosperity and security of nations and communities in every corner of the world.

The decisions we make now will re-shape our societies, in all probability for decades and more. And we have a choice – to retreat or advance, to turn inwards or to look outwards, to be cowed by our fears or led by our hopes.

The world today can seem a daunting place. And when people feel buffeted or bewildered by the scale of the changes, it can seem easy to retreat into the outworn and failed responses of yesterday – to a time of pessimism, protectionism and retrenchment. But we could make a far better choice.

I want this to become the moment when together we rise to the new challenges by purposeful visionary and international leadership, leaving behind the orthodoxies of yesterday and embracing new ideas to create a better tomorrow – not as victims of history but as shapers of an open, free-trade, flexible globalisation that is also inclusive and sustainable.

For while today so much looks grey or dark in the global economy, we should not forget that we are in the midst of an economic transition to a new global age – whatever happens now, it is likely that in the next two decades the world economy will double in size. And that means twice as many opportunities for good businesses and twice as many opportunities for men and women with new ideas to market. And as many as one thousand million new jobs for skilled workers will be created. So this is the other side of globalisation – not just the insecurities we know about but the opportunities, the promise it holds for tomorrow.

And it is, indeed, possible to see the threats and challenges we face today as the difficult birth pangs of a new global order – and our task now nothing less than making the transition through a new internationalism to a more collegial, collaborative and opportunity-rich global society, not muddling through as pessimists but as optimists, making the necessary adjustment to a better future.

Since the financial crisis began it has dominated the agenda. I have travelled perhaps more than I had planned to. But all in the protection of the British economy, British jobs and firms, British living standards – knowing the livelihoods of British families and businesses are shaped in an ever more interdependent world.

And so we can see this year as definitive in another way – the year where we not only came to recognise our deep and irreversible interdependence, each nation with other nations, but acted upon it. Nations agreeing not just on high aspirations but on practical actions; governments ready to act collectively and quickly to take radical, indeed previously unthinkable, measures to avert global meltdown; discovering a common purpose amid the necessity of dealing with the financial crisis – a common approach forged first to deal with the financial crisis but one that will, I believe, enable us to respond positively also to climate change, conflict and poverty. And in doing so to build the confidence in the future that is key to bringing back confidence today.

So while I see a world that is facing financial crisis and still diminished by conflict and injustice I also see the chance to forge a new multilateralism that is both hard-headed and progressive. And I believe that in our international cooperation on finance, climate change, terrorism and ending conflict there is evidence of this new multilateralism at work in the world – fairer, more stable and more prosperous because it is rooted in cooperation and justice.

And if we learn from our experience of turning unity of purpose into unity of action, together we can seize this moment of profound change to create, for the first time, the age of the truly global society. One where progressive multilateralism, not narrow unilateralism, is the norm; one where people find that what unites them is far greater than whatever divided them and where it is cooperation, not confrontation, that flourishes in answer to age-old challenges – the challenge to reassert our faith in the advance of democracy as the most effective weapon in our arsenal against terrorism and tyranny; and, as we mark Armistice Day tomorrow and remember the sacrifices made in darker times, the challenge to build for peace; the challenge to build consensus for a new global financial system; the need to confront the realities of global climate change by building a sustainable low-carbon economy and to make a reality of the vision of a global society by creating global partnerships across public, private and voluntary sectors to address poverty and move toward economic justice.

I believe that we in the West should approach these great challenges of our time with some humility. The West certainly does not have all the answers to them. We need more than the G8, for the time when just a few powers could sit around the table and set the global agenda is over.

Quite rightly, the emerging powers of the twenty-first century will want to, and must, play their part. And so the G8, the IMF and the World Bank must change to meet the new realities.

But my central argument this evening is that the alliance between Britain and America and, more broadly, between Europe and America, can and must provide leadership in this, not in order to make and impose the rules ourselves but to lead and broaden the global effort to build a stronger, secure and more equitable international order.

Rightly, people talk of a special relationship, but that special relationship is also a partnership for a purpose. The transatlantic relationship has been the engine of effective multilateralism for the past 50 years. Together, we faced down aggression and dictatorship; in a few short years we built the great international post-war institutions – the World Bank, the International Monetary Fund, the United Nations; and we led the drive for trade, enterprise and dynamic markets.

Now, unprecedented events have brought a turn of history that few would once have foreseen or expected.

Just days ago across the Atlantic, our closest ally gave new meaning to its founding creed that all 'are created equal', gave new strength to the notion that the American dream is for all Americans.

More than 140 years after the abolition of slavery and more than 40 years on from the civil rights and voting rights acts, America has chosen Barack Obama to be President.

And as we have seen from reaction in America, Europe and around the globe, whatever one's politics, it can surely only be a source of hope and inspiration that a nation which once would have looked at Barack Obama and defined him only by his colour today sees in him the man they want to be their president and commander-in-chief.

And when Barack Obama, four months ago, followed in President Kennedy's footsteps and went to Berlin, he called on the world to stand together as one.

Winston Churchill described the joint inheritance of Britain and America as not just a shared history but a shared belief in the great principles of freedom and the rights of man – of what Barack Obama described in his election night speech as the enduring power of our ideals: democracy, liberty, opportunity and unyielding hope.

And as America stands at its own dawn of hope, so let that hope be fulfilled through a pact with the wider world to lead and shape the twenty-first century as the first century of a truly global society.

And I believe that, with the far-sighted leadership we have in Europe, the whole of Europe can and will work closely with America and with the rest of the world to meet the great challenges which will illuminate our convictions and test our resolution.

First, we must reassert our faith in democracy and be confident in our belief that open, plural, diverse societies are those most likely to stay rich, strong and free. So we must step up and win the battle of ideas against terrorism and extremism, not by sacrificing the liberties that they scorn but by securing new international means of achieving stability, reconstruction and democracy in failed and fragile states. And we must promote greater tolerance and understanding within and between communities. Later this week I will join King Abdullah of Saudi Arabia, alongside President Bush and other world leaders, for his interfaith dialogue at the United Nations, deepening understanding between religions and countering extremist ideologies.

Second, let us move quickly to complement the role of peacekeepers and aid workers through civilian as well as military assistance, to rebuild conflict-ridden and fragile states. Just as we will continue to offer immediate help and advance the cause of peace in Darfur, Burma and Zimbabwe – and stand up for the democracies of Georgia and Ukraine – we will stand by the people of the Democratic Republic of Congo as they face new conflict and turmoil. We will get aid to those who need it. We will protect those who are threatened, by ensuring that UN peacekeepers, already the largest force of its kind in the world, are properly led, trained and enabled. And we will work relentlessly to build the political settlement that is the only guarantee of long-term peace.

Ultimately, our shared security should be based not on the increased use of weapons but on their reduction. At this same occasion last year, I described the leading role I saw for our country in reducing the proliferation of weapons. I am pleased that 100 countries have joined us in banning cluster bombs and that the idea of a multinational fuel bank to help non-nuclear states acquire nuclear energy is gaining support.

And working with our allies, we are ready to do more – having extended export prohibitions on trafficking in small arms, we are ready to promote a new arms trade treaty. And I say to Iran, which has signed the Non-Proliferation Treaty: in these new circumstances, rejoin global society and benefit from help in acquiring civil nuclear power or face new sanctions and growing isolation.

Conflict in the Middle East and the failure to restore a Palestinian state is a festering wound that has for generations poisoned relations between the West and the Arab and Islamic world. But I believe, and I have heard for myself, that the elements that can constitute a settlement are now well understood by those on all sides who want to come together to end the divisions of the past. It has often been said that a historic hard-won and lasting peace is now within our grasp. But what I do know is that, building on the work of President Bush, that durable and just settlement is an urgent priority for the new US administration, and the UK will stand firm in support.

A Middle East settlement has the potential to transform the future of the Middle East. In Iraq we continue to defend a new democracy, and last summer we set out the remaining tasks to be achieved there to make possible a fundamental change of mission and the transition to a long-term bilateral partnership with Iraq, similar to the normal relationships which our military forces have with other countries in the region. And we are making good progress with each of our objectives.

And I welcome the reaffirmed commitment from both President Bush and President-elect Obama to defend a stable and democratic future for Afghanistan and to review the best ways of achieving this through better burden-sharing – America at its best, leading a broad international effort underpinned by shared values; working more effectively with the grain of Afghan society, including the tribes; working with our allies to double the size of the Afghan army; working with President Karzai to tackle corruption; and supporting the democratic Afghan government in its slow but steady attempts to build peace. And we will support the Afghan and Pakistan governments in working together to tackle the security issues across the border, which, the last decade has shown, are crucial to our own security at home. Afghanistan is a test the international community cannot afford to fail. And we will not fail.

Third, 75 years ago, at a time of recession, nations met in London in a World Economic Conference, and because the talks broke up in failure, the world entered a long decade of protectionism and retrenchment.

In Washington this weekend, the British government will work with its G20 partners to establish consensus and begin to build a new Bretton Woods with a reformed, modern IMF that offers, by its surveillance of every economy, an early-warning system and a crisis-prevention mechanism for the whole world.

This will require the recapitalisation of banks and their resumption of lending to families and businesses; immediate action to stop the spread of the financial crisis to middle-income countries – building agreement for a new facility and new resources for the IMF; urgent agreement on a trade deal and rejection of beggar-thy-neighbour protectionism that has been a feature in turning past crises into deep recessions; a restoration of confidence, by addressing the root causes of the instability through reform of the global financial system based on the principles of transparency, integrity, responsibility, sound banking-practice and global governance, with coordination across borders and every nation playing its part; better international coordination of fiscal and monetary policy – recognising the immediate importance of this coordination for stimulating economic activity.

At the heart of this is a growing agreement that, at a time of change and massive uncertainty, people look to governments for action. This is no time for conventional, old thinking or tired, old orthodoxies.

In Britain, we have already cut taxes to help families this year. And as the Chancellor has said, we will maintain our essential public investments while continuing to increase the value for money of every pound spent. This is no time for the old approach of short-term spending cuts in a downturn that would hurt families and businesses today and damage the long-term productivity of the economy.

Since this is a global downturn, it requires a global solution. As was the case with the bank stabilisation plan, the benefits of any individual country's fiscal actions will be all the greater if this is part of a concerted and fairly distributed international response to maintain global demand. There is now a growing international consensus that, especially for those countries with low debt, like the UK, maintaining essential public investment is the right and sensible approach, while allowing a temporary and affordable increase in borrowing to support economic growth.

Yesterday, China announced that it was injecting almost $600 billion to support its economy. The European Union has said that flexibility in the stability pact – to recognise exceptional and temporary conditions – will be used. Last week, Germany announced their plans for a fiscal stimulus. President-elect Obama has already signalled his intention to do likewise. With Britain continuing to lead the debate, economic recovery will work better if we all work together.

The fourth imperative is tackling climate change. For it is clear now that, if left unchecked, climate change will have catastrophic worldwide effects on our future prosperity.

The G8 has already agreed we must at least halve global emissions by 2050. But this also means emissions must peak by 2020.

So we cannot afford to put climate change into the international 'pending' tray because of the present economic difficulties, as some might urge. On the contrary, we must use the imperative to act for our future prosperity through the transition to a low-carbon economy and reduced oil dependency – as a route to creating jobs and economic opportunity for our peoples today.

This is why, as we prepare for an ambitious post-2012 climate change agreement in Copenhagen – for which I pledge our government's unbending commitment – the European Union must, and I believe will, agree in December its '2020' programme for energy and climate change and show European leadership at its best. And I want the World Bank to become a bank for the environment as well as for development, helping developing countries move towards sustainable energy paths of their own.

And a truly global society cannot, of course, exist without the vital humanitarian and development assistance and support for self-sustaining growth that keeps millions of people alive and meets basic needs for education, food and health. For we cannot claim to be a truly global society, or one world, when 30,000 children die every day from diseases we know how to cure.

This is not the time to abandon helping the poorest countries. For now, more than ever, it is both our duty and in our interest to help meet the Millennium Development Goals. For we cannot solve climate change without Africa; nor can we solve the food crisis without Africa. We need a fully financed 'energy for the poor' initiative, where commercial sources of capital dry up support from the international institutions, and we need to support agricultural development. In Africa in the past, 'feed the world' meant that we helped to feed Africa. In future, if we do things right, we will do best by enabling Africa to feed the world.

And I am proud that, even as the world came to terms with the financial crisis, Britain has continued to drive forward the vital effort to meet the Millennium Development Goals.

Tonight, I have argued that, uniquely in this global age, it is now in our power to come together, confer and decide and that we must be guided by one clear truth – that we need solutions that can no longer be defined in terms of 'us' and 'them' but can be achieved only together as 'us' with 'them'. I believe that people do not only cooperate out of need. There is a human need to cooperate. But I believe also that all our efforts reflect what people find when they can communicate across continents with each other – that there is a shared moral sense that we are responsible each to the other, country to country as much as person to person. And because of this, no injustice can last forever, and even in the most desperate of circumstances people can journey with hope.

So my message is that we must be internationalist, not protectionist; interventionist, not isolationist; progressive, not paralysed by events; and forward-thinking, not trapped in the solutions of the past.

And if we do so, 2008 will be remembered not just for a financial crash that engulfed the world but for the decisiveness and optimism with which the world faced the storm, endured it and prevailed. And remembered, too, for how in doing so we discovered and refashioned the global power of nations working together.

President Roosevelt famously said, 'The only thing we have to fear is fear itself.' When fear overwhelms our perceptions of reality, the effect is paralysing; it leaves people frozen into inaction, helpless at a time of great risk and even at a time of great opportunity, too.

But confidence in the future – that most precious asset of all – is the key to bringing back confidence today. It is dynamic; it heralds action. And for reasons I have laid before you this evening, I am confident. Confident that we can seize the moment, grasp it together and use it to lay the foundations – optimistic, multilateralist and inclusive – on which we can build the first truly global society.

3

Tackling the Urgent Challenges

Introduction by Kofi Annan

Over 2,000 years ago, the Roman poet Publilius Syrus declared that 'Speech is the mirror of the soul; as a man speaks, so is he'. Alas, rare are the political speeches today that meet this standard. But there are exceptions – including the two speeches Prime Minister Gordon Brown delivered at the United Nations in 2008 and 2009, (included here in Chapters 3 and 10).

Too many speeches at the UN represent routine repetitions of tired formulae and vacuous injunctions to action, politicians playing to the gallery of their peers or responding to short-term political demands at home. But the two speeches included in these chapters are not about such political grandstanding. They are an impressive testimony to the Prime Minister's genuine commitment to the principles of international cooperation and solidarity, basic principles upon which the UN was built 65 years ago; basic principles which we are now in need of more than ever.

The speeches naturally vary in tone and substance, given the specific circumstances in which they were delivered.

In 2008, leaders met at the brink of global financial and economic crisis. In addition to the anxiety and hardship this was creating in richer countries, the crisis threatened the lives and livelihoods of hundreds of millions, if not billions, of people in the developing world. Progress on the achievement of the Millennium Development Goals was in danger of being reversed.

In 2009, the 192 members of the General Assembly were meeting amidst the first signs of recovery. A near-disaster had been averted, and the world was taking stock of what must be done to stimulate collective action to prevent another crisis and address other shared challenges.

Delivered at different times and in different moods, a simple but powerful thread runs through both – and indeed, many of the Prime Minister's speeches included in this book. That is the imperative of human solidarity, the importance of standing by our fellow human beings in times of need and of working together to overcome challenges we all face, such as climate change or international terrorism.

But even more important than the Prime Minister's expressed support of and advocacy for global solidarity and cooperation is that he acted upon his words and used the UN pulpit to urge others to do the same. At a time when Britain faced tough economic decisions and many other countries were trying to wriggle out of commitments they had made in better times by redefining them or abandoning them altogether, the Prime Minister stood by Britain's generous pledges of international development assistance and resisted the isolationist tendencies of so many around him. For this, I commend him.

If anything, the last two years have shown that we need more such leadership, greater attention to the basic principles of humanity and more effective action.

❦

On the eve of the G20 September 2009 meeting in Pittsburgh, the Prime Minister addressed the UN General Assembly. His speech reflects on what he calls 'the unprecedented unity that has defined the past year', as action was taken to tackle the global economic crisis. But in this forceful address, he urges the world's leaders not to be complacent, saying that much more action is required across five urgent challenges that demand momentous decisions – climate change, terrorism, nuclear proliferation, poverty and shared prosperity.

His urgent message is that we need world agreement: 'If we do not reach a deal at Copenhagen . . . we cannot hope for a second chance some time in the future . . . Not later, at another conference, in another decade, after we have lost ten years to inaction and delay. And if in Afghanistan we give way to the insurgency, al-Qaeda and other terrorist groups will return and from that sanctuary once again plot, train for and launch attacks on the rest of the world. There can be no chance of a nuclear-free world, if we allow Iran to develop nuclear weapons and in doing so set off a new arms race. There can be no global compact for jobs and growth if we choke off recovery by failing to follow through on the coordinated global fiscal expansion we agreed and put in place. And, if we do not act together to fight preventable illness, there can be no plan to save tomorrow the 12,000 children who are dying in Africa today and every day.'

The Prime Minister ends the speech with an appeal to all world leaders to recall the motivation of the founding fathers of the UN: 'Let us remember how, in 1945, nations facing a multiplicity of challenges summoned up the energy and vision not just to rebuild from the rubble and ruin of war but to establish a new international order for shared security and progress. The same principles must now inspire new and better, more representative and more effective ways of working together.' This is important so that we can find 'within ourselves and together, the qualities of moral courage and leadership that, for our time and generation, can make the world new again and, for the first time in human history, create a truly global society'.

SPEECH TO THE UN GENERAL ASSEMBLY
New York, 23 September 2009

We met a year ago on the brink of a global crisis, and as national leaders spoke in turn at this podium, the full scale of the danger became clear – a threat not just to jobs, businesses and life savings but, with the imminent risk of failure of the world's banking system, the prospect of entire countries failing, as nations across Eastern Europe, Asia and Latin America struggled to access credit.

The crisis demanded global action. As never before, the fate of every country rested on the actions of all. And as the fear of the unthinkable took hold, we reached a clear choice – to fail separately or to succeed together.

At the G20 in Washington and again in London, we made our choice. Governments came together to begin the fight back against the global recession. We acted in concert, recognising that national interests could be protected only by serving the common interest; that in this new global age the economy is indivisible and recession anywhere can threaten prosperity everywhere; that for growth to be sustained it has to be shared; and that global challenges can only be mastered through global solutions.

So, today, we can draw strength from the unprecedented unity that has defined the past year – but we cannot be complacent. For while it may seem strange to say so after a time of such intense global action, our world is entering a six-month period which may prove even more testing for international cooperation.

We face five urgent challenges that demand momentous decisions – decisions that I would argue are epoch-making – on climate change, terrorism, nuclear proliferation, poverty and shared prosperity.

Once again, we are at a point of no return. And just as the collapse of the banks focused our minds a year ago, so we must now grasp this next set of issues.

If we do not reach a deal at Copenhagen – if we miss this opportunity to protect our planet – we cannot hope for a second chance some time in the future. There will be no retrospective global agreement to undo the damage we will have caused. This is the moment, now, to limit and reverse the climate change we are inflicting on future generations. Not later, at another conference, in another decade, after we have lost ten years to inaction and delay.

And if in Afghanistan we give way to the insurgency, al-Qaeda and other terrorist groups will return and from that sanctuary once again plot, train for and launch attacks on the rest of the world.

There can be no chance of a nuclear-free world if we allow Iran to develop nuclear weapons and in doing so set off a new arms race. There can be no global compact for jobs and growth if we choke off recovery by failing to follow through on the coordinated global fiscal expansion we agreed and put in place. And if we do not act together to fight preventable illness, there can be no plan to save tomorrow the 12,000 children who are dying in Africa today and every day. So I say we need world agreement.

First, on climate change. Despite the promises we have all made, the road to a successful outcome on climate change in Copenhagen is not assured. Why? Above all, because a robust and long-term climate change deal requires money. If the poorest and most vulnerable are going to be able to adapt, if the emerging economies are going to embark on low-carbon development paths, if the forest nations are going to slow and stop deforestation, then the richer countries must contribute financially.

That is why I have proposed a new approach to financing our action against climate change, which will provide substantially increased, additional and predictable flows, from both public and private sectors, of around $100 billion a year by 2020. We must make progress on this in the coming days.

A post-2012 agreement on climate change at Copenhagen is the next great test of our global cooperation. Each of us has a duty of leadership to make it happen. We must build on our discussions at Secretary General Ban's meeting here this week, and I have said I will go to Copenhagen to conclude the deal. This is too important an agreement – for the global economy and for the future of every nation represented here – to leave to our official negotiators. So I urge my fellow leaders to commit themselves to going to Copenhagen, too.

Second, terrorism. A safer Afghanistan means a safer world. But none of us can be safe if we walk away from that country or from our common mission and resolve.

NATO and its partners from Australia to Japan must agree new ways to implement our strategy, ensuring that Afghanistan, its army, its police and its people assume greater responsibility for the security of their own country.

So, too, must we unite against every source of terror and injustice in our world. It shames us all that the people of Somalia and Sudan are still subject to the most terrible violence; that Israel and Palestine have still not found a way to live side by side in security and peace; and that, for the people of Burma, their elected leader is subjected to a show trial and decades of incarceration.

There is more we can do; there is more we must do. And we must carry forward our efforts to take a more strategic, coherent and effective approach to peacekeeping and peace-building.

Third, nuclear proliferation. Once there were five nuclear armed powers. Now there are nine, with the real and present danger that more will soon follow. And the risk is not just state aggression but the acquisition of nuclear weapons by terrorists. So we are at a moment of danger, when decades of preventing proliferation could be overturned by a damaging rise in proliferation.

If we are serious about the ambition of a nuclear-free world, we will need statesmanship not brinkmanship. Tomorrow's Security Council Resolution will be vital as we move forwards towards next year's Global Nuclear Security Summit in April and the Review Conference in May.

My proposal is a grand global bargain between nuclear weapon and non-nuclear weapons states. And there are three elements to it, where careful and sober international leadership is essential and in which Britain will play its part – on the responsibilities of non-nuclear states, on the rights of non-nuclear states and on the responsibilities of nuclear weapons states.

First, let there be no ambiguity – Iran and North Korea must know that the world will be even tougher on proliferation and we are ready to consider further sanctions. Britain will insist that the onus on non-nuclear states is that in future it is for them to prove they are not developing nuclear weapons.

Second, Britain will offer civil nuclear power to non-nuclear states ready to renounce any plans for nuclear weapons, helping non-nuclear states acquire what President Eisenhower so memorably called 'atoms for peace'. With others, we will be prepared to sponsor a uranium bank outside these countries to help them access civil nuclear power. And Britain is ready to launch a new nuclear centre of excellence to help develop an economic, low-carbon, proliferation-resistant nuclear fuel cycle.

Third, all nuclear weapons states must play their part in reducing nuclear weapons as part of an agreement by non-nuclear states to renounce them.

This is exactly what the Non-Proliferation Treaty intended. In line with maintaining our nuclear deterrent, I have asked our National Security Committee to report to me on the potential future reduction of our nuclear weapon submarines from four to three.

Fourth, while economic cooperation has stabilised the international banking system and forged a foundation for the resumption of economic growth, recovery is neither entrenched nor irreversible. The great lesson of the last year is that only bold and global action prevented a recession becoming a depression. We have delivered a coordinated fiscal and monetary response that the ILO estimates has saved seven to eleven million jobs across the world.

So at Pittsburgh tomorrow we must cement a global compact for jobs and growth, a compact to bring unemployment down and bring rising prosperity across the globe by maximising the impact of the stimulus measures we have agreed, with proper planning of exit strategies to make sure the recovery does not falter – that we do not turn off the life support for our economy prematurely; facilitating agreement – setting clear objectives on how each of us can best contribute to worldwide growth in the future; and ensuring that such growth is balanced and sustainable.

We need strong economic coordination, now, as we navigate the uncertainties of recovery. I therefore propose that we launch the compact by agreeing that we are committed to high levels of growth on a sustainable and balanced basis.

This must be backed up by comprehensive reform of the financial sector, including international principles on bonuses. And we must strengthen our targeting of tax havens with, from next March, real sanctions against those jurisdictions which fail to meet global standards.

But the voice of Africa will have to be heard and heeded to bring recovery in areas devastated by the events of the past year and to assure that we do not put the Millennium Development Goals beyond reach, as a result of a wider failure of global responsibility.

In London, the G20 agreed measures to result in $50 billion for poor countries – to help them weather the crisis. Because of London, the IMF can lend $8 billion instead of $2 billion over this year and next. This is already helping Kenya and Tanzania to increase government spending in response to the crisis.

For amid all the challenges we face, we must remember a promise we made ten years ago. And this is the fifth and final imperative – to achieve a vision for 2015 we are now in danger of betraying. On present trends it will take not five years, as we pledged, and not even fifty years, but more than a hundred years to deliver on some of the Millennium Development Goals.

The unyielding, grinding, soul-destroying, so often lethal poverty I saw in Africa convinced me that, unless empowerment through trade justice is matched by empowerment through free education and free health care, then this generation in sub-Saharan Africa will not have the opportunity to rise out of poverty and will never be fully free. The greatest of injustices demands the boldest of actions.

Today, at this United Nations General Assembly, we will see the beginnings of universal free health care in Africa and Asia as Burundi, Sierra Leone, Malawi, Nepal, Liberia and Ghana all make major announcements that extend free care and abolish fees.

As a result of these actions, more than ten million more people in Africa and Asia will now have access to free health services. Ten million who will now, for the first time, get the treatment they need without being turned away or fearing how they will pay.

I urge you all to match the leadership of these countries with your own support. And I commit the UK to doing so.

Let us remember how in 1945 nations facing a multiplicity of challenges summoned up the energy and vision not just to rebuild from the rubble and ruin of war but to establish a new international order for shared security and progress.

The same principles must now inspire new and better, more representative and more effective ways of working together.

And as we learn from the experience of turning common purpose into common action in this, our shared global society, so we must forge a progressive multilateralism that depends on us finding, within ourselves and together, the qualities of moral courage and leadership that, for our time and generation, can make the world new again and, for the first time in human history, create a truly global society.

4

FIVE GIANTS TO DO BATTLE WITH

INTRODUCTION BY NICK ANSTEE

The Lord Mayor's Banquet is one of the most significant events in a Lord Mayor's year and in the civic year of the City of London. Held in the Great Hall of Guildhall, it is an opportunity for the newly elected Lord Mayor to set out his priorities and for the Prime Minister to deliver a major speech, usually on foreign affairs.

The Banquet has had this status since the mid-nineteenth century. Disraeli, Gladstone, Salisbury and Rosebery, unburdened by the relentless demands of a modern premiership, could spread themselves; these were speeches which could, then, easily last an hour and a half. Before that period, however, Pitt the Younger, shortly after the Battle of Trafalgar, delivered the shortest recorded speech of any premier at the Banquet – a speech consisting of just 41 words.

Today, the Lord Mayor's Banquet remains an event which attracts considerable attention in the world's media, and it remains an important engagement in any prime minister's diary.

Lord mayors of London today, as in 1189, from when the office dates, act as head of the City of London – the world's oldest continuous municipal democracy, which delivers local government services. But a lord mayor's principal role today is in promoting all UK-based financial and business services – the City in the widest sense. In my Banquet speech delivered on 16 November 2009, I called upon the City to re-establish trust with wider society in the wake of the financial crisis. We need to do this to face and help form the future with confidence. That has continued to be my theme in my mayoral year.

In his annual speech to the Lord Mayor's Banquet on 16 November 2009, the Prime Minister used the global financial crisis as a backdrop to explore the global challenges he saw facing the world. Like a modern-day Beveridge, in this speech he brings together his thoughts on the threats posed to the world by what might be termed the five giants of the global age that need to be slain

– climate change, terrorism, nuclear proliferation, poverty and the threat of worldwide economic collapse.

Early on in the speech, the Prime Minister draws attention to the tension that some see between the defence of our national interests and multilateralism. He rejects the view that these are 'mutually incompatible' or that 'a strong partnership with Europe weakens our capacity to pursue our national goals'. Indeed, he goes on to argue that, in a world where the historic challenges we face are so profoundly global, this view is dangerous and threatens the security and prosperity of our country: 'To equate the national interest with a flight to unilateralism, when so many challenges can be met only by collective actions, is to condemn our nation to marginalisation, irrelevance and failure.'

Indeed, the Prime Minister's case is that we in Britain 'must have confidence in our distinctive strengths – our global values, global alliances and global actions … because with conviction in our values and confidence in our alliances, Britain can lead in the construction of a new global order'. He concludes that our foreign policy must be 'hard-headed, patriotic and internationalist – a foreign policy that recognises and exploits Britain's unique strengths and defends Britain's national interests strongly, not by retreating into isolation but by advancing in international cooperation'.

And in his confident concluding summary, Gordon Brown says, 'Usually only in retrospect do people see dramatic sets of events as turning points, but I believe that historians will look back on the sheer scope, speed and scale of the global change that perhaps no peacetime generation has ever before experienced and conclude that, faced with climate change, worldwide economic collapse, terror and the nuclear threat – and surrounded by new means of global communications that allow people to connect across frontiers – we took the first steps towards a truly global society.'

SPEECH TO THE LORD MAYOR'S BANQUET
Guildhall, London, 16 November 2009

We live in no ordinary times. A year into dealing with the greatest economic challenge for generations – the first global financial recession; a few weeks before the most important climate change decisions in human history; a few months ahead of nuclear negotiations that could, for the first time, genuinely bind the world to cooperate and not proliferate; and we meet just as America and NATO are making vital choices about how to continue and win the fight against global terrorism.

These are the four great issues of our time, and what they have in common is that, global in nature, they require global solutions. None can be answered by one country or one continent in isolation. What they demand of us is a shared vision and the creation of new and effective global institutions with the mandate and the authority to make that vision real.

And the great questions of the day call not for hard power or soft power but the power of people working together. Because none, too, can be resolved by national politicians pronouncing from on high, while failing to listen to the citizens they serve, but only by great social movements which create the conditions for common action around the world.

So tonight I want to talk about the problems we face. But, much more than that, I want to talk about why I am an unremitting optimist, about Britain's future and the world's and about why I believe this generation, if we make the right choices, can create an unprecedented century of progress.

Tonight I want to talk about how together we can forge and then legislate, for the first time, a truly global climate change agreement to save our planet from catastrophic climate change; how together, by tough and practical multilateralism, we can shape global rules for prosperity to ensure that never again will a wave of economic crisis sweeping across the world threaten millions with unemployment and poverty; how together we can, with a new Non-Proliferation Treaty, contain and then banish the risk of the development of nuclear weapons; and how together we can agree a strategy for Afghanistan and Pakistan – as a 43-nation coalition in Afghanistan, together with Pakistan and other countries in the region and elsewhere – including a stronger counter-insurgency strategy, to deny the terrorists and extremists the space and freedom to threaten the safety and security of the innocents they target in our streets and thousands of miles away.

Some may regard these challenges as beyond the reach of a world which has, for so long, cast international affairs as competition between national interests rather than the coordination of common interests.

But the events we have witnessed have taught us that there are great causes – causes worth fighting for even when people say the odds are too great, that the hill is too steep. Events we have witnessed in just half a generation, events previously only imagined and apparently impossible, yet so swiftly realised – the fall of the Berlin Wall and the end of the cold war, the release of Nelson Mandela and the end of apartheid.

All these teach us that we should use the word *impossible* with greater care, and we learn that what was yesterday's dream and today's impossibility can become tomorrow's reality.

And I believe that there is no other country, by its history, values and global reach, better placed to shape a safer and more secure world. Ours is an open, free-trading, democratic nation – for centuries internationalist in its instincts and actions – committed to persuasion whenever possible, to force only when necessary and, most of all, to a belief in liberty, fairness and responsibility.

And it is these values, these moral imperatives, that equip us for a role that encompasses diplomacy, conciliation, firmness and, yes, where necessary, armed intervention.

And in leading the debate and doing so in the light of our ideals, Britain brings the influence that comes from being right at the heart of great international institutions and alliances – the EU, NATO, the UN, the Commonwealth, the G8 and G20.

That unique position is an awesome privilege and a great responsibility, and no one – whether narrow nationalist or instinctive isolationist – should consider themselves patriots if they would sacrifice or diminish our influence.

In the nineteenth century, Palmerston talked of a British national interest best served by the strength of those permanent interests but not by permanent allies.

In a very different century, I see our national interest best served in a new way – by the strength of our permanent values and interests and by our strong alliances.

Of course, there are those who believe that multilateral cooperation and the defence of our national interests are mutually incompatible and that a strong partnership with Europe weakens our capacity to pursue our national goals. This view has always been short-sighted. Indeed, in a world where the historic challenges we face are so profoundly global, this view has never been more dangerous and threatening to the security and prosperity of our country.

To equate the national interest with a flight to unilateralism, when so many challenges can be met only by collective actions, is to condemn our nation to marginalisation, irrelevance and failure.

Can anyone today seriously believe we can tackle the recession better without the European Union and the G20? Does anyone now seriously believe we can protect ourselves from international terrorism on our own; in a 'fortress Britain'; without America, NATO, the European Union and our coalition allies?

Does anyone still believe that we can defeat climate change without international action across the European Union, without the nations of our Commonwealth from Africa to Australasia, without challenging the United Nations?

Even to advocate a measure of withdrawal from international cooperation immediately weakens our trade, our economy and our influence.

So let me set out how, by leading in global cooperation in the coming months, we can shape the world of the future.

First, climate change. In just three weeks' time countries will gather at the UN conference in Copenhagen to forge a new international agreement to combat global warming. And let us be clear what such an agreement must involve. Britain is prepared to lead the way, proposing a financial plan to ensure all countries can cut carbon emissions. And this should form part of a comprehensive agreement based on politically binding commitments of all countries, which can be implemented immediately and which can act as the basis for an internationally legally binding treaty as soon as possible. The agreement must contain the full range of commitments required on emissions reductions by both developed and developing countries, on finance and on verification.

We need the same degree of international cooperation to return the world economy to a secure prosperity and to address the global plague of poverty. And we have already seen what international cooperation can do – with the restructuring of the banks and the coordination of a fiscal stimulus. The world has acted together to stop a recession becoming a depression. And I believe that, while we are only halfway through dealing with the causes of the crisis, we also have reason to be confident because, in the next two decades, the world economy will double in size, creating twice as many opportunities for business, for jobs, for exports. And as this new economy moves forward, I want Britain to be right at its centre, making the most of the unprecedented opportunities.

Were we to retreat now from international cooperation and the commitments each country has made to revive and sustain our economies, that would not just put the global recovery at risk but put at risk British jobs, British growth, British prosperity for years and even generations to come. The equation here is clear – trade abroad means jobs at home.

There are no 'Britain-only', 'Europe-only' or 'US-only' ways to manage a global financial system. A new contract of trust is needed between banks and the societies they serve across the world. And whether it is insurance fees, resolution funds, contingent capital arrangements or a global financial levy – measures that can only be implemented at a global level – common sense suggests we must agree internationally how we will mitigate the risks to the economy from financial failure and redress the balance of risk and reward between the public and the financial sector.

And we will never walk away from our global role in the campaign against poverty and injustice. We do not give up hope of a Burma unchained or of a Zimbabwe liberated. And we will continue to work to ensure that every child in the world has schooling and that we reduce the shocking levels of avoidable infant and maternal mortality. The world will not for long endure half prosperous and half poor. Poverty violates conscience even as it invites conflict.

And five months from now we will meet in Washington to confront another source of potential conflict – the proliferation of nuclear weapons and nuclear nations. Britain must continue to lead the renewal of a grand global bargain between nuclear weapon and non-nuclear weapons states, a fair and balanced deal in which non-nuclear weapons states must accept clear responsibilities to end proliferation – by renouncing nuclear weapons in return for the right to access civil nuclear power – and in which nuclear-armed nations must accept the responsibility to work together on a credible road map to nuclear disarmament, towards a world without nuclear weapons.

Never again should any nation be able to deceive the international community and conceal with impunity its pursuit of proliferation. We face critical test cases in Iran and North Korea, with attention focused most recently on Iran. In September, the truth about their secret facility at Qom was revealed. And on 1 October, we again offered Tehran engagement and negotiation. Over the last six weeks that offer has been comprehensively rejected. So it is now not only right but necessary for the world to apply concerted pressure to the Iranian regime. President Obama set an end-of-the-year deadline for Iran to react. If Iran does not reconsider then the United Nations, the EU and individual countries must impose tougher sanctions.

The greatest immediate threat to our national security – the greatest current risk to British lives – is that of international terrorism. We know that from New York, Bali, Baghdad, Madrid, Mumbai, Peshawar and Rawalpindi to London men and women – Muslim, Christian, Jewish, Hindu, of every faith and none – have been victims of international terrorism. I will never compromise when it comes to the safety and security of the British people. We have trebled our domestic security budget, doubled our security-service staff and increased by over two-thirds the numbers of police dealing day to day with terrorism in the UK, and will always do what is necessary.

And I know from my four visits to Afghanistan in the last fifteen months that our armed forces understand our security priority and share that commitment. Let me say that the courage, skill and professionalism of our forces serving there are truly inspiring. In some of the hardest conditions, they have enhanced their already peerless reputation as the finest in the world. And we pay tribute to each and every one of them this evening.

Tonight I want to explain in more detail the relation between the work of our armed forces in Afghanistan and the domestic terrorist threat; to remind people that, despite our successes against al-Qaeda, they and their associates still have active plans to commit terrorist atrocities in the United Kingdom; and to make it clear why it is only by standing up to this terrorist threat at its source that we can properly defend our shores.

Tonight I can report that, methodically and patiently, we are disrupting and disabling the existing leadership of al-Qaeda. Since January 2008, seven of the top dozen figures in al-Qaeda have been killed, depleting its reserve of experienced leaders and sapping its morale. More has been planned and enacted with greater success in this one year to disable al-Qaeda than in any year since the original invasion in 2001. Today, 28,000 Pakistan security forces are inside South Waziristan, again narrowing the scope for al-Qaeda to operate. And our security services report to me that there is now an opportunity to inflict significant and long-lasting damage to al-Qaeda.

We understand the reality of the danger and the nature of the consequences if we do not succeed. We will never forget the fatal al-Qaeda-led attacks in London on 7 July 2005, the unsuccessful al-Qaeda-inspired attacks two weeks later and the al-Qaeda-sanctioned plot to capture and behead a British soldier in the Midlands in January 2007.

Some plots remain under investigation, and so for obvious reasons I cannot elaborate. On others I can. In 2007, five individuals were found guilty of what we now know was an al-Qaeda-inspired conspiracy to cause explosions, with possible plans to target shopping centres or clubs in London and the South East.

And in total since 2001 nearly 200 persons have been convicted of terrorist or terrorist-related offences; almost half of those convicted pleaded guilty. And day by day, we are continuing to track a large number of suspicious individuals and potential plots. Make no mistake – al-Qaeda has an extensive recruitment network across Africa, the Middle East, Western Europe and in the UK. And we know that there are still several hundred foreign fighters based in the Fata area of Pakistan and travelling to training camps to learn bomb-making and weapons skills.

It is because of the nature of the threat, and because around three-quarters of the most serious plots the security services are now tracking in Britain have links to Pakistan, that it does not make sense to confine our defence against terrorism solely to actions inside the UK. Al-Qaeda rely on a permissive environment in the tribal areas of Pakistan and – if they can re-establish one – in Afghanistan. Al-Qaeda has links to the Afghan and Pakistan Taliban. We must deny terrorists the room to operate which the Taliban regime allowed the 9/11 attackers. So that is why I say the Afghan campaign is being prosecuted not from choice but out of necessity.

So vigilance in defence of national security will never be sacrificed to expediency. Necessary resolution will never succumb to appeasement. The greater international good will never be subordinated to the mood of the passing moment. That is why 43 governments around the world now understand the importance of defeating al-Qaeda and of preventing them ever again being able to flourish in Afghanistan. America, with 60,000, and Britain, with 9,000, are the largest troop contributors, but the rest of the international coalition has increased its numbers from 16,000 in January 2007 to over 27,000 today and I am confident that they will be prepared to do more.

But this coalition does not intend to become an occupying army; it is building the capacity of Afghanistan to deal, themselves, with terrorism and violent extremism – what we mean by 'Afghanisation'. Today the army has published its new counter-insurgency doctrine. Partnering the Afghan army and police is fraught with danger, as we have seen in recent weeks, and building up local-level Afghan governance in areas which have not known the rule of law for decades, if at all, is daunting. But as I have emphasised in recent weeks, we have not chosen this path of Afghanisation because it is a safer or easier option but because it is the right strategy.

Following the inauguration this week of President Karzai, I have urged him to set out the contract between the new government and its people, including early action on corruption. And I welcome today's announcement that the new government in Afghanistan will dedicate the next five years to fighting corruption. I have pledged full UK support in this effort. The international community will meet to agree plans for the support we will provide to Afghanistan during this next phase. I have offered London as a venue in the New Year. I want that conference to chart a comprehensive political framework within which the military strategy can be accomplished. A strong political framework should embrace internal political reform to ensure representative government that works for all

Afghan citizens, at the national level in Kabul and in the provinces and districts. It should identify a process for transferring district by district to full Afghan control and, if at all possible, set a timetable for transferring districts starting in 2010.

For it is only when the Afghans are themselves able to defend the security of their people and deny the territory of Afghanistan as a base for terrorists that our strategy of Afghanisation will have succeeded and our troops can come home.

So tonight I want to leave you with a clear summary of Britain's case and that of the coalition as a whole. We are in Afghanistan because we judge that if the Taliban regained power al-Qaeda and other terrorist groups would once more have an environment in which they could operate. We are there because action in Afghanistan is not an alternative to action in Pakistan but an inseparable support to it. As I have shown, the world has succeeded in closing down much of the space in which al-Qaeda can operate, and we must not allow this process to be reversed by retreat or irresolution.

Usually only in retrospect do people see dramatic sets of events as turning points, but I believe that historians will look back on the sheer scope, speed and scale of the global change that perhaps no peacetime generation has ever before experienced and conclude that, faced with climate change, worldwide economic collapse, terror and the nuclear threat – and surrounded by new means of global communications that allow people to connect across frontiers – we took the first steps towards a truly global society.

In meeting each of the four challenges I have talked about tonight, Britain's future is a future shared with our international partners. So we in Britain, who are serious, we have a crucial responsibility to seize this moment.

I believe that Britain can inspire the world, I believe that Britain can challenge the world, but, most importantly of all, I believe that Britain can, and must, play its full part in changing the world.

And to do so we must have confidence in our distinctive strengths – our global values, global alliances and global actions – because, with conviction in our values and confidence in our alliances, Britain can lead in the construction of a new global order. We must never be less than resolute in fighting for British interests because, as you in this room know better than anyone, Britain has nothing to fear in the world's marketplace of ideals and ideas, nor from the world's most destructive ideologies.

At every point in our history where we have looked outwards we have become stronger. And now, more than ever, there is no future in what was once called 'splendid isolation'. When Britain is bold, when Britain is engaged, when Britain is confident and outward-looking, we have shown time and again that Britain has a power and an energy that far exceeds the limits of our geography, our population and our means. And that is why I say our foreign policy must be hard-headed, patriotic and internationalist – a foreign policy that recognises and exploits Britain's unique strengths and defends Britain's national interests strongly not by retreating into isolation but by advancing in international cooperation.

So we will stand with countries that share our values and vision. We will engage with those who disagree with us but who are ready for dialogue. And we will isolate those who are motivated by the will to destroy the structures and principles on which a just global society must depend.

As a nation we have every reason to be optimistic about our prospects – confident in our alliances, faithful to our values and determined as progressive pioneers to shape the world to come. Britain can be, and Great Britain must be, in the vanguard of a new progressive force for change, architect of a new world that honours our hopes and defeats our fears – a new world that can become a truly global society.

PART II

THE GLOBAL CHALLENGES

In the speeches collected in Part I, Gordon Brown sets out a convincing case for a new global order. Even before the global economic crisis hit us, he was articulating this approach and, in addition, suggesting that only by developing a new paradigm of interdependence can we tackle the global challenges facing the world.

In his December 1942 report, *Social Insurance and Allied Services*, Sir William Beveridge set out a plan to put an end to what he called the 'five giants' – want, disease, ignorance, squalor and idleness. In a similar vein, Gordon Brown characterises the problems facing the global community as five evil giants that need to be slain – climate change, terrorism, nuclear proliferation, poverty and the threat of worldwide economic collapse.

As the Prime Minister says, we will only really be able to judge this period once enough time has elapsed, when it will be possible to assess whether this has been one of the great turning points in our national story. But, he goes on, 'we do not need the benefit of hindsight to know that the sheer scale, scope and speed of today's global changes is throwing up problems which, if we do not address, will condemn millions around the world to a life that is unsustainable, insecure and unfair'.

The speeches collected in this section focus on each of the great challenges of this new global age – financial and economic instability in a world of global capital flows; environmental degradation in a world of changing energy need; violent extremism in a world of mass communications and increased mobility; extreme poverty in a world where there are still growing inequalities; and the threat of nuclear proliferation.

And the Prime Minister suggests that 'Answering these questions will determine whether people have continued faith in globalisation, in multilateralism, in modernity itself – whether they will have confidence in the future. And what all these challenges have in common is that none of them can be addressed by one country or one continent acting alone. None of them can be met and mastered without the world coming together. And none of them can be solved without agreed global rules informed by shared global values.'

5

MARKETS NEED MORALS

INTRODUCTION BY KEVIN RUDD

'Let me say something in direct support of my good friend and colleague Gordon Brown. I said this to the United Nations last September. This bloke has been on the question of the Millennium Development Goals, the collective conscience of the West, well before they were ever popular or trendy. Gordon has kept this alive, both as Chancellor and as Prime Minister, and his continued engagement with the likes of me around the world always has that on the agenda. I do not know whether to describe it as a "still, small voice", but in the theological tradition of the "still, small voice", this loud, booming Scottish voice is always on people about this. Advocacy is necessary. That is my first point.

'The second also builds on one of his. He [speaks] about the oxygen of confidence. What we are on about in this summit today is to try to restore the balance in terms of the rules of the global financial system and, underpinning that, do something towards restoring the balance on the values that underpin that system. The other part of the enterprise is this: then having about us not just a strategy for global economic recovery but also, importantly, a narrative of global economic recovery in which we can all be confident. What we say and how we speak about the challenges that lie ahead is as important as that which we do as well. Therefore, on the building and rebuilding of confidence in the institutions that we have spoken about, the policies on which we are deliberating and on the outcomes that we will see on Thursday, let us have about us the habit of rebuilding hope, optimism and confidence. A rational basis for hope, a rational basis for confidence, a rational basis for optimism and anchored in the rebalancing of the values which I fear, in sadness, that we in recent decades may have lost.'

⟨≋⟩

The day before the April 2009 G20 London Summit got under way, the Bishop of London, Dr Richard Chartres, chaired a high-level debate in St Paul's

Cathedral, dealing with moral questions raised by the global economic crisis. The speakers were Prime Minister Gordon Brown and the Prime Minister of Australia, Kevin Rudd, and the debate was open to the public with questions taken from the audience. The comments from Kevin Rudd quoted above are taken from some of his answers. The event was the first in the St Paul's Institute 2009 major programme – *Money, Integrity and Wellbeing*. The Institute is the cathedral's forum for contemporary ethics and aims to recapture the cathedral's ancient role as a centre of education and public debate.

In his address, Gordon Brown suggests that what he calls the first financial crisis of the global age has 'confirmed the enduring importance of the most timeless of truths – that our financial system must be founded on the very same values that are at the heart of the best of our family lives.

'Instead of a globalisation that threatens to become values-free and rules-free, we need a world of shared global rules founded on shared global values.' But he admits that 'the globalisation that has done so much to improve choice, driven down the cost of everything from computers to clothes and lifted millions out of poverty has also unleashed forces that have totally overwhelmed the old national rules and the systems of financial oversight'.

Invoking the writings of Adam Smith, the Prime Minister points out that Smith recognised, in the eighteenth century, that the 'invisible hand' of the market had to be accompanied by the 'helping hand' of society – that, in truth, Adam Smith argued that the flourishing of moral sentiments comes before, and is the foundation of, the wealth of nations. Gordon Brown deduces from this that the challenge for our generation is whether or not we can formulate global rules for our global financial and economic systems – global rules that are grounded in our shared values.

So, rejecting the idea that the only thing we can do in the face of a recession is to let it run its course and do nothing, the Prime Minister concludes, 'the battle the leaders of the G20 are fighting is not the old one against old enemies, but it is a new one against global recession, against climate chaos, unemployment, insecurity, poverty and hopelessness. And leaders meeting in London must supply the oxygen of confidence to today's global economy to give people in all our countries renewed hope for the future.'

SPEECH TO THE ST PAUL'S INSTITUTE
St Paul's Cathedral, London, 31 March 2009

With my friend Kevin Rudd, the Prime Minister of Australia, I come here to St Paul's – a church of enormous beauty and monumental history, a place of sanctuary which, amidst the passing storms of time, has always been a rock of faith at the centre of our national life. St Paul's is a place to which, over the centuries, people have come in hope and in faith – a great national institution standing between Westminster and the City, midway on the horizon between the world of politics and the world of finance and with a lot to teach us both.

Today, you will be pleased to know, we do not want to talk about the details of specific or technical financial programmes or policies, but instead we want to talk about enduring values – indeed the enduring virtues – that we have inherited from the past, which must infuse our ideals and hopes for the future.

And I want to suggest to all of you here today that this most modern of crises, the first financial crisis of the global age, has confirmed the enduring importance of the most timeless of truths – that our financial system must be founded on the very same values that are at the heart of the best of our family lives.

Instead of a globalisation that threatens to become values-free and rules-free, we need a world of shared global rules founded on shared global values. Now I know it's hard to talk about the future when you're having a tough time in the present – you don't redesign a boat in the middle of a storm – but we need to talk about the future because it falls to us to shape it. When Martin Luther King talked about the fierce urgency of now, he asked us to awaken to a tide in human history which, if missed, means you can end up being literally too late for that history.

It is usually only in hindsight that people can interpret the forces which have so transformed their lives – only in the classrooms of the future that the people of a country can stand back to identify and analyse the great turning points in their national story.

But we do not need the benefit of hindsight to know that the sheer scale, scope and speed of today's global changes is throwing up problems which, if we do not address, will condemn millions around the world to a life that is unsustainable, insecure and unfair.

There are four great challenges of this new global age which our generation must address urgently – financial and economic instability in a world of global capital flows, environmental degradation in a world of changing energy need, violent extremism in a world of mass communications and increased mobility, and extreme poverty in a world where there are still growing inequalities.

Answering these questions will determine whether people have continued faith in globalisation, in multilateralism, in modernity itself – whether they will have confidence in the future. And what all these challenges have in common is that none of them can be addressed by one country or one continent acting alone. None of them can be met and mastered without the world coming together. And none of them can be solved without agreed global rules informed by shared global values.

The oil price crisis last year, the financial crisis this year, a climate change crisis every year – it means that we are not at a moment of change; we are in a world of change. Twenty years ago, only one billion people were part of the world's industrial economy; now the figure is four billion. For centuries people rarely moved even from their home town; now every single year 200 million people – the equivalent of the whole populations of Britain, Germany and France – move from their country of birth, and next year another 200 million will do so again.

In one decade, the majority of the world's manufacturing – for two centuries focused in Europe and America – has shifted to Asia. The global sourcing of goods, services and capital means we now depend so much on each other that what happens anywhere can have an impact on what happens everywhere.

And this raises anxieties and questions for people about what will happen to them and what it means for their dream that their children – the children of the next generation – will do better than the children of the last. I recognise that for too many families, anxious about jobs, worried about mortgages, uncertain about their future, the most important financial summits are those that take place around their kitchen table.

And I understand that people feel unsettled and that the pain of this current recession is all too real. And the danger is that in every country workforces will become so worried that they will try to pull up the drawbridge, turn the clock back and retreat into a dangerous protectionism that, in the end, protects no one. If people's fears are not addressed, they may choose to walk away from the benefits that the opening up of this world can bring. Managed well, the same globalisation that has brought us so much global insecurity can also bring great opportunity.

Over the next two decades, millions of people in emerging markets will move from simply being producers of their goods to being consumers of our goods, leading to the world economy doubling in size – with twice as many opportunities for businesses, twice as many round-the-world middle-class jobs and incomes. That is why I am an avowed supporter of open markets, free trade, private capital and a flexible, inclusive and sustainable globalisation.

Let us be honest – the globalisation that has done so much to improve choice, driven down the cost of everything from computers to clothes and lifted millions out of poverty has also unleashed forces that have totally overwhelmed the old national rules and the systems of financial oversight.

I have always said I take full responsibility for my actions, but I also know that this crisis is global, its source is global, its scope is global and its solution will be global. We've seen worldwide changes so fast that they have outpaced people's understanding of them – so that managers sitting in boardrooms were selling financial products they didn't know the value of to traders and investors who didn't know what they were trading and investing in, covered by insurers who didn't know what they were insuring. Complex products like derivatives and securitised loans, which were supposed to disperse risk right across the world, instead spread contagion across that world. The sensible limits to markets agreed in one country became undermined by global competition between all countries and then a race in standards to the bottom. Instead of banks being, as they should be, stewards of people's money, too many of them became speculators with people's futures.

I say to you plainly: this old world of the old Washington Consensus is over, and what comes in its place is up to us. Instead of a global free market threatening to descend into a global free-for-all, we must reshape our global economic system so that it reflects and respects the values that we celebrate in everyday life. For I believe that the unsupervised globalisation of our financial markets did not only cross national boundaries; it crossed moral boundaries too.

You know, in our families we raise our children to work hard, to do their best, to do their bit. We don't reward them for taking irresponsible risks that would put them or others in danger. We don't encourage them to seek short-term gratification at the expense of long-term success. And in Britain's small businesses, managers and owners are the enterprising people our country depends on and we rightly celebrate. But they do not train their teams to invest recklessly or behave in an underhand way or keep their biggest gambles off the books.

Most people who have worked hard to build up their firm or shop understand responsible risk-taking but don't understand why any company would give rewards for failure or how some people have grown fabulously wealthy making failed bets with other people's money. So it is absurd for those on the extremes to blame the private sector for our problems. What we actually need is the practice of most of our private sector to be adopted by all of our private sector.

And our task today is to bring our financial markets into closer alignment with the values held by families and businesspeople across the country. Yesterday I said there were five tests for our G20 meeting, and the first of these is to clean up the global banking system.

Most people want a market that is free but never values-free, a society that is fair but not laissez-faire. And so, across the world our task is to agree global economic rules that reflect our own enduring values.

That means rules that make transparent the risks that banks take; rules that bring hedge funds and shadow banking inside the regulatory net; rules that force global banks to hold sufficient capital and ensure their liquidity; rules that require boards to understand their businesses and take responsibility for the decisions they take; and systems of pay and bonuses that reward people for long-term value and not short-term risk-taking. This is the world in which we will have trust and in which we can genuinely say again, 'My word is my bond.'

Now, let me put markets in context. They can create unrivalled widening of choices and chances – harnessing self-interest to produce results transcending self-interest. When they work, they will fulfil the promise of Adam Smith that individual gain leads to collective gain, that even when people are pursuing private interests and private wishes they can nevertheless deliver public good.

But as we are discovering to our considerable cost, the problem is that without transparent rules to guide them free markets can reduce all relationships to transactions, all motivations to self-interest; as Jonathan Sacks has said, they can reduce all sense of value to consumer choice, all sense of worth to a price tag. So, unbridled and untrammelled, they can become the enemy of the good society.

And we can now see also that markets cannot self-regulate, but they can self-destruct, and, again, if untrammelled and unbridled, they can become not just the enemy of the good society; they can become the enemy of the good economy. Markets are in the public interest but they are not synonymous with it.

And the truth is that the virtues that all of us here admire most and the virtues that make society flourish – hard work, taking responsibility, being honest, being enterprising, being fair – these are not the values that spring from the market; these are the values we bring to the market. They don't come from market forces; they come from our hearts, and they are the values nurtured in families and in schools, in our shared institutions and in our neighbourhoods.

So markets depend upon what they cannot create. They presuppose a well of values and work at their best when these values are upheld. And that is why I argued controversially some time ago, in a view that is now, I think, more generally agreed, that there are limits to markets just as there are limits to states.

Just as in the 1970s and '80s people felt government was too powerful – in the grip of vested interests that had to be channelled to work in the public interest – so, too, it is now clear that financial markets can become too powerful, come to be dominated by vested interests of their own, and so it falls to us, supporters of free markets, to save free markets from the most dogmatic of free-marketeers.

To say this is not anti-business, it is not anti-private sector, it is not anti-market. Quite the contrary – my point is that strong rules rooted in shared values are the best way to serve both ourselves and our market systems. Markets need morals.

The reason I have long been fascinated by Adam Smith, who came from my home town of Kirkcaldy, is that he recognised that the invisible hand of the market had to be accompanied by the helping hand of society – that, he argued, the flourishing of moral sentiments comes before and is the foundation of the wealth of nations.

So the challenge for our generation is now clear: whether or not we can formulate global rules for our global financial and economic systems – global rules that are grounded in our shared values.

Now that people can communicate so easily and instantaneously across borders, cultures and faiths, I believe we can be confident that across the world we are discovering that there is a shared moral sense. It is a sense strong enough to ensure the constant replenishment of that well of values upon which we depend and which must infuse the shared rules of our society.

And when people ask, 'Can there be a shared global ethic that can lie behind global rules?' I answer that through each of our heritages, traditions and faiths there runs a single powerful moral sense demanding responsibility from all and fairness to all.

Christians do not say that people should be reduced merely to what they can produce or what they can buy – that we should let the weak go under and only the strong survive. No. We say, 'Do to others what you would have them do unto you.'

And when Judaism says, 'Love your neighbour as yourself'; when Muslims say, 'No one of you is a believer unless he desires for another what he desires for himself'; when Buddhists say, 'Hurt not others in ways that you yourself find hurtful'; when Sikhs say, 'Treat others as you would be treated yourself'; and when Hindus say, 'The sum of duty is not do unto others what would cause pain if done to you', they each and all reflect a sense that we share the pain of others, we believe in something bigger than ourselves, that we cannot be truly content while others face despair, cannot be completely at ease while others live in fear and cannot be satisfied while others are in sorrow. I believe that we all feel, regardless of the source of our philosophy, the same deep sense – a moral sense – that each of us is our brother's and sister's keeper.

Call it as Adam Smith did 'the moral sentiment'. Lincoln called it 'the better angels of our nature'. Winstanley called it 'the light in man'. Call it 'duty' or simply call it 'conscience' – it means we cannot and will not pass by on the other side when people are suffering and when we have it within our power to be both responsible and to support fairness and endeavour to help.

So I believe that we have a responsibility to ensure that both markets and governments serve the public interest, to recognise that the poor are our shared responsibility and that wealth carries unique responsibilities too.

I know that there is one analysis which says that we must seize the opportunity of this crisis to reject materialism in all its forms – and crass materialism is unacceptable. But for me the answer does not lie in asking people to forswear all material things or give up on aspirations for the future but instead in remembering what our pursuit of growth and prosperity is really all about – spreading freedom, that ever more people can live the lives they choose and do so with responsibility and by being fair to others.

But it is no repudiation of wealth to say that wealth should help more than the wealthy, it is no criticism of prosperity to say that our first duty is to those without it and it is no attack on the life-long attachment I have to aspiration to say that each of us has a responsibility also to ensure no one is left behind.

I believe that today we must reaffirm these age-old truths about society – that when those with riches help those without, it enriches us all, and the truth that when the strong help the weak, it makes us all stronger.

Our meeting tomorrow is only the start and world leaders only a part. I am still humbled by the memory of one of the protestors' signs at the Make Poverty History rally I saw in Edinburgh in 2005. It said, 'You are

G8. We are 6 billion.' The campaigning groups, the faith communities, the companies, the social enterprises and trades union represented here rightly demand a lot of us as leaders in the coming days. But you, too, are part of the solution, and I believe that religious leaders, business leaders and leaders of the financial sector, charities and trades union, teachers at our schools and universities must begin a conversation – a national debate as serious as anything I have entered into in my lifetime – about the shape of the economy and the society we have now to renew.

Let me conclude – the battle the leaders of the G20 are fighting is not the old one against old enemies, but it is a new one against global recession, against climate chaos, unemployment, insecurity, poverty and hopelessness. And leaders meeting in London must supply the oxygen of confidence to today's global economy to give people in all our countries renewed hope for the future.

Our first test, as I said, is that we must clean·up the banking system, curb the use of tax havens and introduce principles for pay and bonuses, so instead of banks serving themselves, they serve the people.

Our second test is that we must take the action necessary to prevent any suffering, as we have seen in the past, of mass long-term unemployment, and we must create and save more than 20 million jobs.

Third, by international economic cooperation we must reshape the global financial system for new times, so that with early warnings and proper precautions we can prevent crises like this happening again.

Fourth, we must avoid the mistakes of the 1930s and not descend into protectionism and isolationism.

Fifth, we must press ahead with the low-carbon revolution. And we must never, ever, forget our obligations to the poor.

Just yesterday I received a letter from Pope Benedict, reminding the G20 that positive faith in the human person and, above all, as he said, 'faith in the poorest men and women of Africa and other regions of the world affected by extreme poverty' is what is needed if we are going to get through the crisis.

I can confirm today that, even while others may use this financial crisis as an excuse to retreat from their promises to the poorest, nothing will divert the United Kingdom from keeping to our commitments to the Millennium Development Goals and to our promises of development and aid.

So today I think I speak for all the leaders of the G20 when I say the duty of leadership is to identify, to name and then help shape the changes of this new global age in the interests of all people. And so we completely reject the idea that the only thing we can do in the face of a recession is to let it run its course and do nothing, as if the economy operated according to iron laws and the only role of men and women is to live by these laws and what these laws dictate. This is to demean our humanity, because there are always options, always choices, always solutions that human ingenuity can summon.

A few years ago, when economists were pressing the most dogmatic of free-market policies on some of the poorest countries in the world they argued for it by saying 'TINA' – There Is No Alternative. But African people came up with shorthand of their own, not 'TINA' but 'THEMBA' – short for There Must Be An Alternative. In that cry, THEMBA, we hear everything that must guide us today, because while it was an acronym, it was also the Zulu word for the most important thing that humans can have – hope.

Themba – the confidence, conviction and certainty that where there are problems there are always solutions and we do not need to accept the defeatism of doing nothing. It is the conviction that, through pursuing cooperation and internationalism, we need never return to the isolationism and protectionism of the past. It is the certainty that there is always an alternative to fear of the future and what conquers fear of the future is our faith in the future – faith in who we are and what we believe, in what we are today and what we can become; faith, most of all, in what together we can achieve.

So, we are not here to serve the market; it is here to serve every one of our communities. Governed by rules which reflect our morality, it is our best hope of a better world. Let us imagine that world together. Let us fight for it together, and then, with faith in the future, let us build it together, for the world we build tomorrow will be born in the hopes we share and agree upon today.

6

The Global Economic Crisis

Introduction by Alan Greenspan

Gordon Brown was an exemplary steward of the economy of the United Kingdom for over ten years and, indeed, throughout that period was without peer among the world's economic policy makers.

Since he became Prime Minister of the United Kingdom, he has had to face what will surely be remembered as one of the most dramatic and lethal economic downturns in history. The economic crisis swept round the globe in a matter of weeks and had to be dealt with promptly, firmly and decisively. History may well judge that the right man was in the right place at the right time.

The disastrous response to the economic crisis of the early 1930s led to a cycle of self-defeating protectionism that brought the global economic system to its knees. Gordon Brown has always recognised that modern economies, to thrive and prosper, must participate in a global market that, to function, must be competitive and flexible. There is no international sovereign that can oversee such a vast enterprise. Only nations recognising their own self-interest, in cooperation, can provide that oversight.

In my experience, I know of very few world leaders whose grasp of global economic affairs equips them to lead national policy makers. Gordon Brown stands almost alone in having that capability.

The global economic crisis emerged with incredible speed in the summer of 2008, as if from nowhere, and had to be dealt with promptly, firmly and decisively. The Prime Minister recognised quickly that it would require action on a global scale if we were going to deal successfully with the problems facing the world economy and that, in addition to restoring growth and jobs, action would also be required to rebuild confidence and trust in our financial system, to establish liquidity and then to secure an ongoing supply of credit.

Because this was an all-encompassing issue with almost daily events and decisions to take, there are few set-piece speeches focusing specifically on this issue. At the same time, the impact of the global economic crisis and a description of the actions being taken by the government to protect jobs, homes and public services appear in most speeches made in this period, in some form or other.

The speech selected for this section is the address given by the Prime Minister at the conclusion of the G20 meeting in London in April 2009, summarising succinctly the historic and comprehensive agreement reached at that event. As the Prime Minister says, a few years ago meetings such as this simply could not have happened, far less could there have been an agreement hammered out amongst the countries represented. And the precedents were not encouraging. As he says, 'When the Wall Street Crash happened in 1929, it took 15 years for the world to come together to rebuild and renew our economies.'

But this time, largely due to the Prime Minister's leadership and determination to get an agreement, it was different, and in London in April 2009 there was a historic agreement. As Gordon Brown says, 'This is the day that the world came together to fight back against the global recession not with words but with a plan for global recovery and for reform and with a clear timetable for its delivery.' Although there are 'no quick fixes', for the first time 'we have a common approach around the world to cleaning up banks' balance sheets and restoring lending. We are engaging in a deep process of reform and restructuring of our international financial system for now and for the future, and we have maintained our commitment to help the world's poorest, and we have put more money aside for that and also for a green recovery. These are not just a single collection of actions. This is collective action – people working together at their best.'

SPEECH TO THE G20 PRESS CONFERENCE
London, 2 April 2009

This is the day that the world came together to fight back against the global recession not with words but with a plan for global recovery and for reform and with a clear timetable for its delivery. And our message today is clear and certain – we believe that in this new global age our prosperity is indivisible. We believe that global problems require global solutions. We believe that for growth to be sustained it must be shared and that trade must once again become an engine of growth.

The old Washington Consensus is over. Today we have reached a new consensus – that we take global action together to deal with the problems we face; that we will do what is necessary to restore growth and jobs; that we will take essential action to rebuild confidence and trust in our financial system and to prevent a crisis such as this ever happening again.

There are no quick fixes, but with the six pledges that we make today we can shorten the recession and we can save jobs.

First of all, for the first time we have come together to set principles to reform the global banking system. This is a comprehensive programme of measures that includes for the first time bringing the shadow banking system, including hedge funds, within the global regulatory net. We have agreed that international accounting standards will have to be set. We will regulate credit-rating agencies in order to remove their conflicts of interest. We have agreed that there will be an end to tax havens that do not transfer information on request. The banking secrecy of the past must come to an end.

The Organisation of Economic Cooperation and Development are this afternoon publishing a list of tax havens that are non-compliant and where action must immediately be taken, and we have agreed tough standards and sanctions for use against those who don't come into line in the future.

We will create a new financial stability board to ensure cooperation across frontiers, to spot risks to the economy and, together with the International Monetary Fund, provide the early-warning mechanism that this new global economy needs. We will complete the implementation of international colleges of supervisors of financial institutions, and we will implement new rules on pay and bonuses at a global level that reflect actual performance with no more rewards for failure. We want to encourage corporate responsibility in every part of the world.

Second, we will clean up the banks so that they increase lending to families and businesses, and to enable this we've agreed for the first time a common global approach to how we deal with impaired or toxic assets.

Third, we've agreed to do what it takes to restore global growth and hasten recovery. Since our last meeting in Washington, and as part of this process from Washington, G20 countries have announced and are now implementing the largest macroeconomic stimulus the world has ever seen. We are in the middle of an unprecedented fiscal expansion which will by the end of next year amount to an injection of $5 trillion into our economies, and it will save or create millions of jobs in a period where we must combat unemployment. In addition to the dramatic interest-rate cuts, our central banks have pledged to maintain expansionary policies – as we state in the communiqué, expansionary policies as long as they are needed, using the full range of options available to them.

We have also agreed today additional resources of $1 trillion that are available to the world economy through the International Monetary Fund and other institutions. This includes $250 billion from special drawing rights – the reserve currency of the IMF – drawing rights that will be issued to countries who are part of the International Monetary Fund. This is available to all IMF members. And at the same time we will treble the resources of the International Monetary Fund itself with up to an additional $500 billion.

Together these actions give us confidence that the global economy can return to trend growth even faster than the International Monetary Fund is now predicting. And we have today called on the International Monetary Fund to monitor our progress towards this objective and to report on whatever further actions may be necessary.

Fourth, alongside these extra resources we will ask the international institutions to strengthen their independent surveillance of the world economy and to promote growth and the reduction of poverty. We are agreed that the mandates of these institutions that were created in 1945 must now be reformed to make them more accountable, more representative and more effective, and this includes giving emerging markets and developing countries greater voice and greater representation. And we will also enable the heads and senior staff of these institutions to be appointed on merit.

Fifth, we are going to act decisively to kick-start international trade. Trade is the crucial driver of growth in the global economy. We are agreed to work urgently with leaders discussing, meeting and preparing for a conclusion to the Doha trade round, and this has the potential to boost the global economy substantially.

To address what is a huge shortfall in finance for trade – 90 per cent of all trade depends on this finance – we have today agreed to make available not the $100 billion which was originally called for but $250 billion of trade finance. This will be provided over the next two years through our export, credit and investment agencies and through the multilateral development banks, and this will include $50 billion through the new World Bank programme that is being established.

We will act also to make our global recovery fair and more sustainable. This time of financial crisis is no time to walk away from our commitment to the world's poorest. So, when people are suffering and yet it is within our capacity to help, we will not pass by on the other side. We remain firmly committed to meeting our Millennium Development Goals and our pledges on aid. And, to deal with this crisis for the poorest countries, we have asked the International Monetary Fund to bring forward proposals to use the proceeds of agreed sales of gold to support low-income countries. And so, in total, we have reached agreements worth $50 billion for the poorest countries alongside our support for a World Bank vulnerability fund.

In mobilising the world's economies to fight back against recession, we are resolved to seize the opportunity of our fiscal stimulus programmes, to promote low-carbon growth and to create the green jobs on which our future prosperity depends. And we have committed to building on this by working together to seek agreement on a post-2012 climate change regime at the UN conference in Copenhagen in December. And we have asked our finance ministers to complete the reforms of the regulatory system, and we will meet again as G20 leaders later this year to take stock of progress.

When the Wall Street Crash happened in 1929, it took 15 years for the world to come together to rebuild and renew our economies. This time, I think people will agree that it is different. We will not hesitate, as long as people are losing their jobs and their homes, to make what difference we can by improving their prosperity.

Today's decisions, of course, will not immediately solve the crisis, but we have begun the process by which it will be solved. A few years ago, meetings such as this could not have happened with so many different countries from diverse continents involved, far less could there have been an agreement amongst them. But today the largest countries of the world have agreed a global plan for recovery and reform. This involves the biggest interest-rate cuts in history, the biggest fiscal stimulus we have ever seen, the biggest increase in resources in the history of our international institutions, with $250 billion, more money than ever before, for trade finance as well.

For the first time, we have a common approach around the world to cleaning up banks' balance sheets and restoring lending. We are engaging in a deep process of reform and restructuring of our international financial system for now and for the future, and we have maintained our commitment to help the world's poorest, and we have put more money aside for that and also for a green recovery. These are not just a single collection of actions. This is collective action – people working together at their best.

I think a new world order is emerging and with it the foundations of a new and progressive era of international cooperation. We have resolved that from today we will together manage the process of globalisation to secure responsibility from all and fairness to all, and we've agreed that in doing so we will build a more sustainable and more open and a fairer global society.

7

THE ROAD TO COPENHAGEN

As Chancellor of the Exchequer, Gordon Brown commissioned the Stern Report, which concluded that, inter alia, failure to avoid the worst effects of climate change could lead to global GDP being up to 20 per cent lower than it otherwise would be – an economic cost greater than the losses caused by two world wars and the Great Depression. Acceptance of the report by the government laid the foundations for the substantially revised energy and climate change policies the government has pursued, particularly since 2007. With the formation of the Department of Energy and Climate Change, under Ed Miliband, momentum in this area has been maintained, with an impressive agenda including firm carbon-reduction targets, an enhanced renewables strategy, a renewed commitment to nuclear power generation and revised plans for clean coal and carbon capture in conventional power generation.

However, the main focus of attention in this area in the past two and a half years has been the planning for and deliberations at the UN Climate Change Conference held in Copenhagen in December 2009. Gordon Brown was the first world leader to commit to attending this summit, and the two speeches collected in this chapter show the Prime Minister's commitment to the cause and his vision of how the industrialised world, the developing world and the private sector should combine to create a legally binding commitment to save the planet.

By October 2009, the dividing lines on Copenhagen were beginning to become clear, and, indeed, most commentators were now predicting a lack of formal agreement at the conference. The Major Economies Forum on Energy and Climate was set up to facilitate a candid dialogue among major developed and developing economies, help generate the political leadership necessary to achieve a successful outcome at the December UN Climate Change Conference in Copenhagen and advance the exploration of concrete initiatives and joint ventures that increase the supply of clean energy while cutting greenhouse gas emissions. The Prime Minister spoke to members of the forum at their meeting in London in October 2009, in stark terms. He said that he believed agreement at Copenhagen was possible, but he was worried that the negotiators were not getting close to an agreement quickly enough.

The speech sets out the principal issues that the Prime Minister felt were necessary for any agreement at Copenhagen – binding economy-wide caps in the mid term for developed countries and nationally appropriate mitigation actions for developing ones; finance, including for adaptation, forestry, technology and capacity building; technology cooperation, including specific action plans in areas such as solar power and carbon capture and storage; and national communications and monitoring, reporting and verification. And the Prime Minister reaffirms his commitment to go to Copenhagen to work for agreement – and encourages other leaders to join him there.

FOR THE PLANET THERE IS NO PLAN B
Major Economies Forum, London, 19 October 2009

Let us be in no doubt then that this is a profound moment for our world – a time of momentous choice.

Down one path is a business-as-usual future of high carbon and low cooperation. And, yes, down this path we could see economic growth for a while, powered by traditional energy sources. But such growth would be unsustainable and soon overwhelmed by its inevitable consequences – greater energy insecurity; greater pollution and ill health; and as a result of climate-induced migration and poverty in the poorest countries, almost inevitably, greater conflict.

The other path leads to a low-carbon, high-cooperation future. A future, too, of economic growth, but growth powered by new energy sources and energy efficiency and bringing with it huge economic opportunities for developed and developing countries alike – new jobs and businesses, new technologies and exports.

This will not stop climate change. Already some change is inescapable. But we can slow climate change to a rate to which we have a chance to adapt.

And low carbon means high cooperation – cooperation over technology development and assistance; cooperation in providing finance for adaptation; and cooperation in a global carbon market which fosters efficient emissions reduction and creates investment flows to developing countries.

Taking this path will not be easy for any of us. It involves changing long-held assumptions about the nature of the economic development we will pursue, about the kind of energy we will use and how our societies and economies will be organised. We will all face formidable political constraints and challenges, and the first step – one we must take here in this forum – is to acknowledge all this and resolve that the barriers shall be overcome.

But the signs of momentum, of forward movement, are now unmistakeable. It was at the Bali conference two years ago that the international community agreed to secure the new agreement in Copenhagen this year. And at the G20 in April, at the Major Economies Forum in July and at the Secretary General's summit at the UN last month world leaders reaffirmed their determination to meet this timetable.

In just the last few weeks new commitments and announcements have spurred new progress – including the target announced by the new government of Prime Minister Hatoyama in Japan to cut emissions by 25 per cent on 1990-levels by 2020; President Hu's speech to the United Nations; and President Yudhoyono's announcement that Indonesia would seek to reduce emissions by 26 per cent on business-as-usual by 2020. I welcome these developments, which build on commitments already announced by many countries represented at this meeting and beyond it. And I believe that in many other nations, too, momentum is building towards further announcements before Copenhagen.

So I believe agreement at Copenhagen is possible. But we must, frankly, face the plain fact that our negotiators are not getting to agreement quickly enough. Before Copenhagen there is just one more negotiating week – in Barcelona.

So I believe that leaders must engage directly to break the impasse. We cannot compromise with the earth. We cannot compromise with the catastrophe of unchecked climate change, so we must compromise with one another.

I urge my fellow leaders to work together to reach agreement amongst us, recognising both our common and our differentiated responsibilities and the dire consequences of failure.

We urgently need convergence on the principal issues for any agreement – binding economy-wide caps in the mid term for developed countries and nationally appropriate mitigation actions for developing ones; finance, including for adaptation, forestry, technology and capacity building; technology cooperation, including specific action plans in areas such as solar power and carbon capture and storage; and national communications and monitoring, reporting and verification.

In particular we must make progress on finance. That requires developed countries to come forward with finance offers and developing countries to come forward with the plans and actions that such finance would support – practical commitments which both must make and keep.

As you know, I have put forward a package of proposals for how such climate finance could be organised, with a working figure of $100 billion per year in predictable public and private funding by 2020. Let us match what developed countries can raise with what developing countries can do to combat climate change.

I believe that we can do this. And I also believe that such an agreement not only must but can put the world on a trajectory to a maximum average global temperature increase of two degrees.

Lord Stern has shown that, with annual global emissions currently at 50 gigatonnes, a '2-degree' deal requires emissions to fall to around 20 gigatonnes by 2050. To get there he suggests we will need to reach 44 gigatonnes by 2020 and 35 by 2030.

Already countries are undertaking actions or have put forward offers which would reduce emissions to 48–49 gigatonnes in 2020. So we are looking for a further 4–5 gigatonnes. And I am convinced we can achieve this through a combination of efforts in developed countries, in developing countries and in global reduction in aviation and maritime emissions.

So, over the remaining seven weeks to Copenhagen and in the two weeks of the conference itself I will work tirelessly with my fellow leaders to negotiate a deal. I have said I will go to Copenhagen to conclude it, and I am encouraging them to make the same commitment.

I ask you, as our representatives, to devote this meeting not to parsing disagreements but to pursuing the common interests and global imperatives that are the only path to agreement and the only sure way to make the world safe for human survival.

For this is a test of our ability to work together as nations facing common challenges in the new global era. We have shown this year, in our approach to the global economic crisis, how cooperation from all can benefit each. Now we must apply the same resolve and urgency to the climate crisis also facing us.

We cannot afford to fail. If we act now, if we act together, if we act with vision and resolve success at Copenhagen is still within our reach. But if we falter, the earth itself will be at risk. And for the planet there is no Plan B. In the words of a former President: 'If not us, who? If not now, when? If not together, how?'

So this is the moment. Now is the time. And we must be the people who act.

In this next speech, given during the UN Climate Change Conference in Copenhagen, the Prime Minister returns to his warning that, if the conference does not reach a deal, we should all be in no doubt that once we fail to stem the growth in emissions no retrospective global arrangement can undo that damage.

The Prime Minister puts more flesh on the bones of the emerging financial package that was pursued in the run-up to the conference with European and G20 leaders. Under this, developed countries commit to immediate finance for developing countries and the world sets a goal of $100 billion a year to come from public and private sources, including from innovative financing mechanisms, 'to address the gaping sorrows of left-out millions in Africa, to address our island states, to address the fear gripping the planet's most vulnerable communities and to address the urgent need that we must build, not destroy, the precious forests of our world'.

And he concludes on this point: 'people rightly say to us, if we can provide the finance to save the banks from our bankers, we can, with the right financial support, save the planet from those forces that would destroy it'.

Although the Copenhagen Conference was widely reported as having failed, the accord reached by the main players had many of the elements required for an effective working agreement, and it may well turn out to have been the turning point in this hugely important policy.

SPEECH TO THE UN CLIMATE CHANGE CONFERENCE
Copenhagen, 17 December 2009

I come to this, the largest ever global conference, facing the greatest global challenge of our time, to appeal to you to summon up the highest level of ambition and will. The success of our endeavours depends upon us forging a new alliance not one bloc against another, not north against south, not rich against poor but the first global alliance of 192 countries – a new alliance for the preservation of our planet.

Scientific truths know no boundaries of ideology or politics, and I believe that no one can honestly deny that, without common action, rising sea levels could wipe whole nations from the map. And without common action, extreme temperatures will create a new generation of poor, with climate change refugees driven from their homes by drought, climate change evacuees fleeing the threat of drowning, the climate change hungry desperate for lack of food.

Hurricanes, floods, typhoons and droughts that were once all regarded as the acts of an invisible god are now revealed to be also the visible acts of man. And I say to this conference: informed by science, inspired by common purpose, moved by conscience, the leaders of this fragile world must affirm that every country and every continent will now build their future not at the expense of other countries' futures but in support of our common future.

And we will not condemn millions to injustice without remedy, to sorrow without hope, to deprivation without end. The task of politics is to overcome obstacles even when people say they are too formidable. And the task of statesmanship is to make the essential possible, to make ideals real even when critics tell you they are impractical and unachievable.

And my talks this week convince me that, while the challenges we face are difficult and testing, there is no insuperable barrier of finance, no inevitable deficit of political will, no insurmountable wall of division that need prevent us from rising to the much-needed common purpose and, on the following plan, reaching agreement now – a long-term goal of a global temperature increase by 2050 of no more than two degrees.

On the way to an emissions cut of at least 80 per cent by 2050 all developed countries move to their highest possible level of ambition by 2020.

In recognition of their common but differentiated responsibilities, developing countries commit to nationally appropriate mitigation actions at their highest possible level of ambition, achieving a significant reduction from business-as-usual and standing behind their actions as developed countries must stand behind their emissions cuts.

To make this possible, developed countries commit to immediate finance for developing countries, starting from January 2010, of $10 billion annually in 2010, 2011 and 2012.

And, for long-term finance by 2020, the goal of $100 billion a year – to come from public and private sources, including international and national budgets, with a process to agree how such sums can be raised, including from innovative financing mechanisms, and with fair and effective financial arrangements – to address the gaping sorrows of left-out millions in Africa, to address our island states, to address the fear gripping the planet's most vulnerable communities and to address the urgent need that we must build, not destroy, the precious forests of our world.

We must commit, therefore, to additionality in our support so that we do not ever force a choice between meeting the needs of the planet and meeting our Millennium Development Goals. For people rightly say to us: if we can provide the finance to save the banks from our bankers, we can, with the right financial support, save the planet from those forces that would destroy it.

A commitment also to turn the agreement into a legally binding instrument within six months to a year – as we build on the Kyoto Protocol – with transparency in accounting for both developed and developing countries, including international discussion and without diminishing national sovereignty.

Friends, I do not ask my country or your country to suspend its national interest but to advance it more intelligently, for nothing matters to any nation's interest more than the fate of the one world we have.

To the developed world, I say also: environmental action is the most powerful engine of job creation in an economy urgently in need of millions of jobs.

To the developing world, I say: the technology now exists to gain the dividends of a high-growth economy without incurring the damage of a high-carbon economy.

And to all nations, I say: it is not enough to do the least we can get away with when history asks that we demand the most of ourselves. As one of the greatest of world leaders warned at a different time of peril, 'It is no use saying "We are doing our best." You have got to succeed in doing what is necessary.'

So let us demonstrate a strength of resolve equal to the greatness of our cause. Let us prove today and tomorrow the enduring truth that is more telling than any passing setback – that what we can achieve together is far greater than whatever we can achieve unilaterally and alone. In these few days in Copenhagen, which will be blessed or blamed for generations to come, we cannot permit the politics of narrow self-interest to prevent a policy for human survival, because, for all of us and for all our children, there is no greater national interest than the common future of this planet.

8

The Middle East

Introduction by Shimon Peres

'My family arrived in Israel when it was still under British mandate. In our pockets were British–Palestinian passports, in our hearts the Balfour Declaration. The State of Israel began to take shape as Great Britain, under the leadership of Winston Churchill, saved the world from the Nazi threat. It was a time when many countries closed their gates to Holocaust survivors. The nascent Jewish state was alarmed. The urgency of building a Jewish state with open gates to absorb the displaced was crucial.

'Under the leadership of David Ben-Gurion, it became our top priority – an entire nation's calling. The words of the great poet Isaac Rosenberg, killed by the last shrapnel on the last day of the First World War, convey the spirit of the time:

> They see with living eyes
> How long they have been dead.

'When discussing Israeli–British relations, we must always look to history. It affected our past; it may guide our future. The British people were early to adopt the Bible, to explore it, teach it to their children. Biblical values were integrated into their lives and prayers. They served as a moral compass. The Ten Commandments resonate in the Magna Carta: "To no one shall we sell, to none deny or delay, right or justice."

'Israel would not have a vibrant democracy if it hadn't been for the British legacy. The way in which Great Britain ran the Mandate, and its courageous fight against the Nazis, inspired the state of Israel. David Ben-Gurion, my mentor, was in London during the Blitz. He was in awe of the unforgettable sight of fathers and mothers, the elderly and infants, remaining fearless under the rain of the V-2 rockets. He wrote home: "One can say that if England, with all its humanity, were to survive the Nazi disaster, it would be due to the rule of democracy and freedom that has taken root."

'The United Kingdom proved that no missile can destroy freedom. Our relationship was mostly illuminated, though shadows were cast from time to time, like the White Paper of '38. The great light of the Balfour Declaration will never be dimmed.

'We shall remember the many British leaders who stood by Israel even in hard times. As Churchill told the Parliament during a debate about the Jewish National Home in Israel: "You have no right to support public declarations made in the name of your country in the crisis and heat of war and then afterwards, when all is cold and prosaic, to turn around."

'This was the voice of Great Britain – a bastion of reason throughout human history.'

Address to Joint Houses of Parliament, 20 November 2008

Gordon Brown is the first British prime minister to have addressed the Knesset, and at the beginning of this speech he explains his long interest in Israel – his father was a minister of the Church of Scotland who learned Hebrew and was for three decades a member of the Church's Israel Committee, travelling back and forth to Israel at least twice every year and taking cine-film records to show his family on his return!

In the early part of this fine speech, the Prime Minister says that he will tell his children the story that for two thousand years, until 1948, the persistent call of the Jewish people was 'Next year in Jerusalem'. And he goes on, 'Yet, for two thousand years, nothing – no prison cell, no forced migration, no violence, no massacres, not even the horror of the Holocaust – could ever break the spirit of a people yearning to be free. And you proved that while repression can subjugate, it can never silence; while hearts can be broken, hope is unbreakable; while lives can be lost, the dream could never die.'

Gordon Brown also mentions the support given by the government to the Holocaust Education Trust and its highly effective scheme under which every year two teenagers from each secondary school in Britain travel to Auschwitz. When they return home they share their experiences, and he recounts hearing one such visitor use the experience gained on the trip to argue to fellow pupils that discrimination, persecution, anti-Semitism and racism should be banished for ever.

After describing himself as 'a constant friend of Israel', the Prime Minister says he wants 'to offer the comfort of my support and the support of the British government and also my honest analysis.

'I believe that a historic, hard-won and lasting peace that can bring security on the ground is within your grasp; that the Palestinian Authority – under the courageous leadership of President Abbas and Prime Minister Fayyad – offers Israel the best partner of a generation; that these men share with you a vision of peace and reconciliation and that they understand that they can never achieve their goals for the Palestinian people at the expense of Israel's security.' And he confirms that 'to ensure this historic, hard-won peace is lasting, Britain is also ready to lead the way in supporting an economic road map for peace. Not money for guns but money for jobs, for businesses, for small firms, for housing and for prosperity – to underpin the political road map for peace and give all people in the region an economic stake in the future. As we did in Northern Ireland – to make the cost of returning to violence too high and too unacceptable a price to pay.'

SPEECH TO THE KNESSET
Jerusalem, 21 July 2008

To be able to come here at the invitation of your Speaker and of your Prime Minister Olmert – and to applaud you and the citizens of Israel for the courage you have shown in the face of adversity, resolution in the face of conflict, resilience in the face of challenge – is, for me, a singular honour indeed.

Every day you meet in this Knesset you live out the hopes, the promises, of centuries.

And I am especially pleased, as the first British prime minister to address the Knesset, to congratulate you at this 60th anniversary on the achievement of 1948. The centuries of exile ended, the age-long dream realised, the ancient promise redeemed – the promise that, even amidst suffering, you will find your way home to the fields and shorelines where your ancestors walked.

And your 60-year journey from independence is evidence for all to see that good can come out of the worst of times and that the human spirit is indeed indomitable.

And let me tell the people of Israel today – Britain is your true friend, a friend in difficult times as well as in good times; a friend who will stand beside you whenever your peace, your stability and your existence are under threat; a friend who shares an unbreakable partnership based on shared values of liberty, democracy and justice. And to those who mistakenly and outrageously call for the end of Israel let the message be – Britain will always stand firmly by Israel's side.

My home town – where I grew up not long after your independence in

1948 – is the small industrial town of Kirkcaldy, on the eastern coast of Scotland. Kirkcaldy is two thousand miles from Jerusalem, but for me they are closely linked. Not in their landscapes, and certainly not their weather, but in the profound impact of your early statehood years on my childhood.

My father was a minister of the Church who learned Hebrew and had a deep and lifelong affection for Israel. For three decades he was a member of, and again and again chairman of, the Church of Scotland's Israel Committee. And he travelled back and forth to Israel twice every year, often more.

After each trip he would roll out the old film projector, plug it in and load the film. More often than not the projector would break down, but he would always get it back up and running. And I will never forget those early images of your home in my home and the stories my father would tell.

So, as I learned to listen and to read, I followed the fortunes of an age-old people in your new country. And there was never a time as I was growing up that I did not hear about, read about or was not surrounded by stories of the struggles, sacrifices, tribulations and triumphs as the Israeli people built their new state. And I am proud to say that for the whole of my life I have counted myself a friend of Israel.

My sons are still young children; they are just two and four. They have not yet made that journey to Jerusalem made by their grandfather and then his son. But one day soon I look forward to bringing them here to see what their grandfather first came to see in the early years of statehood.

I will walk with them here and tell them the story that for two thousand years, until 1948, the persistent call of the Jewish people was, 'Next year in Jerusalem'. Yet for two thousand years there was not one piece of land anywhere in all the world that you could call your own. For two thousand years, not one piece of land of your own to follow your faith without fear.

For two thousand years you had history but not a home. For two thousand years you lifted the artistic and cultural life and the scientific and political development of every continent but had no home. For two thousand years you endured pogroms, and then the horror of the Holocaust, because you had no home.

Yet for two thousand years nothing – no prison cell, no forced migration, no violence, no massacres, not even the horror of the Holocaust – could ever break the spirit of a people yearning to be free. And you proved that while repression can subjugate, it can never silence; while hearts can be broken, hope is unbreakable; while lives can be lost, the dream could never die; that, in the words of the prophet Amos, justice would 'roll down like a river and righteousness like an ever-flowing stream'.

Never free of trouble, always facing adversity, yet what remarkable success Israel has achieved during these last few years. You have created modern Hebrew as the language of your daily life. Eight of your citizens have been awarded Nobel Prizes and, alongside Silicon Valley, you now have 'Silicon Wadi'. You have world famous hospitals, like Hadassah, and leading centres of learning and research, like the Weizmann Institute of Science. With 8 per cent of your national income spent on education, you have one of the highest-skilled populations on earth. From draining the swamps in the twentieth century to pioneering electric cars in the twenty-first, your history of ingenuity is a lesson in the boundless capacity of mind and spirit.

No nation has achieved so much in so short a period of time. And to have accomplished all this in the face of the war, the terror, the violence, the threats, the intimidation and the insecurity is truly monumental.

To paraphrase what one poet once said, you were born against the odds, you survived against the odds, you grew against the odds, you have prevailed and flourished against all odds, you have proved that men and women of idealism, bravery and perseverance can succeed whatever the odds.

And I am proud that the British Jewish community and the British people have had a distinguished place and a part in your great endeavour. And today our partnership is strong and getting stronger.

From pharmaceuticals to telecommunications to electrical equipment, we are agreeing new cooperative ventures. The best minds in our two countries are working together in academia and the arts, in sport and music, in science and technology, and Prime Minister Olmert and I were able to announce yesterday path-breaking academic and cultural partnerships. And I want to make clear that the British government will stand full-square against any boycotts of Israel or Israeli academics and their institutions.

Yesterday my wife, Sarah, and I visited Yad Vashem. And even though I was familiar with the harsh and horrific facts – even though I have studied, indeed written about, the fight against the Holocaust and Jewish persecution by Dietrich Bonhoeffer; described the rescue of Jews by men like Raul Wallenberg; spoken about help given to Jews facing the death march by a young Scots prisoner of war, Tommy Noble; given lectures on women who came to the aid of Jewish girls, like Jane Haining; and visited the old Yad Vashem and, indeed, the memorials in Washington and Berlin – I can tell you that nothing fully prepared me for what I saw at Yad Vashem: the full truth of the murders that no one prevented, the indignities that should have never happened, the truth which everyone who loves humanity needs to know.

The last of those who outlasted the Holocaust are now growing old. And this year Israel lost a distinguished member of this Knesset – Tommy Lapid. No one who heard Tommy talk about his bar mitzvah in a Budapest cellar at the end of 1944 – as the fascists hunted and murdered the Jewish population – will ever forget his passion for history's truth. As he said, 'My whole life is a response to the Holocaust.'

And, as the survivors leave us, let me tell you how vital it is that in every continent the next generation learn their story. That is why in Britain we fund the Holocaust Education Trust, so that each year and every year two teenagers from every secondary school travel to Auschwitz. And when they return home they share their experiences – raw and direct and powerful. I have seen the profound effect their message has on their classmates – that discrimination, persecution, anti-Semitism and racism should be banished for ever.

And I can tell you that when young children in my home town of Kirkcaldy returned from Auschwitz they organised a memorial week in honour of those who had died in the Holocaust and raised funds to erect a lasting memorial in our town's gardens – 2,000 miles away in distance but a link between my home and your home, so close that it will never be broken.

And why? Because in the words of a rabbi who having done a great deal for Holocaust education was asked why, when he himself wasn't a survivor, he said, 'But I am a survivor – we all are, not just all Jews, but all of humanity.'

You are the children of the sacrifices of your parents and grandparents. And today, and in the future, the people of Britain and Israel will continue to stand together in believing that history sides with those who fight for liberty. And if the great conflict of ideas of the twenty-first century is between those who believe in closed societies, who would turn back the clock of progress, and those who believe in open societies, then we are together on the side of openness – moving the world forward to what Winston Churchill called the 'sunlit uplands' of prosperity, justice and democracy.

The British people see the threat your people encounter every day when they climb aboard a bus, have a cup of coffee at the café or buy a sandwich. In our homeland, 2,000 miles from your streets, we too have learned the grief when lives are lost through terror on a bus or at the airport or on a crowded underground train on the way to work.

So to those who question Israel's very right to exist and threaten the lives of its citizens through terror we say: the people of Israel have a right to live here, to live freely and to live in security.

To those who are enemies of progress we say: we condemn anti-Semitism and persecution in all its forms.

And to those who believe that threatening statements fall upon indifferent ears we say in one voice that it is totally abhorrent for the President of Iran to call for Israel to be wiped from the map of the world.

And I promise that, just as we have led the work on three mandatory sanctions resolutions of the UN, the UK will continue to lead, with the US and our EU partners, in our determination to prevent an Iranian nuclear weapons programme. The EU has gone beyond each of these resolutions. Last month we took action against an Iranian bank involved in proliferation. We stand ready to lead in taking firmer sanctions and ask the whole international community to join us. Iran has a clear choice to make – suspend its nuclear programme and accept our offer of negotiations or face growing isolation and the collective response not of one nation but of many nations.

And we will do more than oppose what is wrong. We will show those who would give licence to terror the way home to what is right, too – showing them that the path to a better future runs not through violence, not by murder and never with the killing of civilians but by liberty's torch, through justice's mighty stream and across tolerance's foundation of equality.

And to build that peace, stability and prosperity, and to work as one world to eradicate the worst evils of poverty, environmental degradation, disease and instability, I believe that we should work together to summon up the best instincts and efforts of humanity in a cooperative endeavour to build new international rules and institutions for the new global era – a renewed United Nations that can deliver stability, peacekeeping and reconstruction; a new IAEA-led international system to help non-nuclear states who renounce nuclear weapons acquire, through an enrichment bond or bank, the new sources of energy their peoples need; a new World Bank that is a bank for the environment as well as development; to bring global financial stability, a new International Monetary Fund that is an early-warning system for the world economy.

And I hope that together we can write a new chapter in history that will, for this new global age, honour our truest ideals.

But today there is one historic challenge you still have to resolve so that your 60-year journey into the future is complete – peace with your neighbours and throughout the region.

Over 60 years I believe that you have shown the greatest of ingenuity in solving the greatest of problems. I think of David Ben-Gurion, who, from humble beginnings in Poland, built up the Jewish National Institutions and in 1948 said it was not enough for the Jewish state simply to be Jewish, it had to be fully democratic, offering equal citizenship to all residents – a democracy not just of one people but of all your peoples. I think of Menachem Begin, who reached out to Anwar Sadat, an old adversary, and who stood by him in this Parliament when in 1977 he made his historic speech offering himself as a partner for peace. I think of Yitzhak Rabin, who, having served Israel on the battlefield from the war of independence, made peace with Jordan and who was cruelly struck down in his prime as he committed himself to the path of peace with the Palestinians.

Peace with Egypt in 1979. Peace with Jordan in 1994. Today talks with Syria under way. And now is the time to construct the last building block of peace – peace with the Palestinians.

My father taught me that loyalty is the test of a real friendship – easy to maintain when things are going well but only really tested in hard times. And as a constant friend of Israel, I want to offer the comfort of my support and the support of the British government and also my honest analysis.

I believe that a historic, hard-won and lasting peace that can bring security on the ground is within your grasp; that the Palestinian Authority, under the courageous leadership of President Abbas and Prime Minister Fayyad, offers Israel the best partner of a generation; that these men share with you a vision of peace and reconciliation and that they understand that they can never achieve their goals for the Palestinian people at the expense of Israel's security.

And I believe that a historic, hard-won but lasting peace is within your grasp, by seizing the opportunity opened up by Annapolis, now taken forward by Prime Minister Olmert and President Abbas, and built on fundamentals – a two-state solution based on 1967 borders; a democratic state of Israel, secure from attack, recognised by and at peace with all its neighbours; alongside a peaceful, democratic and territorially viable state of Palestine that accepts you as its friend and partner; with Jerusalem the capital for both and a just and agreed settlement for refugees.

So because I believe that historic, hard-won and lasting peace is within your reach, I urge you to take it by the hand. And to deliver this historic, hard-won and lasting peace, it is vital also that both sides now create the conditions for a final agreement – the Palestinians acting with persistence and perseverance against the terrorists who attack your country, Israel freezing and withdrawing from settlements. And, like many of your friends, I urge you to make these decisions.

And let me tell you today that, to ensure this historic, hard-won peace is lasting, Britain is also ready to lead the way in supporting an economic road map for peace. Not money for guns but money for jobs, for businesses, for small firms, for housing and for prosperity – to underpin the political road map for peace and give all people in the region an economic stake in the future. As we did in Northern Ireland, to make the cost of returning to violence too high and too unacceptable a price to pay. And, without compromising your needs for security, we need your help in easing the obstacles to Palestinian economic growth, including the reopening of the Chamber of Commerce in East Jerusalem. You, Israel, drawing upon your deep wells of hope and aspiration to give hope and aspiration to others.

No one people in history has more global reach and global connections for good than the Jewish people. You are truly global citizens – often the first to offer help or medical aid or engineering assistance when there is a disaster.

One hundred and six years ago Theodor Herzl – under whose portrait I am proud to stand as I speak today – set out his vision of the future in his book *Old New Land*. He said that he saw Jerusalem as the centre of a global educational, medical and scientific endeavour with, at its heart, a unique centre for all kinds of charitable and social ventures where work is done not only for Jewish land and Jewish people but for other lands and other peoples, too.

And he went on to say, 'Wherever in the world a catastrophe occurs – earthquakes, flood, famine, drought, epidemic – the stricken country telegraphs to this centre for help.'

And if the nineteenth century was the century of industrialisation and the twentieth century the century of war, the Holocaust and a world divided, then we should make the twenty-first century the century of the global community – a century where out of competing interests we find common interests; a time when, by moving from conflict to harmony, we make a reality of the vision of a global society in which we create global civic institutions that turn words of friendship into bonds of human solidarity, stronger than any divisions between us.

And how do we champion this dream when so much seems to defy it? How do we ensure that the march of progress and justice is always toward those 'sunlit uplands'? We engage those who will lead after us. We reach out to the generations to come.

Already, around a thousand young people come from Britain to Israel on volunteering programmes every year. I want hundreds more young people who do voluntary service in Britain to link up with the thousands who do voluntary service here in Israel – bringing young people together, increasing understanding and realising the potential for the greater good.

And what I want to propose today is in that spirit: a global citizenship corps – men and women from all nations coming together in a peaceful civilian force to offer help in conflict-ridden or disaster-ridden or disease-ridden homelands that need reconstruction, development and stability.

Britain will contribute 1,000 experts and professionals to this global corps. And in this way we will be able to ensure that where homelands suffer from strife, conflict or natural disasters there will be people ready to serve a neighbour or even a stranger in need of help and hope.

So some day in the not too distant future another boy will watch his father prepare to show pictures of his travels. This time they will be on a digital camera, not an old projector. But I hope the pictures of a distant land, and of people working to build something worthy and proud, will inspire another young person to feel a deep and abiding friendship with Israel – this most promised of lands.

And when, in these next 60 years, my sons follow in the steps that their grandfather and their father have taken, I also hope they will be able to see neighbours once enemies now friends. Then 'Next year in Jerusalem' will mean not only 'home at last' but 'free from war at last', the greatest victory of all achieved – the victory of peace. And not only peace secured but prosperity achieved so that, in the words of the prophet Isaiah, we turn swords into ploughshares so that there is never a need for swords again – the ancient dream given new life in a new age.

And the story of Israel's beginning and perseverance will speak not just to Jews but to all who believe in the victory of hope over despair, home over wandering in the desert, peace over war and the everlasting promise and power of the human spirit.

If we work hard enough, together we can achieve this. Or, in the words of Theodor Herzl, 'If you will it, it is no dream.'

9

AFGHANISTAN

This speech was given in the week before Armistice Day and just before the annual remembrance ceremony at the Cenotaph. As the Prime Minister says, at these ceremonies 'we remember the sacrifices made by generations of our armed forces who have given their lives in the service of this country. We celebrate their courage, we honour their extraordinary dedication and we remember them with pride. For the sacrifice and the great achievements of our armed forces are defining features of our nation, a testament to the strength and irrepressible spirit of a Britain always prepared to do what is necessary to protect the liberty and security of its people – a Britain that fights for its values, that stands up against the things we know are wrong.'

At the time of this important and influential speech, it was known that many members of the coalition of over 40 countries, including, most notably, the US, had been reviewing their commitments in Afghanistan. Moreover, in a tragic attack earlier that week, three British guardsmen and two military policemen had been killed while mentoring local Afghan police servicemen – an incident which brought the death toll in Afghanistan to ninety-three, with over one hundred injured.

At the start of the speech, the Prime Minister reminds people that 'In the last decade, in hundreds of attacks across the world, al-Qaeda and those associated or inspired by them have killed thousands. These victims of terrorism were Muslim, Christian, Jewish, of every faith and none. This is a reality all the world has witnessed in New York, Bali, Baghdad, Madrid, Mumbai, Rawalpindi and, of course, right here on the streets of London.

'So when people ask why we are in Afghanistan – why are over 40 countries there with troops on the ground? – I ask them to look at this list of terrible atrocities, and I ask them to remember that in Britain alone since 2001 more than 200 people have been convicted of planning terrorist plots – plots that were prevented by the vigilance of our security forces. We all face the same threat; we all agree on the need to take action to meet that threat. We must all agree on the strategy to meet it and the resources necessary to carry out that strategy.'

The Prime Minister explains that the starting point for the strategy is that the main terrorist threat facing Britain emanates from the mountains of Pakistan and Afghanistan, so it is right that our first line of defence is there. In Pakistan, our role is to support the Pakistan army. In Afghanistan, our role is necessarily different, as the Afghan army is not yet able to mount the same kind of offensive as the Pakistan army. Gordon Brown goes on to explain that 'Our forces are, by necessity, playing a front-line role, but our objective is the same – if the Taliban insurgency succeeds in Afghanistan, al-Qaeda will once again cross the border and re-establish themselves in sanctuaries in Afghanistan from where they will plan, train and launch attacks on the rest of the world. This is what our security services report to me, and this is the basis for our assessment that our presence in Afghanistan is justified and that our strategy, that we set out in detail in the spring, is the right one for the future. Our strategy emphasises the need to strengthen the legitimate authorities in both Afghanistan and Pakistan and recognises that we cannot succeed in one country without succeeding in the other.'

And the Prime Minister also raises the question of timing: 'What people here in Britain ask for is the same as our forces on the ground ask for – it's a clear sense of what success in Afghanistan would look like and how we will get there. My answer is this: we will have succeeded when our troops are coming home because the Afghans are providing security themselves – continuing the essential work that we have started of denying the territory of Afghanistan as a base for terrorists.

'The right strategy – for Britain and for the international community as a whole – is the one that enables the Afghans to take over from international forces sooner, at a higher level of capability and with a greater level of assurance, so that the pressure on al-Qaeda and other terrorist groups will be maintained – so that a safer, more stable and better-governed Afghanistan will contribute to a safer Britain and a safer world.'

SPEECH TO THE ROYAL COLLEGE OF DEFENCE STUDIES
London, 6 November 2009

This weekend, as we do each year, we remember the sacrifices made by generations of our armed forces who have given their lives in the service of this country. We celebrate their courage, we honour their extraordinary dedication and we remember them with pride. For the sacrifice and the great achievements of our armed forces are defining features of our nation: a testament to the strength and irrepressible spirit of a Britain always prepared to do what is necessary to protect the liberty and security of its people – a Britain that fights for its values, that stands up against the things we know are wrong.

And this is not just an essential part of British history. It is at the heart of modern Britain and epitomised today by the immense service and sacrifice of our armed forces engaged in operations across the world and especially – as I have seen myself on each of my visits – in Afghanistan today. So, as this weekend we rightly remember and honour many generations of British servicemen and women, I want to pay a personal tribute to all those who have been killed or wounded serving in Afghanistan.

As a nation we share the sorrow and we share the grief that comes from the loss of their lives. Ninety-three men have been killed this year, and that ninety-three is not just a number – ninety-three families whose lives will never be the same again; ninety-three families without a dad or a husband, a brother or son; ninety-three families this Christmas with a place at their table no one else will ever be able to fill. More than 100 have been seriously wounded this year in Afghanistan and wounded in ways that will change their lives, and the lives of their families, for ever.

In the tragic attacks earlier this week, three guardsmen and two military policemen were killed carrying out work which is so vital to our strategy – the work that is so feared by our enemies: the work of being alongside the Afghan army and police, training and mentoring them so that the Afghan security forces fighting against the Taliban can be strengthened and so that one day they will be able to take responsibility for the security of their own country.

These men are our heroes today. Our nation will pay tribute to their memory this Sunday and every Remembrance Sunday, and, though we owe them a debt of gratitude we can never repay, we will remember them. And just as in the past we learned of the bravery and sacrifice of British soldiers in the First and Second World Wars in their fight to protect freedom both in our nation and the world, so our children will learn of the heroism of today's men and women fighting in Afghanistan, protecting our nation and the rest of the world from the threat of global terrorism. Fighting there so that we are safer at home. Joined by countries from all over the world so that terrorism can be combated – a campaign of 43 countries prosecuted out of necessity, not of choice.

In the last decade in hundreds of attacks across the world, al-Qaeda and those associated or inspired by them have killed thousands. These victims of terrorism were Muslim, Christian, Jewish, of every faith and none. This is a reality all the world has witnessed in New York, Bali, Baghdad, Madrid, Mumbai, Rawalpindi and, of course, right here on the streets of London.

So when people ask why we are in Afghanistan – why are over 40 countries there with troops on the ground? – I ask them to look at this list of terrible atrocities, and I ask them to remember that in Britain alone since 2001 more than 200 people have been convicted of planning terrorist plots – plots that were prevented by the vigilance of our security forces. We all face the same threat; we all agree on the need to take action to meet that threat. We must all agree on the strategy to meet it and the resources necessary to carry out that strategy.

Britain has consistently shouldered its fair share of this burden and more, especially in the last three years since we deployed into Southern Afghanistan – the heartland of the Taliban. But when the main terrorist threat facing Britain emanates from Afghanistan and Pakistan; when, although the sustained pressure in Pakistan, combined with military action in Afghanistan, is having a suppressive effect on al-Qaeda; when we know that they continue to train and plot attacks on Britain from the region, our mission must not fail. It is not easy; the choices are not simple. There is no strategy that is without danger and risk. But that is the responsibility of leadership, of government and of our armed forces – to do what is necessary, however difficult, to keep the British people safe. We cannot, must not and will not walk away.

Investment, of course, in our borders and our domestic counterterrorism capability is vital, but, when three-quarters of terrorist plots originate in the Pakistan–Afghan border regions, investment at home of itself cannot insulate us entirely from the new terrorist threat we face. Only by tackling this threat at source can we prevent it reaching our shores, and it is the combined effort of our armed forces, police, security services, border agency and other agencies both at home and abroad which are our best protection against further attack.

So I reject any suggestions that our efforts to tackle the terrorist threat abroad have distracted us from mounting the strongest possible defence against the threat at home. Our investment in domestic counterterrorism has continued to increase throughout the Afghan campaign. The number of police working in counterterrorism is up from 1,700 in 2003 to over 3,000 today. Today, the security services are doubled in size, with a budget that has risen from £1 billion in 2001 to over £3 billion by next year. There is stronger protection at the border and for our crowded places, and there is an increasingly sophisticated approach to preventing radicalisation.

At present the biggest domestic threat continues to come from the mountains of Pakistan and Afghanistan, so it is right that our first line of defence is there. We have to build up the capacity, and help do so, of the Pakistani security forces, to support their efforts and the efforts of the civilian government in Pakistan in taking the fight to the terrorists and extremists. They have already taken decisive action in the Swat Valley, and Britain is supporting them with a package of aid covering humanitarian help for displaced persons. We are also supporting them with a comprehensive development and reconstruction plan.

The Pakistan military have now moved 28,000 troops into South Waziristan, and, as a reminder of the link between extremism in these mountains on the Afghan–Pakistan border and the terrorist threat to Britain, we have recently seen reports of a passport found as part of this recent offensive, allegedly belonging to an individual known to be associated with the 9/11 hijackers.

In Afghanistan our role is necessarily different. The Afghan army is not yet able to mount the kind of offensive that the Pakistan army is doing. Our forces are, by necessity, playing a front-line role, but our objective is the same – if the Taliban insurgency succeeds in Afghanistan, al-Qaeda will once again cross the border and re-establish themselves in sanctuaries in Afghanistan from where they will plan, train and launch attacks on the rest of the world. This is what our security services report to me, and this is the basis for our assessment that our presence in Afghanistan is justified and that our strategy that we set out in detail in the spring is the right one for the future. Our strategy emphasises the need to strengthen the legitimate authorities in both Afghanistan and Pakistan and recognises that we cannot succeed in one country without succeeding in the other.

The Taliban's original plan, when the American, British, Canadian, Dutch, Danish, Australian, Estonian and other countries deployed to southern and eastern Afghanistan three years ago, was to defeat us through conventional warfare. This plan of the Taliban has failed. The Taliban's hope now is that – even if they cannot win outright through asymmetric warfare – through intimidating the population and through preventing economic progress they can undermine morale and erode public support back home and persuade us to give up before the Afghan people get to see the benefits of legitimate governance or share in the benefits of greater prosperity.

So our strategy has moved from straightforward counterterrorism to more complex counter-insurgency – protecting the people, helping the government win their support and providing them with a stake in the future. And that is how our strategy in Afghanistan differs from previous foreign interventions, including the intervention of the Soviet Union, which lacked the support of the population and did not seek to empower Afghans in maintaining their own security.

So our progress is not to be measured in enemies killed or battles won, alone; it must be measured in the progress made each season – in improving the capability of the Afghans to protect themselves, in improving the quality of life of Afghan citizens, by improving the governance of Afghanistan – as we slowly but surely make it more and more difficult for the Taliban and al-Qaeda to rebuild their bases in Afghanistan and the wider region.

Tuesday's tragic loss of life happened as British troops were mentoring the Afghan army and police. The Royal Military Police and Service Inquiry Board is currently investigating in detail this event. In parallel, an investigation is being carried out jointly by ISAF and the Afghan authorities. The investigations will cover all angles of the incident, and from its findings lessons will be identified and acted upon.

The truth is, as we have always been clear, that we have not chosen the path of training and mentoring the Afghan forces because it is an easier or safer alternative – often it may be the opposite – but because it is the right strategy. The Taliban and others who seek to undermine the work our forces are doing will not divert us from that strategy. The Taliban understand that our efforts represent our commitment to leaving a lasting legacy in the ability of local security forces to resist the Taliban.

Four hundred of our armed forces are already dedicated to mentoring the Afghan army. Over 100 are dedicated to mentoring the Afghan police. They are working together with British and European specialist police trainers. But all our forces are working increasingly closely with Afghan counterparts as we move towards the approach that we call 'partnering'. I saw this partnership in action in August in the Joint Operational Coordination Centre in Lashkar Gah, bringing together the Afghan army, police and security services – all with British monitors and working well. I heard how the Afghan police are often on the front line, taking heavier casualties often than the Afghan army, and also that the challenge for their mentors here is even tougher than for the Afghan army because of the problems of illiteracy, drug abuse and corruption.

But despite these very serious challenges the Afghan police have played some role this summer, involved in holding the Babaji area in Operation Panther's Claw and in the security effort around the elections – led out of the joint operations centre I visited – which ensured that over 100 polling stations were opened and stayed open despite the Taliban threats. We will not give up this strategy of mentoring. It is what distinguishes a liberating army from an army of occupation – not an army in opposition to local Afghan people but an army supporting local Afghan people. And this approach of 'Afghanisation' that we recommended more than a year ago is now the strategy of the whole coalition. It is essential for the whole coalition to implement it across the whole of Afghanistan.

It is well known that President Obama is considering his response to General McChrystal's report. It is clear that he sees that the response must come from the international coalition as a whole. For, as we consider the nature of the threat we face, it is not just the US that is being tested in Afghanistan; nor is it just Britain – it is the whole international community. We entered together, more than forty nations, eight years ago. We must persist together; in our different ways we must all contribute. In the end we will succeed or fail together, and we will succeed.

I have made clear to President Obama that the UK will play its full part. In July I indicated that the temporary deployment of 700 troops, for the period of the presidential election, would remain beyond the elections. Last month I announced that if key conditions are met, including burden-sharing across the international community, then the UK would send an extra 500 troops. This would bring the total number of British troops to 9,500. It is proof that we will not be deterred, dissuaded or diverted from taking whatever measures are necessary to protect our security. But we will also rightly insist, every time a single soldier is deployed to Afghanistan, that we have the reassurance of the military chain of command that they have the best possible equipment; that they are there in support of a clear strategy; it is agreed across the international community; and that an Afghan government is in place which will be asked and forced to live up to its side of the bargain.

The sad news from yesterday's loss of life reminds us that, despite the tragic incident earlier in the week, the deadliest challenge still facing our forces remains that of detecting the new Taliban tactic of IEDs – mines and roadside bombs. These attacks, as many of you here know, have more than doubled over the last year. Casualties have increased across the coalition; three-quarters of coalition casualties are now due to electronic devices.

Responding to this growing threat requires not one response but many. It requires new equipment, better surveillance, specialised troops, offensive operations – not just to find and dismantle the IEDs but also to identify and target the networks who lay them. British forces have dismantled over

1,000 of these electronic devices, these explosive devices, this year, and the proportion detected compared with those that exploded has almost doubled since spring last year.

In August I announced that we would increase the surveillance assets targeted on the bomb-makers; last month these increases came on stream. I also announced, and last week the Chief of the Defence Staff confirmed, further increases in helicopters – ensuring by next spring we will have increased the number of helicopter hours, including commercially leased freight helicopters, more than threefold over the last three years.

But let us be clear – what separates successful counter-insurgency from unsuccessful counter-insurgency is that it is won on the ground and not in the air. We are committed to giving our commanders more options for road moves as well – we have bought another 20 Ridgeback mine-protected patrol vehicles to ensure that more will be going into action this autumn, joining the world-class Mastiff vehicles, and since 2006 we have spent over £1 billion from the reserves on new vehicles for Afghanistan.

All this equipment has, of course, to be manufactured, delivered, adapted and the personnel trained to operate it. It is simply wrong to question our commitment as we adapt to the new tactics of the Taliban or to doubt our willingness to pay for it. That is why we are speeding up the deployment of vital equipment but also making its delivery a condition for further troop increases. And I am determined that, while it is inevitable that conditions change and our strategy must respond, the fundamental principle must remain – that every soldier and unit deployed to Afghanistan is fully equipped for the operations they are asked to undertake.

Let me also be clear – people are right to ask whether our soldiers should be placed in harm's way if the government of Afghanistan is unable or unwilling to meet its obligations to the Afghan people. And this is the second condition I placed on any increases in British troops. In all my conversations with President Karzai – and we have already spoken on a number of occasions this week – I have said that he needs swiftly to set out his positive agenda for the second term. He needs a contract with the Afghan people – a contract against which the Afghans, as well as the international community, can judge his success. When President Karzai takes the oath of office for the second term later this month I hope he will be able to set out his plans in detail. International support depends on the scale of his ambition and the degree of his achievement in five key areas – security, governance, reconciliation, economic development and relations with his neighbours.

Now, take security and the Afghanisation of the security effort. The first priority of any government is to provide security for its people. It is not sustainable to subcontract that task indefinitely to the international community. So the expansion and training of the Afghan army and police must be the new government's first priority. We have made clear for some months that Britain accepts General McChrystal's recommendation to accelerate the expansion of the Afghan army from 90,000 to 134,000 by this time next year. To achieve this, Afghanistan has to provide up to 5,000 army recruits per month. The international community will help with funding and training, but it is the job of the Afghan government to find the recruits. I have welcomed the Afghan intention to set up an army corps headquarters in Helmand. British forces, as part of our strategy of Afghanisation, will be ready to partner 5,000 Afghan troops in Helmand – not just embedding mentors with Afghan units but working closer together right up the command chain.

Better governance is the second strand of our Afghanisation strategy. Sadly, the government of Afghanistan had become a byword for corruption. And I am not prepared to put the lives of British men and women in harm's way for a government that does not stand up against corruption. So President Karzai agreed with me yesterday that the first priority of his new government would be to take decisive action against corruption. I proposed that there should be a new anti-corruption law, that a new anti-corruption commission be formed with powers of investigation and prosecution, that the commission appoint an international adviser of standing and substance and that there be new rules for the more transparent award of contracts.

Good governance is more, of course, than the absence of corruption. It is about having properly qualified men and women in the key jobs. The world will be monitoring the new government's appointments – cabinet ministers and provincial governors – to ensure they are based on merit. Cronies and warlords should have no place in the future of a democratic Afghanistan.

Constitutional arrangements in Afghanistan were clearly severely tested by the presidential election. Malpractice was exposed, and it was dealt with. But as we approach next year's Afghan parliamentary elections, the flaws that have been exposed must be rectified. Neither we nor Afghanistan can afford a repetition of the quarantined ballot boxes from August's first round.

Nowhere is democracy a perfect system. But I firmly believe that everywhere democracy is the best option. In an infant democracy it will function imperfectly. Faltering beginnings, however, are not a reason to give up. All commentators have noted what was a setback in Afghanistan's presidential election – and I accept that – but more might acknowledge that, even up against the insurgency, millions of people did go to the polls in the first presidential election organised by Afghans themselves. A people who for so long were denied a say in their future are now beginning to take the destiny of their country into their hands.

We also need a more inclusive political settlement. We commend President Karzai for reaching out to his defeated opponent. More challenging still is to reach out to those who have been outside the political process. Reconciliation and reintegration are now central to future security, stability and prosperity. So there needs to be an agreed process for bringing those who reject violence back into the political fold. That process needs to be led by Afghans, and we are ready to provide the support to whatever process they adopt.

An ambitious but realistic plan for economic development to give the Afghan people a stake in the future is a fourth condition. As Douglas Alexander, our International Development Secretary, set out yesterday, Helmand is one of the most aid-supported places in the world. The United Kingdom is alone spending over £80 million in Helmand on development this year; it's part of the international community's wider efforts that total £200 million. That means Helmand will receive some £200 in aid per person this year – around double the Afghan average.

So just as it's wrong to say that we are not giving the fullest possible backing to our troops it is also a myth to say that our development effort is not directly supporting our military campaign. The challenge is to Afghanise that part of our strategy also – with an emphasis on identifying long-term growth areas and investing in education and skills to match them, to create economic opportunities.

Outside the cities, of course, the key to this must lie in agriculture. In the last 12 months there has been a 38 per cent reduction in the poppy harvest in Helmand. Wheat has become the crop of choice in Governor Mangal's food zone. Such changes must be entrenched in Helmand and then across the country. And at the same time President Karzai's government must deliver safe drinking water, reliable electricity, schooling for girls as well as boys and for everyone a primary health-care centre within walking distance. We can help, but only he and his government can deliver.

The final test for the Karzai government is to build stronger regional partnerships. There are welcome indications that President Zardari will come from Pakistan to attend President Karzai's inauguration, just as Karzai attended Zardari's inauguration. Relationships between the leaderships of Afghanistan and Pakistan are better than for many years. But this has yet to translate into closer cooperation between key institutions. The problems of extremism and terrorism straddle these borders and so too must the solutions.

I commend the European Council and the United Nations for the leadership they have shown. When I met Secretary Ban this week I offered our support and help in the face of the recent attacks on their staff. They have assured us that their withdrawal of some staff is a temporary measure while security arrangements are reviewed.

If we are to help the Afghan government to deliver against these five tests that we have set, stronger international coordination is crucial – as well as clearer metrics to measure progress. In devising these metrics the international community and the sovereign Afghan government must listen to what the Afghan people want. As well as being very clear that they do not want the Taliban back, what they say they want above all – as I heard myself at a shura in Lashkar Gah earlier this year – is security, justice and opportunity, which correspond to the first, second and fourth of the five tests I set out today.

Measuring security is difficult. The perceptions of the Afghan people are crucial and so are the capabilities of the Afghan security forces. This year we have conducted increasing numbers of joint operations, building their capabilities by fighting alongside them. Kabul has been handed over to Afghan overall control. Over time, other areas should follow and be handed over, province by province, to Afghan control. We are making progress, too, in training Afghans in counterterrorist and counternarcotics operations.

As I argued in September, what we need, above all, is to encourage the advance of Afghan autonomy and responsibility in all of these areas. The more Afghans can take responsibility in the short term the less international intervention will be needed in the long term. If with our help the new Afghan government meets these five tests, it will have fulfilled an essential contract with its own people. And it will have earned the continuing support of the international community, despite the continuing sacrifice. If the government fails to meet these five tests, it will have not only failed its own people, it will have forfeited its right to international support.

What people here in Britain ask for is the same as our forces on the ground ask for – it's a clear sense of what success in Afghanistan would look like and how we will get there. My answer is this – we will have succeeded when our troops are coming home because the Afghans are providing security themselves, continuing the essential work that we have started of denying the territory of Afghanistan as a base for terrorists.

The right strategy for Britain and for the international community as a whole is the one that enables the Afghans to take over from international forces sooner, at a higher level of capability and with a greater level of assurance so that the pressure on al-Qaeda and other terrorist groups will be maintained – so that a safer, more stable and better-governed Afghanistan will contribute to a safer Britain and a safer world.

10

THE MILLENNIUM DEVELOPMENT GOALS

The Lambeth Conference of Anglican Bishops takes place every ten years at the invitation of the Archbishop of Canterbury. Also invited are bishops from other churches in communion with the Anglican Communion, bishops from the United Churches and a number of ecumenical guests. In July 2008, the Prime Minister addressed the audience of 650 Anglican bishops, their spouses and representatives from other faith groups and churches in the courtyard of Lambeth Palace, following a Walk of Witness through central London, where some 1,500 faith leaders, diplomats, parliamentarians and NGO heads highlighted the urgent need for more action on tackling poverty through sustainable solutions.

This impressive speech, given without notes, builds from the Walk of Witness and is primarily focused on the lack of progress to date in achieving the UN Millennium Development Goals. For, as the Prime Minister says, 'we need a march not just on Lambeth, we need a march also to New York, to 25 September when the United Nations will meet in emergency session. It is a poverty emergency that needs an emergency session. And I ask you to go back to your countries, and I ask you to ask your governments, and I ask you to ask all of civil society to tell people that on 25 September we have got to make good the promises that have been made, redeem the pledges that have been promised, make good the Millennium Development Goals that are not being met.'

During the speech, the Prime Minister argues that we need the determination to act: 'We used to be able to say if only we had the technology, if only we had the medicines, if only we had the science, if only we had the engineering skills then we could meet the Millennium Goals. But we know that with the technology we have, the medicine we have, the science we have, it is the will to act that now must be found.'

And he ends with the hope that people will be energised by what, acting together, they have achieved: 'if people say to me that these are unrealisable goals, that we are just dreamers, that we are just idealists with illusions, let us remember that 20 years ago they said it was an impossible dream that apartheid would end, they said it was an impossible dream that Nelson Mandela would be free, they said it was an impossible dream that the cold war would be over, they said it was an impossible dream that the Berlin Wall would come down. But, because men and women of faith and religious belief fought hard for these changes, these changes happened.'

SPEECH TO THE LAMBETH CONFERENCE OF ANGLICAN BISHOPS
London, 24 July 2008

Let me say first of all that I am privileged and I am humbled to be at a conference of so many men and women for whom I have the utmost respect, the greatest admiration and the highest affection. And let me immediately thank the Archbishop of Canterbury, let me thank Cardinal O'Connor, let me thank Dr Sacks, Dr Singh, Dr Sacranie, Helen Wangusa – who have all been on the platform – and all those members of the different denominations who are here today. Let me thank you on behalf of the whole of this country for the work that you do for justice and humanity. And let me thank all men and women, bishops, archbishops, families from the 130 countries who are represented here today.

Let me tell you there are millions of people, whom you may never meet, who owe you a debt of gratitude for the work that you do in upholding the cause of the poor, and I want to thank every person from every country for what you do to remind the world of its responsibilities.

This has been one of the greatest public demonstrations of faith that this great city has ever seen, and you have sent a simple and very clear message, with rising force, that poverty can be eradicated, that poverty must be eradicated and if we can all work together for change poverty will be eradicated.

You know, it was said in ancient Rome of Cicero that when he came to speak at the Forum and crowds came to hear him, they turned to each other after he had spoken and said, 'Great speech.' But it was said of Demosthenes in ancient Athens that when he came to speak and the crowd heard him, they turned to each other and they said, 'Let's march.'

And you have marched today under the leadership of the Archbishop of Canterbury. You have marched to stand up for the ten million children in this world who, because of our failure to act collectively, will die unnecessarily of avoidable deaths from tuberculosis, from polio, from diphtheria, from malaria – all diseases we know we have it in our power to eradicate. You have marched today to speak up for the 77 million children who, tomorrow and every day until we change things, will not be able to go to school because there is no school to go to. And you have marched also, just as 50 years ago many of us marched for the Freedom From Hunger Campaign, for the 100 million people who shamefully and disgracefully today face a summer of starvation and an autumn of famine – all because we cannot yet organise and grow the food we need to meet the needs of the hungry people of this world.

And you have marched because, as Rabbi Sacks once said, 'You cannot feast while others starve, you cannot be happy while others are sad, you cannot be fully at ease while millions suffer, and as long as millions of people are in poverty, our whole society is impoverished.'

And I believe you have marched because whenever you see suffering you want to heal it, whenever you see injustice you want to rectify it, whenever you see poverty you want to bring it to an end. And has that not been the message of the churches and faith groups throughout the ages?

Two hundred years ago was it not men and women of faith and religious convictions who saw an evil and said for the first time that slavery must be brought to an end? Was it not true 100 years ago that men and women of faith and conscience came together with their religious beliefs and said democracy must replace tyranny and every single person should have the vote – a message that we send to Zimbabwe and to other countries where democracy should be flourishing today?

And 50 years ago was it not men and women of conscience and religious faith who, when they saw discrimination and prejudice and racism, said that you cannot live in a world unless every single citizen whatever their colour, their race, their background and their birth enjoys equal rights? And was it not the religious movement for change that made it possible for us to talk about a world of equal rights? And was it not you as individuals in these last ten years – was it not you in the work you did in Make Poverty History – that realised the vision of Isaiah to undo the burden of debt and let the oppressed go free so that, instead of debts being paid to bankers in rich countries, debt relief was used so that there are hospitals and schools now open in the poorest countries of the world, thanks to your activities over these last ten years?

And I want to thank you also because it is because of your efforts in Make Poverty History that there are two million people who are receiving treatment for AIDS today, where otherwise they would not be alive. In the greatest vaccination and immunisation campaign the world has ever seen, as a result of your efforts, 500 million children have been vaccinated. Three million children who would otherwise have died for lack of vaccinations are now living today. And 40 million children are now at school because you have built the schools and you have made it possible for us to employ the teachers in every continent of the world.

But we know that that is not enough, and we know we have only just begun. The Millennium Development Goals that the Archbishop has just mentioned said that by 2015 we would cut infant mortality by two-thirds and maternal mortality by three-quarters. But on present rates of progress, let us be honest, we will not achieve that change in life, not in 2015, not even in 2020 or 2030. We would not under present rates of progress achieve it until 2050, and lives are being unnecessarily lost as a result of our failure to act.

Take the Millennium Development Goal on children – our promise that every child would be in school by 2015 – and on present rates of progress we will not meet that goal in 2015 or in 2050 or even 2100, not before 2115. And take all our Millennium Development Goals to provide water and sanitation and equality and to cut poverty by half, as the slogan said today, and we will not meet that Millennium Development Goal on current rates of progress in this century or in the next.

And I say to you that the poor of the world have been patient, but 100 years is too long for people to wait for justice and that is why we must act now.

We used to be able to say if only we had the technology, if only we had the medicines, if only we had the science, if only we had the engineering skills then we could meet the Millennium Goals. But we know that with the technology we have, the medicine we have, the science we have, it is the will to act that now must be found.

And each of us has our own personal stories of what we have seen. In Kibera, in Kenya, I came out of a camp and I saw a young child who was the only person caring for a mother with AIDS and with tuberculosis, and that child was only five. And then I met in Mozambique young children of 11 and 12 who were begging me to have the chance of education. I met a young man with AIDS in a village hut in Africa who was suffering not just from AIDS but from the stigma of AIDS, and he said to me, 'Are we not all brothers?' I saw the sight of a woman leaving a hospital with a dead newborn baby in a sack.

And perhaps the story that I witnessed that influenced me most was a young girl of 12 called Miriam, and I met her in a field in Tanzania. Her mother had died from AIDS, her father had died from AIDS and she was an AIDS orphan being pushed from family to family, and she herself had

HIV and tuberculosis. And her clothes were in a mess; she was wearing rags. She had no footwear; she was barefoot. Her hair was dishevelled. But what struck me most of all was when you meet a young girl of 12 there is hope in their eyes, there is the feeling that their life is ahead of them – a family ahead, work and all the opportunities of youth. But for that young girl there was an unreachable sadness, hope all but gone. And I decided there and then that if every child is precious – as I believe they are – if, as from my own experience I know, every child is unique and every child is special and every child deserves the best chance in life then we must act as a community to change things.

So we need a march not just on Lambeth, we need a march also to New York, to 25 September when the United Nations will meet in emergency session. It is a poverty emergency that needs an emergency session. And I ask you to go back to your countries, and I ask you to ask your governments, and I ask you to ask all of civil society to tell people that on 25 September we have got to make good the promises that have been made, redeem the pledges that have been promised, make good the Millennium Development Goals that are not being met.

And I ask you to ask governments to pledge three things which I pledge on behalf of our government.

The first is, instead of 100 years of children not getting education, that by 2010 40 million more children are in schools – on the road to every child being in schooling by 2015.

And the second pledge I ask you all to ask your governments to make is, instead of ten million children dying unnecessarily a year, we invest in training four million nurses and doctors and midwives and health workers and provide the equipment so we can do what medicine allows us to do and eradicate polio, tuberculosis, malaria and diphtheria and then go on to eradicate HIV-AIDS in our generation.

And I also ask you to go back to your countries and ask your governments to pledge that, in a world where 100 million are suffering today from famine, we set aside $20 billion for food aid and not only for food aid but to give people the means – free of the old agricultural protectionism for which we should be ashamed, free of that protectionism to grow food themselves – with help from our countries to develop a green revolution in Africa. And it is only by doing this that we can ensure that all people can have the dignity of being able to grow the food they need to sustain themselves and their families and that the world that made the pledge to end poverty can finally keep the promise.

And if people say to me that these are unrealisable goals, that we are just dreamers, that we are just idealists with illusions, let us remember that 20 years ago they said it was an impossible dream that apartheid would end, they said it was an impossible dream that Nelson Mandela would be free, they said it was an impossible dream that the cold war would be over, they said it was an impossible dream that the Berlin Wall would come down. But, because men and women of faith and religious belief fought hard for these changes, these changes happened.

And so I would say to you to have confidence today. Have confidence today that – just as Mandela went free and apartheid came to an end – that while the arc of the moral universe is long, it does bend towards justice. And I would say to you have confidence that just as you managed to achieve debt relief, and just as we have managed to deal with many injustices in the past, that hope, even when trampled to the ground, will rise again and people of goodwill will continue to fight for what is right.

And I ask you finally to have confidence – have confidence that all people round the world of goodwill, people of faith, conviction and religious beliefs will ensure, in the words of Amos, that justice will flow like water and righteousness like a mighty stream, and there is nothing that we cannot do for justice. If what we do for justice is doing it in unison and together, let's work together for the transformation we know together we can achieve.

The Prime Minister begins this next speech to the United Nations with an urgent plea for countries to continue their support of the Millennium Development Goals: 'Some say this time of financial turbulence is the time to put our ambitions on hold – to cut back or postpone the dream of achieving the Millennium Development Goals – but this would be the worst time to turn back.' As he says, 'Every global problem we have requires global solutions, involving all the continents of the world. We cannot solve the food shortages that face many continents without involving Africa and developing countries. We cannot solve climate change without involving Africa and developing countries. We cannot solve the pressure on resources and energy without involving Africa and the developing countries. And Africa and the developing countries are not the problem; they are part of the very solution to today's problem.'

The Prime Minister points the finger at what he regards as the reason for the lack of action on achieving the Millennium Development Goals: 'indifference in the face of soul-destroying poverty, indifference in the face of catastrophic threats to our planet – a casual, uncaring, corrosive, pass-by-on-the-other-side, walk-by indifference'. And his solution is a four-point plan – to recruit and train a million health workers; to agree that we will stop all malaria deaths by 2015; to get 24 million more children into school by 2010 and to aim for universal education by 2015; and to invest $10 billion in Africa so it can help feed the world.

SPEECH TO THE UN EMERGENCY SESSION ON THE MILLENNIUM DEVELOPMENT GOALS
New York, 25 September 2008

I come to the richest city in this, the richest country, to declare on behalf of the poorest citizens of the poorest countries a global poverty emergency that we must now address.

Under Ban Ki-moon's leadership we gather today from the head of the African Union, President Kikwete, to the Prime Minister of China, from Bill Gates to Bono, governments, NGOs, businesses – people of all faiths and societies in a new, unique and historic coalition against poverty to unite the world in an unprecedented effort from now on to secure the Millennium Development Goals. And already this is a historic summit. Even at this time of financial difficulty, already we know that $8 billion has been pledged to reduce poverty.

Now our United Nations chapter begins – 'We, the people.' And I am humbled to stand here and speak for the thousands of our people who are dying because they are too poor to live. And throughout the ages the fate of the hungry, the homeless, the deprived and what we do to help has been the touchstone of compassion – the crucible in which our morality is tested. And we cannot stand aside. We say we are 'one world', but every three seconds we allow one child to die from extreme poverty.

Some say this time of financial turbulence is the time to put our ambitions on hold – to cut back or postpone the dream of achieving the Millennium Development Goals – but this would be the worst time to turn back.

Every global problem we have requires global solutions involving all the continents of the world. We cannot solve the food shortages that face many continents without involving Africa and developing countries. We cannot solve climate change without involving Africa and developing countries. We cannot solve the pressure on resources and energy without involving Africa and the developing countries. And Africa and the developing countries are not the problem; they are part of the very solution to today's problem.

Today, facing famine, we promised we, the United Nations of the world, will come to help, but the hungry are dying while we wait. Facing poverty, we promise that we will come to help, but the poor are dying while we wait. Facing betrayal of the Millennium Development Goals, we say again we will come, but many continue to die while we wait. And I believe our greatest enemy is not war or inequality or any single ideology or a financial crisis. It is too much indifference – indifference in the face of soul-destroying poverty, indifference in the face of catastrophic threats to our planet, a casual, uncaring, corrosive, pass-by-on-the-other-side, walk-by indifference. As Elie Wiesel said, 'To be indifferent to suffering makes the human being inhuman.'

So today, again, it is this United Nations of the world that is on trial. It is our credibility, as representatives of the global community, that is being tested. It is our commitment to one inclusive sustainable world that is under challenge. Our global leadership itself is being questioned, and let us face the shameful truth that while we have made huge advances – forty million more children at school, three million children living who would otherwise have died, three million getting treatment for AIDS – but despite all our promises, with one mother dying in childbirth every minute, the 2015 goal to cut maternal and infant mortality will not be met even in 2020 or 2030, not before 2050. And with 75 million of the world's children still without a school to go to, the goal promising every child schooling will not be met on present trends in 2015 or 2025 or even in 2100.

And I say to the richest countries of the world: the poorest of the world have been patient, but 100 years is too long to wait for justice.

So to seek to make poverty history, we need to make new history today and make it happen now. So I ask you to take today four steps. First, on health – that we recruit and train a million health workers, saving the lives of three million mothers and seven million children; second, on malaria – we agree that we will stop all malaria deaths by 2015, to ensure everyone has a bed net by 2010, to fund the research for the vaccine that can prevent the loss of life; then, on education – to get 24 million more children into school by 2010, to get us back on track to universal education by 2015; and fourth, on famine – to prevent today's starvation in the Horn of Africa, to fund and deliver seeds and fertilisers to 30 countries in time for the planting season, to invest $10 billion in Africa so it can help feed not just Africa but feed beyond Africa with its exports.

In the past 'feed the world' meant that we helped to feed Africa. In future, if we do things right, we will do best by enabling Africa to feed the world.

So let this United Nations, this leadership of the world, today rouse the conscience of the world. Let us summon global citizens to great and common purpose so that millions of men, women and children trapped in the prison of poverty can at last be set free.

II

NUCLEAR ENERGY AND PROLIFERATION

INTRODUCTION BY MOHAMED ELBARADEI

'This is such an important conference because we are witnessing a major increase in the interest of using nuclear energy due to energy security, climate change and many other considerations. With the increase in the use of nuclear energy for power generation, there will definitely be an extensive need for nuclear fuel for powering the reactors and also for assurance of supply.

'It is, in my view, an opportune time to review the whole non-proliferation regime, which we brought into force in the 1970s with the aim that we have to establish a world free from nuclear weapons. There are four clusters, in my view, that we need to work on, thirty-nine years after the treaty came into force, to ensure that at all times nuclear energy is exclusively used for peaceful purposes and that we ensure that the gaps that might exist for the misuse of that technology are plugged. The four clusters that we need to work on simultaneously are nuclear disarmament, verification, physical protection of nuclear material and multinational assurance of supply.'

It may at first sight be a surprise to find the Prime Minister making a major speech on nuclear issues a fortnight or so before the G20 meeting in London, when the international and domestic focus was on tackling the recession and saving jobs, houses and services. But, as he points out in this speech to the International Nuclear Fuel Cycle Conference in March 2009, the global financial crisis may in fact turn out to be the key to unlocking some other seemingly intractable problems – the challenges of global financial instability, global climate change, global poverty and global security.

In this groundbreaking and highly influential speech, Gordon Brown makes the point that the nuclear question is central: 'More than about security, vital as it is; more than about nuclear power and meeting the challenge of energy shortages and climate change, important as they are; it is about the values of the global society we are trying to build, and it is about the very idea of progress itself – about the foundations upon which we build our common security and a sustainable future for our planet. In short, about what kind of world we are and what kind of world we want to be.'

The main purpose of the speech is to propose an international campaign to 'enshrine the right for all nations to access civil nuclear power – safely, securely and subject to proper multilateral verification processes – with tougher sanctions brought to bear on those who break the rules'; and to publish a 'credible road map towards disarmament by all the nuclear weapons states – through measures that will command the confidence of all the non-nuclear weapons states'.

As part of this, the Prime Minister reaffirms the UK's commitment to retaining the minimum force necessary to maintain effective deterrence, while at the same time stating that if it is possible to reduce the number of UK warheads further, consistent with the progress of multilateral discussions, Britain will be ready to do so.

SPEECH TO THE INTERNATIONAL NUCLEAR FUEL CYCLE CONFERENCE
London, 17 March 2009

In just two weeks' time the eyes of the world will turn to London as the leaders of the G20 nations meet here to rebuild our global economy. At stake will be a global new deal for our economic future – with decisions that will remake the rules not just for a global economy but for a global society – and the actions that we take in the coming weeks and months will define the values of our world and the inheritance we will bequeath our children and our grandchildren.

Amid the pressures of a global economic crisis there will be those who argue that other challenges are a distraction, that the global economy is the only concern where there is an urgency to act or the opportunity to seize a historic moment. But I think that is to profoundly misunderstand the world we are in today and the one we can build for tomorrow.

For I believe that history will take a broader view and in due course tell how, in the making of a new global society and in an unprecedented time of change, we had to confront four great and interconnected challenges: the challenges of global financial instability, global climate change, global poverty and, my subject today, global security – momentous challenges but challenges best addressed together. And in this world of change, the task of leadership is to name the challenges, shape them and rise to them.

And the nuclear question is absolutely central to them. More than about security, vital as it is; more than about nuclear power and meeting the challenge of energy shortages and climate change, important as they are; it is about the values of the global society we are trying to build, and it is about the very idea of progress itself – about the foundations upon which we build our common security and a sustainable future for our planet. In short, about what kind of world we are and what kind of world we want to be.

Taxing as these issues are, I am an optimist with faith in the future. For I believe we are witnessing, as nations come together to address the financial crisis, the power of common purpose – nations agreeing not just high aspirations but practical down-to-earth actions, governments acting quickly and collectively to take radical and even previously unthinkable measures, because we know now that we must succeed together or separately fail.

And as we learn from this experience of turning common purpose into common action in our shared global society, so I believe we can together seize this time of profound change to forge for our generation a new internationalism that is both hard-headed and progressive – a multilateralism born out of a commitment to the power of international cooperation, not confrontation; founded on a belief in collaboration, not isolation; and driven forward by a conviction that what we achieve together will be greater than what we can achieve on our own.

And it is this new spirit of progressive multilateralism that gives us hope that we can find within ourselves and together the moral courage and leadership the world now seeks.

Sir Michael Quinlan, who sadly died last month and for whose work we will always be grateful, argued 30 years ago that nuclear weapons cannot be 'disinvented'. Our task now, he said, 'is to devise a system for living in peace and freedom while ensuring that nuclear weapons are never used, either to destroy or to blackmail'.

That pragmatism was right for the dark days of the cold war. But I believe we can and should now aim higher. The only way to guarantee that our children and grandchildren will be free from the threat of nuclear war is to create a world in which countries can, with confidence, refuse to take up nuclear weapons in the knowledge that they will never be required.

I know from President Obama and the new US administration that America shares with us the ultimate ambition of a world free from nuclear weapons. But let me be clear – this will be a difficult path that will be crossed in steps, not in one leap.

With each step we must aim to build confidence – confidence that action to prevent proliferation is working and that states with weapons are making strides to live up to their commitments.

And I believe that this is the time to act to take together the next step in building that confidence, for we are at a decisive moment – facing risks of a new and dangerous nuclear era of new-state and perhaps even non-state nuclear weapon holders.

Once there were five nuclear weapons powers. Now there are nearly twice as many, with the risk that there could be many more. Proliferation is our most immediate concern. And for that reason alone it is time to act.

And there is yet another risk – that of nuclear weapons falling into the hands of unstable or ideologically driven regimes, or terrorist groups like al-Qaeda. We must all commit to prevent this from ever happening.

In 2005 the Non-Proliferation Treaty Review Conference failed. We cannot afford to fail next year.

So as we approach the 2010 Review Conference I want us to renew and refresh for our times the grand global bargain, the covenant of hope between nations, at the heart of the treaty – a bargain under which we reaffirm the rights and responsibilities for those countries which forgo nuclear weapons but also a bargain under which there are tough responsibilities to be discharged by nuclear weapons states. For as possessor states we cannot expect to successfully exercise moral and political leadership in preventing the proliferation of nuclear weapons if we ourselves do not demonstrate leadership on the question of disarmament of our weapons.

Under this bargain there is a right for all states to develop civil nuclear power. But there is a responsibility for these states to reject the development of nuclear weapons. And there is a responsibility, too, on nuclear weapons states to reduce their nuclear weapons.

So in the coming months Britain, working with other countries, will be setting out a 'Road to 2010' plan with detailed proposals on civil nuclear power, disarmament and non-proliferation, on fissile material security and the role and development of the International Atomic Energy Agency. We will be seeking the widest possible international engagement and consultation around this plan.

We will also host a recognised nuclear weapons state conference on nuclear disarmament issues and confidence-building measures, including the verification of disarmament.

For in the same way Britain has led in challenging old orthodoxies by eliminating conventional weapons which cause harm to civilians, such as cluster munitions, I pledge that Britain will be at the forefront of the international campaign to prevent nuclear proliferation and to accelerate multilateral nuclear disarmament.

Article VI of the Non-Proliferation Treaty specifically states that countries that do possess nuclear weapons agree to divest themselves of them over time.

No single nuclear weapons state can be expected to disarm unilaterally. But I know that people have been trying to abolish nuclear weapons almost since their invention in the 1940s. Even during the cold war, when they were central to defence planning, there were efforts to reduce their spread and indeed to initiate disarmament with the introduction of the Non-Proliferation Treaty.

In the 1980s Presidents Reagan and Gorbachev – leaders of the countries with by far the largest arsenals of nuclear weapons – discussed the abolition of their most powerful weapons. And every president of both parties in the USA since the 1960s has reaffirmed the Treaty.

If no single nuclear weapons state can be expected to disarm unilaterally, neither should it. But, step by step, we have to transform the discussion of nuclear disarmament from one of platitudes to one of hard commitments. And we also have to create a new international system to help non-nuclear states acquire the new sources of energy they need, because, whether we like it or not, we will not meet the challenges of climate change without the far wider use of civil nuclear power.

For we must invest in all sources of low-carbon energy – energy efficiency, renewables, carbon capture and storage and nuclear power. Given the scale of global emissions reductions required, and the likely costs, no cost-effective low-carbon technology must be off limits.

The complete life cycle emissions from nuclear power – from uranium mining to waste management – are only between 2 and 6 per cent of those from gas for every unit of electricity generated. And the International Atomic Energy Agency estimates that we must build 32 nuclear reactors globally every year if we are to halve emissions by 2050.

So, however we look at it, we will not secure the supply of the sustainable energy on which the future of our planet depends without a role for civil nuclear power. And we simply cannot avoid the real and pressing challenges that presents. From the safety and security of fissile material to the handling of waste, a comprehensive multilateral strategy to allow nations safe and secure access to civil nuclear power is essential.

So this morning I want to outline the principles that must guide our progress in the months ahead and the practical steps I believe we should consider to strengthen the global non-proliferation architecture by renewing and refreshing the global nuclear bargain for our times.

Let me be clear – we are not asking non-nuclear weapons states to refrain from proliferation while nuclear weapons states amass new weapons; we are asking them not to proliferate while nuclear weapons states take steps to reduce their own arsenals in line with the Non-Proliferation Treaty's requirements.

It is a fair and even-handed bargain that contains two central elements – that we enshrine the right for all nations to access civil nuclear power safely, securely and subject to proper multilateral verification processes, with tougher sanctions brought to bear on those who break the rules; and that nuclear weapons states must set out much more clearly the responsibilities that we, too, must discharge.

So what does this mean in practice? In the first place, we must give every nation the right to access what President Eisenhower so memorably called 'atoms for peace'. But in doing so we must, as an international community, be completely confident that we are able to ensure there are appropriate mechanisms for multilateral control of the entire fuel cycle – ensuring the security of fissile material and preventing unwanted proliferation with clear, tough and immediate sanctions for those who break the rules.

Iran is a test case for this new philosophy of the right to civil nuclear power with sanctions for rule breakers. Let me be unequivocal – Iran has the same absolute right to a peaceful civil nuclear programme as any other country. Indeed the UK and international community stand ready to help Iran achieve it – as the opening of the Bushehr nuclear plant already shows. But let me be equally clear that Iran's current nuclear programme is unacceptable. Iran has concealed nuclear activities, refused to cooperate with the IAEA and flouted UN Security Council Resolutions. Its refusal to play by the rules leads us to view its nuclear programme as a critical proliferation threat.

Iran therefore faces a clear choice – continue in this way and face further and tougher sanctions or change to a UN-overseen civil nuclear energy programme that will bring the greatest benefits to its citizens. I hope that Iran will make the right choice and take advantage of the international community's willingness to negotiate, including President Obama's offer of engagement, rather than face further sanctions and regional instability. So I urge Iran, once again, to work with us rather than against us on this. The opportunity to do so remains on the table; the choice is theirs to make.

For our own part, in Britain we will bring forward detailed plans for the responsible future management of our stocks of fissile material. And as part of the 'Road to 2010' we will consult on how best to deal with these stocks which have accumulated.

But I am committed that the UK will also lead on bringing forward proposals internationally for multilateral control of the fuel cycle.

We will seek an innovative partnership between industry, academia and government for further research and development to tackle the technical challenges involved in developing a proliferation-proof nuclear fuel cycle.

There are a number of proposals that are already being considered. The UK's proposal for a nuclear fuel assurance or uranium enrichment bond is an important contribution to resolving this important matter. However, most of the options proposed are aimed at the front half of the fuel cycle – enrichment and fuel provision.

I believe we should now go further in considering all the options, including those that can address the challenges of handling spent fuel in a secure way.

As countries already operating civil nuclear programmes know, establishing a civil nuclear programme carries both significant costs and technological challenges. So I would encourage countries embarking on civil nuclear programmes for the first time to consider all options. This should include detailed examination of whether a collaborative approach, perhaps at a regional level, could provide a new opportunity to make access to civil nuclear power a reality. Under the oversight of an international body, countries could join together to share in the development of civil programmes. And this approach could be particularly beneficial in regions such as the Middle East, where already the Gulf Cooperation Council has proposed a joint nuclear technology programme for peaceful applications conforming to international regulations.

And I very much hope that this conference will generate further contributions which will inform our proposals as part of the 'Road to 2010' plan this summer.

Just as we must reshape the international financial architecture to meet the challenges of a global economy so, too, we must reshape the international architecture that deals with proliferation in a global society.

This will require new funds from within the international community for a significantly changed global work programme. The changes will be significant – a central role in the security of fissile material; a clear and proactive mandate to inspect, with enhanced powers of inspection to cover not just civil programmes but also, eventually, military programmes; more support and training for an inspectorate that will cover both the extension of civil nuclear power and the monitoring of abuses of the Non-Proliferation Treaty; and binding guarantees about the safeguards in place. For if the International Atomic Energy Agency is to play this enlarged and reformed role, its safeguards regime would also need to be further strengthened. This means everyone should implement the highest level of safeguards possible – such as the Additional Protocol, giving the IAEA the power to ensure that there is no indication of activity designed to turn peaceful nuclear energy programmes into nuclear weapons. Beyond this we also need to look at the development of next-generation safeguards which introduce even greater levels of assurance.

Any material failure to cooperate with inspections and any material breach or withdrawal from the Non-Proliferation Treaty should automatically lead to reference to the United Nations Security Council, and indeed it should be assumed that sanctions will be imposed in response to anything other than the most minor of breaches.

At the moment the international community has to prove an offence against the Treaty, but in future the right to develop nuclear energy should be matched by an acknowledged obligation towards openness and transparency. Having signed the Treaty, it should be that country's responsibility to prove it is adhering to the Treaty and to dispel and disprove any accusations of its being undermined.

And it is vital we also ensure that terrorists cannot get their hands on nuclear material. This requires revised, stronger and universally implemented international standards for the protection of fissile material. And I will bring forward proposals for such standards as part of our 'Road to 2010' plan.

Every nuclear state and prospective civil nuclear state must give security the highest attention. It is an essential component of the investment in nuclear programmes. Since 2003 in the UK we have spent more than £70 million on improving security at our Sellafield site alone, and we are committed to spending a further £220 million on the construction of a state-of-the-art storage facility.

But we understand that to be effective security must meet the highest standards around the world so, in addition to the £270 million the UK has spent on global threat-reduction projects since 2002, and a further £36.5 million we will spend each year for the foreseeable future, we are doubling our contribution to the IAEA's Nuclear Security Fund. And we will work with our partners to identify ways to strengthen the role of the Nuclear Suppliers Group, whose work is of vital importance.

And it is important to note that, in the horrific event of an attack, after-the-fact detection is now an established science that would allow us to attribute the origins of the material used in almost any nuclear device. We are therefore in a position to identify those responsible and thus define liability for providing such assistance to terrorists. The supplier must accept responsibility just as the perpetrator, and thanks to the advance of science there can be no escape from justice.

To achieve our objective we need two major breakthroughs – effective and universal mechanisms to prevent proliferation to non-nuclear weapons states and active steps by nuclear weapons states towards disarmament. Now is the time for serious commitment to both.

So the other core ambition of the 'Road to 2010' proposals we will publish this summer is a credible road map towards disarmament by all the nuclear weapons states – through measures that will command the confidence of all the non-nuclear weapons states.

Of course, we have already seen huge cuts in weaponry – with in total 40,000 warheads destroyed since the end of the cold war. But what we need is more than this – a forward plan for multilateral disarmament, a joint commitment shared by nuclear and non-nuclear weapons states alike.

We must begin by reducing the number of nuclear weapons still out there in the world, and between them the US and Russia retain around 95 per cent.

The START treaty – the mainstay of their bilateral arms control effort – will expire later this year. I welcome their commitment to work for a legally binding successor, which I hope will pave the way for greater reductions to come.

For our part – as soon as it becomes useful for our arsenal to be included in a broader negotiation – Britain stands ready to participate and to act.

The nuclear choices being made today will determine whether we face a future arms race or a future of arms control. Averting the former and promoting transparency in the latter are both vital to our common future.

So the recognised nuclear weapons states must now show unity and leadership and set tirelessly to work on a programme of confidence-building measures.

I will gladly share, for the benefit of all, the pioneering work that we have been doing in the UK on the science of verifying warhead destruction. Our Atomic Weapons Establishment, working with partners from Norway, have been developing techniques that can provide reassurance that nuclear weapons have been destroyed – without giving away sensitive information about warhead design.

Britain has cut the number of its nuclear warheads by 50 per cent since 1997. And we are committed to retaining the minimum force necessary to maintain effective deterrence. For future submarines our latest assessment is that we can meet this requirement with 12 missile tubes, not the 16 on current submarines. In Britain our operationally available warheads number fewer than 160, and the government keeps this number under constant review. If it is possible to reduce the number of UK warheads further, consistent with our national deterrence requirements and with the progress of multilateral discussions, Britain will be ready to do so.

And in the meantime, we must drive forward the multilateral agenda. The first steps of which are to commence urgent negotiations without pre-conditions on a Fissile Material Cut-off Treaty and for all states to sign and ratify the Comprehensive Test Ban Treaty.

States have national interests, but capping the production of weapons-usable fissile material and outlawing the testing of nuclear weapons are two powerful and achievable goals that I believe are consistent with the long-term needs and interests of every state.

So as we stand together against those who would seek to threaten our security and, in some cases, even our existence, I offer today a practical plan to deliver on the pledges we have made.

For today is a time for leadership, confidence and common purpose, not weakness, withdrawal or retreat.

So let us go forward, fully recognising the importance of the task before us. For the sake of future generations across the world, let us ensure that the chapter of history that we write together – our generation, here, today – tells the story of a common journey towards a world that is free from the fear of its own destruction. Let this be a journey of hope in which hard-headed cooperation by friends who were once foes defines our modern age – underpinned by a new covenant of hope that brings us a truly global society not of enemies fearful of each other but of partners with the confidence to work together.

Part III

Towards a New Special Relationship

A reading of the Prime Minister's speeches collected in Parts I and II of this book shows how he has been arguing consistently throughout his premiership for a new global compact, based on a new paradigm of interdependence between nations and blocs, so as to address and resolve the five challenges of the global age – climate change, terrorism, nuclear proliferation, poverty and the threat of worldwide economic collapse. And he argues forcibly that if we do not address these global changes in the very near term, the sheer scale, scope and speed of them will condemn millions around the world to a life that is unsustainable, insecure and unfair.

This approach is premised on a determination to work together with others with whom we share values, 'so that we can fulfil the hopes and dreams of the day' – what he calls a 'partnership of purpose'. In previous generations, bilateral alliances and special relationships, notably that between the UK and the US, did a huge amount to face down the threats and challenges of those periods of history. But, the Prime Minister argues, 'If these times have shown us anything it is that the major challenges we face are global. No matter where it starts, an economic crisis does not stop at the water's edge; it ripples across the world. Climate change does not honour passport controls. Terrorism has no respect for borders. Modern communication instantly spans every continent. The new frontier is that there is no frontier, and the new shared truth is that global problems now need global solutions.'

The main thrust of the Prime Minister's speeches collected in this part of the book is that there should be a new 'special relationship' between Europe and America. In his brilliant speech to the Joint US Congress, the Prime Minister says, 'you now have the most pro-American European leadership in living memory. It is a leadership that wants to cooperate more closely together in order to cooperate more closely with you. There is no old Europe, no new Europe, there is only your friend Europe.'

This point is picked up again in the Prime Minister's address to the European Parliament, in the D-Day address and in his speech on the occasion of the 20th anniversary of the fall of the Berlin Wall. His argument is that, faced with the most difficult of challenges, working with partners also founded on shared ideals and shared values has the best chance of helping to build our world anew, for 'how can we say we have achieved all we set out to do – the promise of peace and justice – when the shadow of nuclear proliferation still spreads across the earth? When Darfur is in the grip of genocide, Burma is in chains, Zimbabwe is in agony? When the enemy is not just violence but the mortal threat of poverty, hunger, illiteracy, disease and want?' There are, he concludes, 'dreams of liberation still to be realised, commitments still to be redeemed and vows to the dead still to be kept'.

13

SHARED VALUES, SHARED FUTURES

INTRODUCTION BY BARACK OBAMA

'Prime Minister Brown and I had a productive discussion this morning. Both of us greatly value the special relationship between our nations. The United States and the United Kingdom have stood together through thick and thin, through war and peace, through hard times and prosperity – and we've always emerged stronger by standing together. So I'm pleased that my first meeting overseas as President is with Gordon Brown, just as I was pleased to host him in Washington shortly after taking office. And I know that we both believe that the relationship between our two countries is more than just an alliance of interests; it's a kinship of ideals, and it must be constantly renewed.'

Pre-G20 Press Conference, April 2009

'In an era of integration and interdependence, it is also my responsibility to lead America into recognising that its interests, its fate, is tied up with the larger world; that if we neglect or abandon those who are suffering in poverty, that not only are we depriving ourselves of potential opportunities for markets and economic growth but ultimately that despair may turn to violence that turns on us; that unless we are concerned about the education of all children and not just our children, not only may we be depriving ourselves of the next great scientist who's going to find the next new energy source that saves the planet but we also may make people around the world much more vulnerable to anti-American propaganda.'

G20 Press Conference, April 2009

⬥

This is an impressive speech that started with the unexpected announcement of a knighthood for Ted Kennedy: 'I know you will allow me to single out for special mention today one of your most distinguished senators, known in every continent and a great friend. Northern Ireland today is at peace, more

Americans have health care, children around the world are going to school, and for all those things we owe a great debt to the life and courage of Senator Edward Kennedy.'

The main theme of this speech is working together for the common good: 'I come in friendship to renew, for new times, our special relationship that is founded on our shared history, our shared values and, I believe, our shared futures.' And the Prime Minister reflects: 'So let it be said of the friendship between our two countries that it is in times of trial, true, that in the face of fear, faithful and amidst the storms of change, constant. And let it be said of our friendship also – formed and forged over two tumultuous centuries, a friendship tested in war, strengthened in peace – that it has not just endured but has renewed each generation to better serve our shared values and fulfil the hopes and dreams of the day. Not an alliance of convenience, it is a partnership of purpose.'

Turning to the present, Gordon Brown says, 'An economic hurricane has swept the world, creating a crisis of credit and a crisis of confidence. History has brought us now to a point where change is essential. And we are summoned not just to manage our times but to transform them. And our task is to rebuild prosperity and security in a wholly different economic world where competition is no longer just local, but it is global, and where banks are no longer national, but they are international.

'And we need to understand, therefore, what went wrong in this crisis – that the very financial instruments that were designed to diversify risk across the banking system instead spread contagion right across the globe.'

And, reminding his audience of the last global recession and the style of leadership employed then, he says, 'In the depths of the Depression, when Franklin Roosevelt did battle with fear itself, it was not simply by the power of his words, his personality and his example that he triumphed. Yes, all these things mattered, but what mattered more was this enduring truth – that you, the American people, at your core, were, as you remain, every bit as optimistic as your Roosevelts, your Reagans and your Obamas. And this is the faith in the future that has always been the story and promise of America.

'So, at this defining moment in history, let us renew our special relationship for our generation and our times, let us work together to restore prosperity and protect this planet and, with faith in the future, let us together build tomorrow today.'

SPEECH TO THE JOINT US CONGRESS
Washington, 4 March 2009

Madam Speaker, Mr Vice President, distinguished members of Congress. I come to this great capital of this great nation, an America renewed under a new president, to say that America's faith in the future has been, is and always will be an inspiration to me and to the whole world.

Two centuries ago your creation of America was the boldest possible affirmation of faith in the future. It is a future that you not just believe in but a future you have built with your own hands. And on 20 January you, the American people, wrote the latest chapter in the American story with a transition of dignity in which both sides of the aisle could take great pride, and on that day billions of people surely looked to Washington DC as 'a shining city upon the hill', lighting up the whole of the world.

And let me thank President Obama for his leadership, for his friendship and for giving the whole world renewed hope in itself.

And I know you will allow me to single out for special mention today one of your most distinguished senators, known in every continent and a great friend. Northern Ireland today is at peace, more Americans have health care, children around the world are going to school, and for all those things we owe a great debt to the life and courage of Senator Edward Kennedy.

I want to announce – awarded by Her Majesty the Queen on behalf of the British people – an honorary knighthood for Sir Edward Kennedy.

Madam Speaker, Mr Vice President, I come in friendship to renew, for new times, our special relationship that is founded on our shared history, our shared values and, I believe, our shared futures.

I grew up in the 1960s as America, led by President Kennedy, looked to the heavens and saw not the endless void of the unknown but a new frontier to dare to discover and to explore. People said it couldn't be done, but America did it. And 20 years later in the 1980s, America, led by President Reagan, refused to accept the fate of millions trapped behind the Iron Curtain and insisted instead that the peoples of Eastern Europe be allowed to join the ranks of nations which live safe, strong and free. People said it would never happen in our lifetime, but it did, and the Berlin Wall was torn down brick by brick.

So, early in my life I came to understand that America is not just the indispensable nation – you are the irrepressible nation. Throughout your history America has led insurrections in the human imagination. You have summoned revolutionary times through your belief that there is no such thing as an impossible endeavour. And it is never possible to come here without having your faith in the future renewed.

Now I want to thank you on behalf of the British people, because throughout a whole century the American people stood liberty's ground – not just in one world war but in two. And I want you to know that we will never forget the sacrifice and the service of the American soldiers who gave their lives for people whose names they never knew and whose faces they never saw, yet people who have lived in freedom thanks to the bravery and valour of the Americans who gave that last full measure of devotion.

Cemetery after cemetery across Europe honours the memory of American soldiers resting row upon row, often alongside comrades in arms from Britain. And there is no battlefield of liberty on which there is not a piece of land that is marked out as American, and there is no day of remembrance within Britain that is not also a commemoration of American courage and sacrifice far from home.

In the hardest days of the last century faith in the future kept America alive, and I tell you that America kept faith in the future alive for all the world.

And let me pay tribute to the soldiers, yours and ours, who today fight side by side in the plains of Afghanistan, the streets of Iraq, just as their forefathers fought side by side in the sands of Tunisia, the beaches of Normandy and then on the bridges over the Rhine.

Almost every family in Britain has a tie that binds them to America. So I want you to know that whenever a young American soldier or marine or sailor or airman is killed in conflict anywhere in the world we, the people of Britain, grieve with you. We know that your loss is our loss, your families' sorrow is our families' sorrow and your nation's determination is our nation's determination that they shall not have died in vain.

And after that terrible September morning when your homeland was attacked, the Coldstream Guards at Buckingham Palace played the Star-Spangled Banner – our own British tribute as we wept for our friends in the land of the free and the home of the brave.

And let me, therefore, promise you our continued support to ensure that there is no hiding place for terrorists, no safe haven for terrorism. You should be proud that in the years after 2001, that whilst terrorists may destroy buildings and even, tragically, lives they have not and will not ever destroy the American spirit.

So let it be said of the friendship between our two countries that it is in times of trial, true, that in the face of fear, faithful, and amidst the storms of change, constant. And let it be said of our friendship also – formed and forged over two tumultuous centuries, a friendship tested in war, strengthened in peace – that it has not just endured but has renewed each generation to better serve our shared values and fulfil the hopes and dreams of the day. Not an alliance of convenience, it is a partnership of purpose.

Alliances can wither or be destroyed, but partnerships of purpose are indestructible. Friendships can be shaken, but our friendship is unshakable. Treaties can be broken, but our partnership is unbreakable, and I know that there is no power on earth that can ever drive us apart.

We will work tirelessly with you as partners for peace in the Middle East – for a two-state solution, proposed by President Clinton and driven forward by President Bush, that provides for nothing less than a secure Israel safe within its borders, existing side by side with a viable Palestinian state. And we will work tirelessly with you to reduce the threat of nuclear proliferation and reduce the stockpile of nuclear weapons. And our shared message to Iran, it is simple – we are ready for you to rejoin the international community, but first you must cease your threats and suspend your nuclear programme.

Past prime ministers have travelled to this capital building in times of war to talk of war. I come now to talk of new and different battles we must also fight together, to speak of a global economy in crisis and a planet imperilled. These are new priorities for our new times. And let us be honest – tonight too many parents, after they have put their children to bed, will speak of their worries about losing their jobs or their need to sell their house. Too many will share stories of friends or neighbours already packing up their homes; too many will talk of a local store or business that has already gone to the wall.

For me this global recession is not to be measured just in statistics or in graphs or on a balance sheet. Instead I see one individual with one set of dreams and fears, and then another, and then another – each with their own stars to reach for, each part of a family, each at the heart of a community now in need of help and hope. And when banks have failed and markets have faltered we, the representatives of the people, have to be the people's last line of defence.

And that is why for me there is no financial orthodoxy so entrenched, there is no conventional thinking so ingrained, there is no special interest so strong that it should ever stand in the way of the change that hard-working families now need.

We have learned through this world downturn that markets should be free but markets should never be values-free. We have learned that the risks people take should never be separated from the responsibilities that they must meet.

And if, perhaps, some once thought that it was beyond our power to shape global markets to meet the needs of the people, we now know that that is our duty. We cannot and must not stand aside.

In our families and workplaces and in our places of worship we celebrate men and women of integrity who work hard, treat people fairly, take responsibility, look out for others. And if these are the principles we live by in our families and neighbourhoods, they should also be the principles that guide and govern our economic life.

And the world has learned that what makes for the good society also now makes for the good economy too.

My father was a minister of the Church, and I have learned again what I was taught by him – that wealth should help more than the wealthy, that good fortune should serve more than the fortunate and that riches must enrich not just some of our communities but all of our communities. And these enduring values are in my view the values we need for these new times.

We tend to think of the sweep of history as stretching across many months and years before culminating in decisive moments that we call history. But sometimes the reality is that the defining moments of history come suddenly, and without warning, and the task of leadership then is to define them, to shape them and to move forward into the new world they demand.

An economic hurricane has swept the world, creating a crisis of credit and a crisis of confidence. History has brought us now to a point where change is essential. And we are summoned not just to manage our times but to transform them. And our task is to rebuild prosperity and security in a wholly different economic world where competition is no longer just local, but it is global, and where banks are no longer national, but they are international.

And we need to understand, therefore, what went wrong in this crisis – that the very financial instruments that were designed to diversify risk across the banking system instead spread contagion right across the globe.

And today's financial institutions are so interwoven that a bad bank anywhere is a threat to good banks everywhere.

But should we succumb to a race to the bottom and to a protectionism that history tells us that, in the end, protects no one? No. We should have the confidence, America and Britain most of all, that we can seize the global opportunities ahead and make the future work for us.

And why? Because, whilst today people are anxious and feel insecure, over the next two decades literally billions of people in other continents will move from being simply producers of their goods to being consumers of our goods. And in this way the world economy will double in size. Twice as many opportunities for business, twice as much prosperity – the biggest expansion of middle-class incomes and jobs the world has seen.

So we win our future not by retreating from the world but by engaging with it. And America and Britain will succeed and lead if we tap into the talents of our people, unleash the genius of our scientists, set free the drive of our entrepreneurs. We will win the race to the top if we can develop the new high-value-added products and services and the new green goods that the rising number of hard-working families across our globe will want to buy.

So in these unprecedented times we must educate our way out of the downturn, we must invest and invent our way out of the downturn, we must re-tool and re-skill our way out of the downturn. And this is not blind optimism or synthetic confidence to console people; it is the practical affirmation for our times of our faith in a better future.

Every time we rebuild a school we demonstrate our faith in the future. Every time we send more people to university, every time we invest more in our new digital infrastructure, every time we increase support for our scientists we demonstrate our faith in the future.

And so I say to this Congress, and this country, something that runs deep in your character and is woven in your history: we conquer our fear of the future through our faith in the future. And it is this faith in the future that means we must commit to protecting the planet for generations that will come long after us. The Greek proverb, what does it say? 'Why does anybody plant the seeds of a tree whose shade they will never see?' The answer is because they look to the future. And I believe you, as a nation that had the vision to put a man on the moon, are also the nation with a vision to protect and preserve our planet earth.

And you know it is only by investing in environmental technology that we can end the dictatorship of oil, and it is only by tackling climate change that we can create the millions of new green jobs that we need and can have.

But the lesson of this crisis is that we cannot just wait for tomorrow, we cannot just think of tomorrow today, we cannot merely plan for tomorrow today – our task must be to build tomorrow today.

And America knows from its history that its reach goes far beyond its geography. For a century you have carried upon your shoulders the greatest of responsibility – to work with and for the rest of the world. And let me tell you that now more than ever the rest of the world wants to work with America.

If these times have shown us anything it is that the major challenges we face are global. No matter where it starts, an economic crisis does not stop at the water's edge; it ripples across the world. Climate change does not honour passport controls. Terrorism has no respect for borders. Modern communication instantly spans every continent. The new frontier is that there is no frontier, and the new shared truth is that global problems now need global solutions.

And let me say to you directly: you now have the most pro-American European leadership in living memory. It is a leadership that wants to cooperate more closely together in order to cooperate more closely with you. There is no old Europe, no new Europe, there is only your friend Europe.

So once again I say we should seize this moment, because never before have I seen a world willing to come together so much, never before has that been more needed and never before have the benefits of cooperation been so far-reaching.

So when people here and in other countries ask what more we can do to bring an end to this downturn, let me say this: we can achieve more by working together. And just think of what we can do if we combine not just in a partnership for security but in a new partnership for prosperity. On jobs you, the American people, through your stimulus proposals, could create or save at least three million jobs. We in Britain are acting with similar determination, but how much nearer an end to this downturn would we all be if the whole of the world resolved to do the same?

And you are also restructuring your banks. So are we. But how much safer would everybody's savings be if the whole world finally came together to outlaw shadow banking systems and outlaw offshore tax havens?

So just think how each of our actions, if combined, could mean a whole much greater than the sum of its parts – all and not just some banks stabilised; on fiscal stimulus, the impact multiplied because everybody is doing it; rising demand in all our countries creating jobs in each of our countries; and trade once again the engine of prosperity, the wealth of nations restored.

No one should forget it was American visionaries who, over half a century ago, coming out of the deepest of depressions and the worst of wars, produced the boldest of plans for global economic cooperation. They recognised that prosperity was indivisible. They concluded that to be sustained it had to be shared.

And I believe that ours, too, is a time for renewal, for a plan for tackling recession and building for the future, every continent playing their part in a global new deal – a plan for prosperity that can benefit us all.

And first, so that the whole of our worldwide banking system serves our prosperity rather than risks it, let us agree at our G20 summit in London in April rules and standards for accountability, transparency and reward that will mean an end to the excesses and will apply to every bank, everywhere and all the time.

Second, America and a few others cannot be expected to bear all the burden of the fiscal and interest-rate stimulus. We must share it globally. So let us work together for the worldwide reduction of interest rates and a scale of stimulus that is equal to the depth of the recession around the world and to the dimensions of recovery and, most of all, equal to the millions of jobs we must safeguard and create.

And third, let us together renew our international economic cooperation – help emerging markets rebuild their banks; let us sign a world trade agreement to expand commerce; let us work together also for a low-carbon recovery. And I am confident that this president, this Congress and the peoples of the world can come together in Copenhagen in December and reach a historic agreement to combat climate change.

And let us never forget in times of turmoil our duty to the least of these – the poorest of the world. In the Rwanda Museum of Genocide there is a memorial to the countless children who were among those murdered in the massacres in Rwanda. And there is one portrait of a child, David. The words beneath him are brief, yet they weigh on me heavily. It says, Name: David, aged 10; Favourite sport: football; Enjoyed: making people laugh; Dream: to become a doctor; Cause of death: tortured to death; Last words: 'The United Nations will come for us.'

But we never did. That child believed the best of us. That he was wrong is to our eternal discredit. We tend to think of a day of judgement as a moment to come, but our faith tells us, as the writer said, that judgement is more than that, 'It is a summary court in perpetual session.'

And when I visit those bare, run-down yet teeming classrooms across Africa they are full of children, like our children, desperate to learn. But, because we have been unable as a world to keep our promises to help, more and more children, I tell you, are being lured to expensively funded madrasas teaching innocent children to hate us. So for our security and our children's security and these children's future, you know, the greatest gift of our generation, the greatest gift we could give to the world, the gift of America and Britain, could be that every child in every country should have the chance that 70 million children today do not have – the chance to go to school, to spell their names, to count their age and perhaps learn of a great generation who are striving to make their freedom real.

So let us remember that there is a common bond that, across different beliefs, cultures and nationalities, unites us as human beings. It is at the core of my convictions, it is the essence of America's spirit, it is the heart of all our faiths and it must be at the centre of our response to this crisis too. Our values tell us that we cannot be wholly comfortable while others go without comfort, that our communities can never be fully at ease if millions feel ill at ease, that our society cannot be truly strong when millions are left so weak. And this much we know – when the strong help the weak it makes us all stronger.

And this too is true – all of us know that in a recession the wealthiest, the most powerful and the most privileged can find a way through. So we don't value the wealthy less when we say that our first duty is to help the not-so-wealthy, we don't value the powerful less when we say our first responsibility is to help the powerless, and we do not value those who are secure less when we say our first priority must be to help the insecure.

These recent events have forced us all to think anew. And, while I have learned many things over these last few months, I keep returning to something I first learned in my father's church as a child. In these most modern of crises I am drawn to the most ancient of truths – wherever there is hardship, wherever there is suffering we cannot, we will not, we will never pass by on the other side.

But, you know, working together there is no challenge to which we are not equal, there is no obstacle we cannot overcome and there is no aspiration so high it cannot be achieved.

In the depths of the Depression, when Franklin Roosevelt did battle with fear itself, it was not simply by the power of his words, his personality and his example that he triumphed. Yes, all these things mattered, but what mattered more was this enduring truth – that you, the American people, at your core, were, as you remain, every bit as optimistic as your Roosevelts, your Reagans and your Obamas. And this is the faith in the future that has always been the story and promise of America.

So, at this defining moment in history, let us renew our special relationship for our generation and our times, let us work together to restore prosperity and protect this planet and, with faith in the future, let us together build tomorrow today.

13

EUROPE

INTRODUCTION BY JOSÉ LUIS RODRÍGUEZ ZAPATERO

I am pleased to introduce the text of the address delivered by Prime Minister Brown to the European Parliament in March 2009, a speech in which he showed the political vision and the social conscience that characterises his leadership.

Gordon Brown stands for what is best in politics. Through his words one immediately senses a man of deep social values, for whom fairness and human dignity are not empty concepts but the keystone of his political compass. A man who deeply believes that, in his own words, 'a good society and a good economy needs a strong sense of values . . . , the solid virtues of honesty, responsibility, fairness and valuing hard work – virtues that come not from markets but actually come from the heart'. A man, thus, deeply committed to a fair and decent society.

As he himself points out, this is a conviction rooted in his experience of post-war Europe. A Europe that has been shaped by the values and lessons we have learned working together over the last six decades and that are the foundations of the European project: the importance of liberty, equality, social protection, cooperation, diversity and openness. It is for these reasons that Gordon Brown stands also for what is best of Europe.

The Prime Minister, however, calls, rightly, for a 'global Europe', a Europe that must open itself to the world and project its values if it is to preserve them. In doing so, the Prime Minister argues – and I could not agree with him more – Europe can and should take the lead in building a just and humane global society. Not only because it is in our enlightened self-interest to do so, but also because after 60 years building coordination among countries, cooperation among peoples and unity out of diversity, Europe is uniquely equipped to foster the new global governance the world needs to address the global challenges we confront.

Yet Gordon Brown stands, above all, as a politician of progressive vision and leadership. A leader deeply committed to progressive values but who also understands that, if they are to remain relevant today, we must apply those same progressive values that have served us so well in the past to the new challenges of globalisation: regulating global markets so that they serve the people and not the other way around, addressing environmental degradation, fighting extremism and, most important of all, making poverty history. Our aim as progressives should be, in short, to build 'a truly global society in a truly progressive way', so that it is sustainable economically, socially and environmentally. An effort in which Europe is already leading the way.

As the Prime Minister rightly says, 'globalisation has been crossing national boundaries but also moral boundaries'. We have now discovered the cost of these trespasses, of unregulated markets, of greed let loose and of the corrosive force of inequality. The time has come for us progressives to lead and build, in the Prime Minister's own words, 'a truly global society which is sustainable for all, secure for all and fair to all'.

A week after his speech on nuclear energy and proliferation, and a week before the G20 Summit in London in late March 2009, the Prime Minister was in Strasbourg, addressing the European Parliament.

The Prime Minister starts this speech by stating his European credentials: 'I stand here proud to be British and proud to be European, representing a country that does not see itself as an island adrift from Europe but as a country at the centre of Europe, not in Europe's slipstream but in Europe's mainstream.'

Gordon Brown goes on to argue that the European Union is uniquely placed to lead in building a truly global society that is sustainable for all, secure for all and fair to all, precisely because we have proved over the last 60 years that we can meet and master the challenges of cooperation across borders, of coordination between peoples and of building unity out of diversity.

The Prime Minister points out that the recent changes in leadership – in America, France and Germany in particular – have brought together progressive partnerships that, he proposes, in a new era of transatlantic cooperation, should work together for a new worldwide climate change agreement; combine to defeat the growing threat of terrorism from Pakistan and Afghanistan; work together for peace in the Middle East, with a secure Israel side by side with a viable Palestinian state; work together to ensure that there will be more jobs, more businesses, more trade as we meet and master the great financial challenges of our times; and, with France joining the centre of NATO again, work together for a world where nuclear weapons do not proliferate and where the nuclear powers agree real reductions in their arsenals of nuclear weapons.

His conclusion is that, faced with the most difficult of challenges, a united Europe, working with partners also founded on shared ideals and based on shared values, has the best chance of helping to build our world anew.

ADDRESS TO THE EUROPEAN PARLIAMENT
Strasbourg, 24 March 2009

Mr President, members of the Parliament. For this special honour of an invitation to speak to you, and for your successful presidency of the Parliament, let me thank you, Mr President. And let me thank you, European parliamentarians and members of the European Commission led by President Barroso – it is thanks to the work of all of you, and the generations whose work we build on, that today we enjoy a Europe of peace and unity which will truly rank among the finest achievements of human history and which is today a beacon of hope for the whole world.

And if anyone in any country or continent is in any doubt about how the human will and the courage of representatives with a mission can build a new future on past decades of despair, let them simply reflect upon how 60 years ago Europeans talked of enemies that were forever entrenched, relationships that could never be repaired. They talked of a hard, long and bitter cold war. They did not believe it possible that our Europe could ever be fully at peace, far less that it could unite and cooperate. And then let them think of how today, after years of cooperation and unity, none but those on the political extremes would question that we are stronger together, safer together than ever we are apart.

On 9 November this year we will celebrate the 20th anniversary of something that surely, for each of us in this chamber, must count as one of the most defining events of our lives – the fall of the Berlin Wall. It was a wall torn down by the resolution of people determined that no barrier, no intimidation, no repression would ever be again allowed to divide the people of Europe. And, friends, today there is no old Europe, no new Europe, no new East or West Europe; there is only one Europe, and it is our home Europe.

So I stand here proud to be British and proud to be European, representing a country that does not see itself as an island adrift from Europe but as a country at the centre of Europe, not in Europe's slipstream but in Europe's mainstream.

And that is why I am also proud that by a large majority our British Parliament ratified the Lisbon Treaty. And I believe that we in Europe are uniquely placed to lead the world in meeting the wholly new and momentous challenges of globalisation ahead. We are uniquely placed because of what we have achieved in our union, and I want to thank the members of this European Parliament. You should all be proud of what together we have achieved: the greatest and biggest single market in the world, now bringing opportunities to 500 million people – the most successful endeavour in economic cooperation anywhere in the world. And you should be proud that this is an achievement of the European Union.

And you should be proud, too, of the comprehensive framework of environmental protection that we are building – a defining achievement of European coordination with this continent the first in the world to set itself unequivocally on the path to becoming a low-carbon economy.

And you should be proud, too, that through the world's biggest programme of aid the most sustained commitment to saving and changing lives anywhere in the world has been made by this European Union.

So many of the consumer rights and workplace rights we all enjoy across Europe have resulted from the campaigns led by individual members and groupings of this House. And let us not forget that the European Union has the most comprehensive social protection anywhere in the world – a set of rights and responsibilities that was enhanced for the people of Britain when, I am proud to say, our government led Britain into the Social Chapter.

Mr President, these successes of Europe would have been impossible without the cooperation between peoples that you and this Parliament have delivered. Yes, we can see unity advanced by officials meeting officials across frontiers. Yes, we can see unity when leaders meet leaders. But the unity that will last is the democratic unity rooted in the common values of people now represented in this Parliament. And more than treaties, more than institutions, more than individuals, it is these defining values that bind us closely together – our belief as a European Union that liberty, economic progress and social justice advance together or not at all.

These are the values rooted in the lessons we have learned by working together – the truth that freedom must never become a free for all; that markets should be free, but never values-free; the belief that being fair is more important than being laissez-faire. And we have learned again in this crisis that wealth is of no great value to society unless it serves more than the wealthy and riches are of value only when they enrich not just some communities but all.

And this is not simply our political philosophy. In Europe we believe these truths because we have lived them in the work that we have done in our countries.

So now, in the midst of a global crisis of a speed and scope and scale quite unprecedented in history, I want to discuss with you how, applying these values that are now part of our DNA, these lessons that we have learned over time in Europe, Europe and the world can rise to the four great challenges of globalisation – financial instability in a world of instant global capital flows; environmental degradation in a world of energy shortages; extremism and the threat it brings to security in a world of unprecedented mobility; and growing poverty in a world of worsening inequality.

And I want to discuss, too, how, with a global economy managed properly by us working together, billions of people in Europe, Asia and elsewhere – many just producers of their goods – can become tomorrow's consumers of our goods; how we can see over the next 20 years the biggest expansion of middle-class jobs and incomes ever seen; and how, despite all the problems we have today, we can see ahead a world economy that will double in size, creating new opportunities for all of us in all our countries.

So I want to discuss how we can build from a world which looks today unsustainable, unsafe and unequal a truly global society which is sustainable for all, secure for all and fair to all.

And let me repeat – I believe that the European Union is uniquely placed to lead in building this future precisely because we have proved over the last 60 years that we as Europe can meet and master the challenges of cooperation across borders, of coordination between peoples and of building unity out of diversity.

Some of you will know that for many years I have advanced the case for a global Europe and for the economic reforms to make it happen. I know that some critics suggested that I was supporting global action more because I supported European action less. But I have made this case so strongly in recent years precisely because I passionately want Europe to be leading on the world stage and because I believe that the countries of Europe, having come together around values of liberty, fairness and responsibility, have so much to offer the world as it, too, comes together. I want to see a globalisation that is open, free trading and flexible but which is also reforming, inclusive and sustainable. And that is the message, at these most testing of economic times, that Europe can send to and shape with the rest of the world.

Today, as you know, an international hurricane is sweeping the world. No European country is immune from its impact. It is hitting every business, every worker, every homeowner and every family, too. And let us be honest with each other. Our global economic system has developed and become distorted in ways that run contrary to the values that we celebrate and uphold in our families, in our communities and in every other part of our lives – values such as being fair to others and taking responsibility, valuing hard work and not rewarding irresponsible excess.

Complex products like banking derivatives, which were supposed to disperse risk around the world, have instead spread contagion. So no longer can we allow risk to be transferred around the world without responsibility. I say every part of what has been a shadow banking system must now come under the supervisory net. Established limits to markets agreed in one country or region are being overtaken by global competition between all countries. And I say it is not enough to promote self-regulation and allow a race to the bottom; we have to agree international standards of transparency, of disclosure and, yes, of remuneration too.

And just as globalisation has been crossing national boundaries, we know it has been crossing moral boundaries too. As we have discovered to our cost, the problem of unbridled free markets in an unsupervised market place is that they can reduce all relationships to transactions, all motivations to self-interest, all sense of value to consumer choice and all sense of worth to a price tag.

Yet a good society and a good economy needs a strong sense of values. Not values that spring from the market but values we bring to the market: the solid virtues of honesty, responsibility, fairness and valuing hard work – virtues that come not from markets but actually come from the heart.

And so starting at our debate today, as we prepare for the London Summit next week, I propose that we as Europe take a central role in replacing what was once called the old Washington Consensus with a new and principled economic consensus for our times.

Faced with all these global problems we cannot stand where we are. We have to act. But, of course, we have a choice. I know the temptation for some is to meet this new insecurity by retreating – to try to feel safe by attempting to pull up the drawbridge, to turn the clock back. But, I tell you, if there is anything we know from past history it is that protectionism is a policy of defeatism – the politics of retreat and the politics of fear – and in the end it protects no one at all.

So instead of heading for the rocks of isolation, let us together chart the course of cooperation. That is in all our national interests. That is why I propose that Europe takes the lead in a bold plan to ensure that every continent now makes the changes in their banking system that will open the path to shared prosperity; that every country participates and cooperates in setting global standards for financial regulation; and every continent injects the resources we need to secure economic growth and jobs.

So what is the agenda? First, the market is there to serve us. We are not here to serve the market. That is why we in Britain, other countries in Europe and, yesterday, America have removed uncertainty from the banking sector – in order to get lending moving again for those people who need it to get on with their ordinary lives in the midst of extraordinary times.

And I believe that the common principles behind the US, the UK and the European plans for cleaning up the banks' balance sheets will help to rebuild confidence and help to restore lending to the wider economy.

And for the first time ever across our world we have a consensus – reflected in the de Larosière report, the G30 report of Paul Volcker, the Turner Report in our country and the Financial Stability Forum – that, in the interests of protecting people's savings, tough regulatory standards should be set across Europe and across the world, be implemented and fully monitored not just in one country but in every continent of the world. And I believe that for the first time we can also agree the big changes necessary for coordinated action that will signal the beginning of the end of offshore tax havens and offshore centres.

So let us together say that our regulations should apply to every bank everywhere at every time, with no opt-out for a shadow banking system, no hiding place in any part of the world for tax avoiders who are refusing to pay their fair share.

Now we know also that a worldwide fiscal and monetary stimulus to our economy can be twice as effective in every country if it is adopted by all countries. I believe that this year we are seeing the biggest cuts in interest rates that the world has ever seen, and we are seeing implemented the biggest fiscal stimulus the world has ever agreed. And I am confident that the London Summit can build on the action that the European Council and the G20 finance ministers agreed a few days ago – that we will do whatever it takes to create the jobs and the growth we need. And the whole of Europe, I believe, will agree with President Obama in saying that our actions should be sustained and robust until recovery is achieved.

We have a responsibility also to the unemployed. I believe that no one should go unemployed for months without the offer of training or a job or help to obtain a job and that no school leaver should be out of school and out of work for long without being offered the chance they need to get the skills for the future. I believe also that in this crisis we must take urgent, serious and large-scale action to build a low-carbon recovery and make our economy sustainable.

Europe led the industrial revolution, and now we can lead a low-carbon revolution through investment in energy efficiency, the expansion of renewables and nuclear power, the demonstration of carbon capture and storage, the development of the Smart Grid, the commercialisation of electric and ultra-low-carbon vehicles. And that is why I am proud to be part of the European 2020 package on energy and climate change that we agreed in December – a decision of this Parliament which has set the highest standards for global leadership on the road to a climate change agreement we all want to see at Copenhagen later this year.

Mr President, what we are now experiencing in some of the countries of Eastern and Central Europe demonstrates why we must build anew the international economic cooperation to help countries whenever they are in times of need. A new, reformed International Monetary Fund in which we welcome greater representation from the emerging economies and which must have at least $500 billion of resources – twice what it has today – must be empowered to help countries who are facing a flight of capital, help them assist restructuring the capacity of the banks and enable them to restore lending to their industries.

And so I want an International Monetary Fund that does not just react to crises but prevents crises, and I want a World Bank that has the resources to prevent poverty and to facilitate amidst the collapse of trade credits the expansion of trade around the world.

So as we remember and celebrate that our European Union, and this Parliament, has so successfully expanded to welcome new members of our family, I say to Union members from Eastern Europe now: we will not walk away from you at any time of need; we will do all that we can to be on your side.

And let us not forget either that for hundreds of millions of people in the poorest countries, thrust into extreme poverty, this crisis is nothing less than a matter of life and death – the grim truth that because banks can fail and markets and trade collapse, half a million extra children, 10.5 million children in all, will die this year because they are literally too poor to live. And 10.5 million children is not just a statistic. It is one child, then a second child, then a third child, then a fourth – each of them not just a child but somebody's child; each a funeral that should never have happened; each a life that could be saved – a tragedy I believe that strikes at the very soul of my being and yours.

And times that are difficult for us must never become the excuse for turning our backs on the poorest of the world or allowing broken banks to lead to, and justify there being, broken promises on aid. So instead of allowing our European aid pledges to drift towards being mere intentions – then vague aspirations and eventually tragically quiet betrayals – we should instead redouble our efforts to make sure that ours is the generation that finally does make poverty history.

Now we can together deliver the biggest fiscal stimulus, the biggest cut in interest rates, the biggest reform in our international financial system, the first international principles governing banking remuneration and banking standards, the first comprehensive action around the world against tax havens and, for the first time in a world crisis, new and additional help to the poor.

But how do we build this global consensus for the global changes we need? Let me say one of the great opportunities ahead of us is for Europe and every other continent to work together, and today I want to emphasise also that Europe and America can work more closely together.

I talked to President Obama yesterday about what I want to talk to you about today – about a new era of heightened cooperation between Europe and America.

Now, never before in recent years have we had an American leadership so keen to cooperate at all levels with Europe on financial stability, on climate change, on security, on development, and seldom has such cooperation been so obviously of benefit to the whole world.

So, starting with the EU–US Summit a few days from now, when President Obama comes to Prague, we can transform that summit from just an annual meeting into an unstoppable progressive partnership to secure the global change that the world now needs.

And think of all the advances we, Europe and America, in a new era of transatlantic cooperation, can work together to achieve. Let us work together for a new worldwide climate change agreement – a climate change agreement initiated at the G8 in 2005 by Chancellor Merkel for the biggest cuts in carbon emissions the world has ever seen.

Let us work together, Europe and America, to defeat the growing threat of terrorism from Pakistan and Afghanistan that can strike any of our countries' streets at any time.

And with France, under the leadership of President Sarkozy, joining the centre of NATO again, let Europe and America work together to achieve something that was once a dream that is now in my view possible – a world where nuclear weapons do not proliferate and where the nuclear powers agree real reductions in their arsenals of nuclear weapons.

And let us work together for an urgent imperative all of us want to see in our lifetimes, something that all parties in this Parliament, I believe, crave – peace in the Middle East, with a secure Israel side by side with a viable Palestinian state.

But, you know, the most immediate and the most urgently needed gift our European and American cooperation could give is that as a result of our actions there will be more jobs, more businesses, more trade – as together we meet and master these great financial challenges of our times.

There is a quote from one of the most famous Europeans of all, Michelangelo, that it is better to aim too high and fall short than to aim too low and succeed. And that is the choice that we face now because, as I look round this chamber today, I see that all of us here today are not just witnesses, not just spectators, but potentially the makers of change, free to shape our own destiny.

The people of Europe need not be mastered by events. No matter what they are, we can be masters of them.

So let it be said of us that in the worst of times, in the deepest of downturns, we kept to our faith in the future and together we reshaped and renewed the world order for our times.

And I believe that only once the history books have been written will we be able to truly grasp the range and scale of the extraordinary challenges each country in every continent is having to deal with as a result of globalisation now. This is more than a moment of change in our common history; this is a world of change, and we should remind ourselves that the most epoch-making decades in European history have never been fully understood as they have happened.

If you look back to the Renaissance – one of the greatest ages the world has ever seen – we cannot attribute its impact on the world to a single date or person or breakthrough. Or the Enlightenment – we cannot say with certainty when or by whom or how it was launched, merely that today's Europe and today's world couldn't exist without it. And when we look back at the industrial revolution we can't point to the day the whistle blew and it began or highlight just one inventor or entrepreneur or a management committee that oversaw it. No. We can only say that, today, events that were not properly understood at the time, that we are all beneficiaries of them.

And so in this generation we face a world of change not yet fully understood, which we can either hasten or delay progress by the myriad of decisions that we take every day. And I say in this world of amazing change – climate change, environmental demand, energy needs, the risk of terror, poverty and inequality that has to be tackled, a financial crisis that has to be dealt with – let us not retreat into protectionism that is the road to ruin.

Let this be our legacy – that we foresaw and then shaped a truly global society for our new times; that, instead of globalisation being a force for injustice and inequality, we make globalisation a force for justice on a global scale. And that, faced with the most difficult of challenges, a united Europe founded on shared ideals, based on shared values, helped build this world anew.

14

D-Day

Introduction by Nicolas Sarkozy

As dawn broke on 7 June on the Normandy beaches, armies of men and women came from England's shores to liberate our country. France knows what she owes the British combatants who made the supreme sacrifice in the face of oppression and barbarity. She is eternally grateful to them. France honours their memory.

It is because they were foremost in my thoughts that the presence at my side of my friend Gordon Brown, Prime Minister of the United Kingdom, in the celebrations of the 65th anniversary of the landings was so important to me. His speech symbolised the duty of remembrance we owe those who died for our freedom. His words echoed in all French hearts the immense gratitude owed to the British combatants for the heroic act they accomplished when landing at the risk of their lives on the Normandy beaches.

What would have happened had the freedom fighters not come? We dare not imagine.

Today, the great totalitarianisms of the twentieth century have been defeated. The infernal cycle of vengeance, which had led the European peoples to the verge of annihilation, has given way to a reunited Europe, founded on peace and the building of a better future.

But grave risks still hang over the future of mankind. More than ever they demand that we, British and French, united by a brotherhood of arms sealed with the blood of our soldiers, act together, as we have in times past.

Together, we are fighting terrorism. Together, our troops are cooperating with all our allies to wrest Afghanistan from the threat of obscurantism and negation of the values of civilisation. Together – and in the framework of a European operation commanded by the United Kingdom – we are fighting piracy in the Indian Ocean. Since defending our continent and its values demands the commitment, capabilities and forces of the United Kingdom and France, the two strongest in Europe.

It's together, too, that we are tackling the challenges to the security of tomorrow's world: non-proliferation and the danger of the Iranian nuclear programme, economic regulation and the return to growth, global warming, energy security, migrations and the fight against poverty.

On all these issues, we are working hand in hand. It's what, during my state visit in March 2008, Gordon Brown called our 'Entente formidable'. He is absolutely right.

Never have the French and British nations been so close. Never have they cooperated to so great an extent at the United Nations, in the European Union and in NATO. We share the same ambitions and are endeavouring to carry our other partners along with us. When Europe follows us, when we succeed together in winning the others over, we carry irresistible weight in the world.

This Franco–British friendship is today possible because, at the darkest moments of our history, the United Kingdom was in the vanguard of the reconquest of freedom and defence of our common values. As Gordon Brown forcefully emphasised in Colleville-sur-Mer on 6 June 2009, it is more necessary than ever to keep these values alive, realise all the dreams of freedom still to come and honour the memory of our soldiers' commitment and sacrifice. We will never forget it.

On 6 June 2009, allied leaders and veterans took part in ceremonies in Normandy to mark the 65th anniversary of the D-Day landings. Gordon Brown, President Nicolas Sarkozy, President Barack Obama and Canadian Prime Minister Stephen Harper each spoke at the ceremony, also attended by HRH Prince Charles, at the Normandy American Cemetery, where more than 9,000 men are interred. The cemetery is close to Colleville-sur-Mer, codenamed Omaha Beach in 1944 – one of five beaches targeted at the start of the allied invasion on German-occupied France. Some 156,000 allied troops took part in the 1944 landings.

In this poignant address, the Prime Minister reminds us that those who risked everything 65 years ago did so in support of freedom: 'They enacted the belief that as long as one of us is not free, no one of us is free. They made real the timeless values enshrined in the Bill of Rights, the Declaration of Independence, the Charter of Liberty and in the call of liberty, equality and fraternity. In doing so they embodied not just the hopes of one age but the dreams of all ages.'

He goes on to stress that it falls to us, their successors, to 'complete our great covenant with the dead of D-Day – our promise that we would build a world worthy of their sacrifice and their heroism'. And he suggests that that line of thinking raises uncomfortable questions – how can we say we have achieved all we set out to do when there are 'dreams of liberation still to be realised, commitments still to be redeemed and vows to the dead still to be kept'?

D-DAY MEMORIAL SERVICE
Colleville-sur-Mer, France, 6 June 2009

Sixty-five years ago, in the thin light of a grey dawn, more than a thousand small craft took to a rough sea on a day that will live forever in bravery. On that June morning the young of our nations stepped out onto these beaches below and into history. And as long as freedom lives, their deeds will never die.

And now, more than half a century on, it is an honour for me to speak for the British people alongside friends – President Sarkozy, President Obama and Prime Minister Harper – each of us representing the peoples of our nations as together we salute the brave fighting men of the largest amphibious operation in the annals of warfare.

We remember those who advanced grain of sand by grain of sand, utterly determined amid the bullets and the bloodshed that freedom would not be pushed back into the sea but would rise from these beaches below to liberate a continent and save a generation.

So this is sacred ground. This day marks the triumph of good over evil and truth over lies and the victory of human decency over hatred and the Holocaust. For it is the only place from which, after five years of total war and forty million dead, Europe could be liberated. The place where breakthrough to victory occurred. The place from where you can chart the war's end and the start of a new world. And this is the place where Britain, America, Canada and the French came together as one.

People talk of Europe and America as continents that are an ocean apart – separated by thousands of miles of water and hundreds of years of different traditions. But on 6 June 1944, at this place and in that moment, Europe and America were bound closer together than at any time in any century, and so we are allies not for a season but for centuries ever more – people now bound for time immemorial by a shared endeavour and an unshakeable faith.

Those who risked everything here 65 years ago demonstrated that although tyranny may suppress, it cannot endure for ever. They proved that dictatorship may, for a time, have the power to dictate but that it will not in the end decide the course of the human journey.

They enacted the belief that as long as one of us is not free, no one of us is free. They made real the timeless values enshrined in the Bill of Rights, the Declaration of Independence, the Charter of Liberty and in the call of liberty, equality and fraternity. In doing so they embodied not just the hopes of one age but the dreams of all ages.

So intense was the allied cooperation that when Winston Churchill regularly asked to see strategists planning D-Day he never knew, until he arrived at 10 Downing Street, whether the officer would be British, Canadian or American.

And so, next to Omaha Beach, we join President Obama in paying particular tribute to the spectacular bravery of American soldiers who gave their lives for people whose names they never knew and whose faces they never saw and yet people who have lived in freedom thanks to their sacrifice and valour.

And I know that the whole of Britain will be proud that Jack Woods is today being decorated by President Sarkozy. And alongside the brave and fearless Canadians, Jack Woods landed on Juno Beach on that 6 June day and with his comrades went on to capture five bridges, and the hand that today receives the Légion d'honneur is the hand which liberated one of the first French villages to be free.

And there is an unbroken line from what happened here through to Arnhem, to the Battle of the Bulge, to the crossing of the Rhine and to the fall of the Third Reich and the end of Europe's enslavement.

On D-Day the sounds of liberation on the march were heard right across Europe. All over France, resistance fighters began to blow up bridges and railway lines. And we have heard before, and millions have read, that in Amsterdam Anne Frank was inspired to write of the news of D-Day as 'too wonderful, almost too much like a fairy tale'. And for her, even at 14, it was an affirmation that humanity could triumph in the midst of carnage. 'In spite of it all,' she wrote, 'I still believe that people are good at heart.'

And these words, written before her short life ended, in a diary she thought nobody would ever read, are perhaps the finest epitaph for these courageous young men of 1944. The immortal truth – that people are good at heart – is now an inspiration for another generation of courageous men and women in our armed forces today, whose goodness is to work for peace around the world. We salute their devotion, and our gratitude to them and their families must always be equal to what they give.

Above all else for you, the remaining few who outlived that day, that battle and that war, who gather here today with your families and children – so our children and our children's children will gather here year after year to honour you, long after you are gone. And far beyond these moments of reflection and remembrance, the threads of your lives and your ultimate victory are already woven into the fabric of the world.

Because if anyone had said on 6 June 1944 that we would create a new age of peace and union in a Europe that had been torn by centuries of conflict; that we would then witness a wall raised up by the hands of totalitarian power torn down brick by brick by the hands of people yearning to be free; if anyone had said such things in 1944, who would have dared to believe all this was possible? But the impossible has happened.

So now we must complete our great covenant with the dead of D-Day – our promise that we would build a world worthy of their sacrifice and their heroism. For how can we say we have achieved all we set out to do – the promise of peace and justice – when the shadow of nuclear proliferation still spreads across the earth? When Darfur is in the grip of genocide, Burma is in chains, Zimbabwe is in agony? When the enemy is not just violence but the mortal threat of poverty, hunger, illiteracy, disease and want?

There are dreams of liberation still to be realised, commitments still to be redeemed and vows to the dead still to be kept. And so we must be as if liberators for our day and for our generation. For today we are only halfway to honouring the pledges we made for a new world – only halfway from these beaches to the shining future, the truly global society, to which they opened the way.

The beacon of hope that was lit with the liberation of Europe must now lead us on – on to a world free of the danger of nuclear weapons, with all assuring the mutual security of each against terror and war. Lead us on to a world finally delivered from the evil of poverty and the sin of prejudice, where intolerance is never tolerated, where no one suffers persecution or discrimination on grounds of race or faith or differences of identity and nationality.

The newer world we reach for is not preordained or predetermined, just as victory at Normandy could not be predicted or presumed.

So, too, the success of our cause today is not inevitable. But neither is it impossible. And if our beliefs are God-given, our path to achieve them is man-made. And this place of all places affirms that free people can bend history in the direction of our best hopes. So it was on D-Day; so it is today.

15

THE BERLIN WALL

INTRODUCTION BY ANGELA MERKEL

On 9 November 2009, we celebrated the 20th anniversary of the fall of the Berlin Wall. That day, Prime Minister Gordon Brown gave an impressive speech in front of the Brandenburg Gate. The 20th anniversary of the fall of the Berlin Wall was a very special occasion for us Germans. It reminded us of the historic dimension of events in 1989, which symbolise the sweeping away of the Iron Curtain that once ran through the heart of Berlin, Germany and Europe. During the period when Germany was divided, the United Kingdom stood shoulder to shoulder with the Federal Republic of Germany. I would like to express my personal thanks, and those of my fellow Germans, to our British friends for their resolve and steadfastness.

At an event marking 20 years since the Berlin Wall fell, the Prime Minister paid tribute to the 'unbreakable spirit' of those who 'dared to dream'. He was taking part in commemorations in Germany hosted by Chancellor Angela Merkel. Also present were President Nicolas Sarkozy, President Dmitry Medvedev and Secretary of State Hillary Clinton.

In this speech, Gordon Brown acknowledges the role of Berliners: 'You tore down the wall that for a third of a century had imprisoned half a city, half a country, half a continent and half the world, and because of your courage two Berlins are one, two Germanies are one and now two Europes are one.' The Prime Minister adds that what, today, 'seems impossible – an end to nuclear proliferation, an end to extreme poverty, an end to climate catastrophe – can become possible and be unstoppable thanks to the power of people united in common endeavour'.

SPEECH AT THE 20TH ANNIVERSARY OF THE FALL OF THE BERLIN
WALL

Brandenburg Gate, 9 November 2009

President, Chancellor, Mayor, let me say first of all to the people of Berlin: the whole world is proud of you. You tore down the wall and you changed the world. You tore down the wall that for a third of a century had imprisoned half a city, half a country, half a continent and half the world, and because of your courage two Berlins are one, two Germanies are one and now two Europes are one, and no one can ever imprison a people who know what it is now to be free.

This wall was torn down not by leaders, not from on high, not by military might; this wall was torn down by the greatest force of all – the unbreakable spirit of the men and women of Berlin. You dared to dream in the darkness. You know that while force has temporary power to dominate, it can never ultimately decide. You proved that there is nothing that cannot be achieved by people inspired by the power of common purpose, and let me thank you, the people of Berlin, for sending a message to every continent that no abuse, no crime, no injury need endure for ever.

Let me thank you, the people of Berlin, for demonstrating that injustice is not the final word on the human condition. Let me thank you, the people of Berlin, for showing that in a troubled world with an Africa in poverty, Darfur in agony, Zimbabwe in tears, Burma in chains, individuals, even when in pain, need not suffer for ever without hope. And let your achievement – the achievement of the people of Berlin and Germany – inspire us that by the power of one united Europe working together we can advance prosperity not just for some but for all.

And I pledge today that Britain will always be at the heart of Europe. We will never give succour to extremism that would drive us apart. And let the celebration of that historic night and the celebration of this night ring out across the world that what seems impossible – an end to nuclear proliferation, an end to extreme poverty, an end to climate catastrophe – can become possible and be unstoppable thanks to the power of people united in common endeavour.

What has happened here in Berlin tells the world that the tides of history may ebb and flow but that across the ages history is moving towards our best hopes, not our worst fears, towards light and not darkness, towards the fulfilment of our humanity, not its denial. So as we stand here – as free people gathered today in the shadow of history – let us pledge that we will work together to write the next chapter of the human story. Let us write a chapter of liberty and of prosperity and of peace.

PART IV

DOMESTIC POLICY

As will be evident from the balance of the speeches collected in this book, the Prime Minister has actively addressed international issues for much of his premiership. These are fine speeches on any comparison, which deserve inclusion on their merits, but this international focus is primarily a reflection of the major global crises that Gordon Brown has had to confront on the economy and on climate change and because of the wars in Iraq and Afghanistan. In simple practical terms, this obviously reduces the time available for making speeches on purely domestic issues, but it does not mean that he has neglected domestic policy, and several excellent speeches on this subject are included in this part.

The Prime Minister's first statement to the House of Commons, in July 2007, shortly after taking over, was on constitutional reform. This was a surprise in the sense that his comments upon appointment and his speeches during the leadership election hustings in June 2007 revealed that education and health were his two main priorities. However, it was a theme that was to recur several times over the course of the following two and a half years, not least because of the parliamentary expenses scandal that dominated the headlines in 2009, following the leak of material to the media.

As demonstrated in the earlier chapters, the economy was the main issue for most of the period covered by this book, and included are three speeches that set out the plans the government made for preserving British jobs, housing and public services – and then for investing in growth and recovery. Gordon Brown has not, of course, ignored health and education, and two keynote speeches are included here, which, taken together, map out the new approach to the reform of public services. He has also made some fine speeches on liberty and citizenship, using his long-standing interest in Britishness and in liberty as the twin starting points.

And this part concludes with a speech on Northern Ireland – a topic to which the Prime Minister has devoted considerable time and effort out of the glare of publicity and which has recently concluded with the successful agreement on the devolution of justice and police powers.

16

CONSTITUTIONAL REFORM

If there had been no global financial crisis, it is possible that the defining issue in Gordon Brown's premiership might have been constitutional reform. Although this issue came to be dominated by the parliamentary expenses scandal, the new Prime Minister's very first statement to Parliament was on this topic, and he returned to it with a powerful new initiative as this book went to press.

This first parliamentary statement largely focused around what the Prime Minister said was the first step on the way towards building a new relationship between citizens and government, proposing changes that will transfer power from the Prime Minister and the executive: 'For centuries they have exercised authority in the name of the monarchy without the people and their elected representatives being consulted. So now I propose that in 12 areas important to our national life the Prime Minister and executive should surrender or limit their powers – the exclusive exercise of which by the government should have no place in a modern democracy.'

This statement set off a substantial programme of consultation across a wide range of issues, which culminated in the Constitutional Renewal and Governance Bill, introduced in the 2008–09 session with the aim that it receive Royal Assent during the fifth session.

CONSTITUTIONAL REFORM STATEMENT
House of Commons, London, 3 July 2007

Mr Speaker, all members of this House and all the people of this country have a shared interest in building trust in our democracy. And it is my hope that, by working together for change in a spirit that takes us beyond parties and beyond partisanship, we can agree a new British constitutional settlement that entrusts more power to Parliament and the British people.

Change with a new settlement is, in my view, essential to our country's future. For we will only meet the new challenges of security, of economic change, of communities under pressure – and forge a stronger shared national purpose – by building a new relationship between citizens and government that ensures that government is a better servant of the people.

Let me pay tribute to the contribution to our thinking – and the wider constitutional debate – already made by parliamentarians on all sides of the House. And because I want this process to be one in which we consult and involve not only all political parties but also all the people of this country, what I propose today is not and should not be seen as the final blueprint for a constitutional settlement but a route map towards it.

This route map seeks to address two fundamental questions – to hold power more accountable and to uphold and enhance the rights and responsibilities of the citizen.

And while constitutional change will not be the work of just one bill or one year or one Parliament, I can today make an immediate start by proposing changes that will transfer power from the Prime Minister and the executive. For centuries they have exercised authority in the name of the monarchy without the people and their elected representatives being consulted. So now I propose that in 12 areas important to our national life the Prime Minister and executive should surrender or limit their powers – the exclusive exercise of which by the government should have no place in a modern democracy.

While constitutional change should never limit our ability to deal with emergencies and should never jeopardise the security of our forces or any necessary operational decisions, the government will consult on a resolution to guarantee that on the grave issue of peace and war it is ultimately this House of Commons that will make the decision. I propose, in addition, to put onto a statutory footing Parliament's right to ratify new international treaties.

We will also consult on proposals that this House of Commons would have to approve a resolution for any dissolution of Parliament requested by the Prime Minister and that – while at present Members of Parliament cannot decide whether the House should be recalled – for the first time a majority of members, and not just the Prime Minister, should have that right subject to your authority, Mr Speaker.

The House of Commons should also have a bigger role in the selection of key public officials. I propose, as a first step, pre-appointment hearings for public officials whose role it is to protect the public's rights and interests and for whom there is not currently independent scrutiny. This includes the Chief Inspector of Prisons, the Local Government Ombudsman, the Civil

Service Commissioner and the Commissioner for Public Appointments. For public offices where appointments are acknowledged to be market-sensitive, the Chancellor will set out today how pre-commencement hearings will apply to new members of the Monetary Policy Committee, including the Governor of the Bank of England and the Chairman of the Financial Services Authority. I propose that we extend pre-commencement hearings to utility and other regulators, that we review, too, the arrangements for making appointments to NHS boards, and it is right that this House of Commons vote on the appointment of the Chair of the new Independent Statistics Board.

Mr Speaker, I can announce that from now on the government will regularly publish, for parliamentary debate and public scrutiny, our national security strategy – setting out for the British people the threats we face and the objectives we pursue. I have said for some time that the long-term and continuing security obligation upon us requires us to coordinate military, policing, intelligence and diplomatic action – and also to win hearts and minds in this country and round the world. So, following discussions over the last few months, I have decided to establish within government a National Security Council charged with bringing together our overseas, defence and security but also our development and community-relations effort – and sending out a clear message that at all times we will be vigilant and we will never yield in addressing the terrorist threat.

As the security agencies themselves recognise, greater accountability to Parliament can strengthen, still further, public support for the work they do. So while ensuring necessary safeguards respecting confidentiality and security, we will consult on whether and how the Intelligence and Security Committee can be appointed by and report to Parliament. And we will start now with hearings, where possible held in public; a strengthened capacity for investigations; reports subject to more parliamentary debate; and greater transparency over appointments to the Committee.

The Church of England is, and should remain, the established church in England. Establishment does not, however, justify the Prime Minister influencing senior church appointments, including bishops. And I also propose that the government should consider relinquishing its residual role in the appointment of judges.

The role of attorney general, which combines legal and ministerial functions, needs to change. And while we consult on reform, the Attorney General has decided, except if the law or national security requires it, not to make key prosecution decisions in individual criminal cases.

To reinforce the neutrality of the Civil Service, the core principles governing it will no longer be set at the discretion of the executive but will be legislated by Parliament – and so this government has finally responded to the central recommendation of the Northcote–Trevelyan report on the Civil Service made over 150 years ago in 1854.

The frameworks for granting pardons and for issuing and withdrawing passports should also be set not by government but by Parliament.

And I propose we reduce the advance sight government departments have of the release of statistical information – from as much as five days currently to just twenty-four hours.

Mr Speaker, even as we reduce the power of the executive, we will also increase its accountability. Following my decision to revoke the provisions which previously allowed special advisors to give orders to civil servants, I am today publishing a new Ministerial Code which provides for a new independent adviser to supervise disclosure and who I can ask to scrutinise ministerial conduct, including conflicts of interest.

I propose we reinforce the accountability of the executive to Parliament and the public with a statement in the summer, prior to the Queen's speech, on the provisional forward legislative programme and annual departmental reports debated in Parliament.

But just as the executive must become more accountable to Parliament, Parliament itself must become more accountable.

Given the vote in this House in March for major reform of the House of Lords as a second and revising chamber with provision for democratic election, a statement will be made before the recess as we press ahead with reform. A statement on the reform of local government will propose a new concordat between local and central government. We will fulfil our manifesto commitment to publish our review of the experience of the various voting systems introduced since 1998, and the House will have a full opportunity to discuss in detail and vote upon the legislation that flows from the European Union amending treaty.

Just as we have appointed ministers for each region of England, I propose that to increase the accountability of local and regional decision-making the House consider creating committees to review the economies and public services of each region, and we will propose a regular question time for regional ministers.

But while we will listen to all proposals to improve our constitution in the light of devolution, we do not accept the proposal for 'English votes for English laws', which would create two classes of MPs – some entitled to vote on all issues, some invited to vote only on some. We will do nothing to put at risk the union.

The right of all the British people to have their voice heard is fundamental to our democracy and to holding public institutions to account. Britain is rightly proud to be the pioneer of the modern liberties of the individual. And I think it right to make it a general rule that in this area there is independent oversight of authorities and accountability to Parliament. I also encourage this House to agree a new process for ensuring consideration of petitions from members of the public.

Disengagement is too often reflected in low turnout in elections. Britain is unusual in holding elections on weekdays, when people are at work, and my Right Honourable friend the Secretary of State for Justice will announce a consultation on whether there is a case for voting at weekends.

The government will also bring forward plans to extend the period of time during which parties can use all-women shortlists for candidate selections and to give more time for all parties in this House to take up this new right if they choose.

And while balancing the need for public order with the right to public dissent, I think it right – in consultation with the Metropolitan Police, Parliament, the Mayor of London, Westminster City Council and civil liberties groups – to change the laws that now restrict the right to demonstrate in Parliament Square.

Mr Speaker, these measures I have just announced represent an important step forward in changing the way we are governed. But it is possible to do more to bring government closer to the people.

While our system of representative democracy – local as well as national – is at the heart of our constitution, it can be enhanced by devolving more power directly to the people, and I propose we start the debate and consult on empowering citizens and communities in four areas.

First, powers of initiative – extending the right of the British people to intervene with their elected local representatives to ensure action, through a new community right to call for action and new duties on public bodies to involve local people.

Second, new rights for the British people to be consulted through mechanisms such as 'citizens' juries' on major decisions affecting their lives.

Third, powers of redress – new rights for the British people to scrutinise and improve the delivery of local services.

And fourth, powers to ballot on spending decisions in areas such as neighbourhood budgets and youth budgets, with decisions on finance made by local people themselves.

At the same time, we must give new life to the very idea of citizenship itself. All of us in this House would acknowledge there are very specific challenges we must meet on engaging young people and improving citizenship education, and I hope there will be all-party support for a commission to review this and make recommendations. And while the voting age has been 18 since 1969, it is right, as part of this debate, to examine, and hear from young people themselves, whether lowering that age would increase participation in the political process. And consultation will take place with you, Mr Speaker – and through the Leader of the House, this House – as to whether the Youth Parliament, and the Youth Parliament alone, should be invited here in this chamber once a year and on a non-sitting day.

What constitutes citizens' rights – beyond voting – and citizens' responsibilities – like jury service – should itself be a matter for public deliberation. And as we focus on the challenges we face and what unites us and integrates our country, our starting point should be to discuss together and then, as other countries do, agree and set down the values, founded in liberty, which define our citizenship and help define our country.

And there is a case that we should go further still than this statement of values to codify either in concordats or in a single document both the duties and rights of citizens and the balance of power between government, Parliament and the people.

In Britain we have a largely unwritten constitution. To change that would represent a fundamental and historic shift in our constitutional arrangements. So it is right to involve the public in a sustained debate whether there is a case for the United Kingdom developing a full British Bill of Rights and Duties or for moving towards a written constitution.

And because such fundamental changes should happen only where there is a settled consensus on whether to proceed, I have asked my Right Honourable friend the Secretary for Justice to lead a dialogue within Parliament and with people across the United Kingdom by holding a series of hearings, starting in the autumn, in all regions and nations of this country – and he will consult with the other parties on this process.

Mr Speaker, the changes we propose today and the national debate we now begin are founded upon the conviction that the best answer to disengagement from our democracy is to strengthen our democracy.

It is my hope that this dialogue of all parties and the British people will lead to a new consensus, a more effective democracy and a stronger sense of shared national purpose.

And I commend this statement to the House.

It is not often recognised that the parliamentary expenses scandal was precipitated by the powers available under the Freedom of Information Act. If a daily newspaper had not published the details first, they would have had to have been made available anyway under an FOI request. Gordon Brown has on a number of occasions said that he supports the FOI legislation: 'Freedom of information can be inconvenient, at times frustrating and, indeed, embarrassing for governments. But freedom of information is the right course because government belongs to the people not the politicians.'

The Prime Minister was the first to recognise that Parliament's failure to act on its expenses would damage the whole fabric of parliamentary democracy in the UK, and his second statement on constitutional reform, in June 2009, centres on the action that needed to be taken to deal with the issue. As the Prime Minister says, 'the public require, as an urgent imperative, higher standards of financial conduct from all people in public life and an end to any abuses of the past'.

However, the Prime Minister also identifies a further set of substantial constitutional changes necessary to restore trust in Parliament and our politicians. As he says, 'all of us have to have the humility to accept that public confidence has been shaken and the battered reputation of this institution cannot be repaired without fundamental change.

'At precisely the moment when the public need their politicians to be focused on the issues which affect their lives – on fighting back against recession and keeping people in their jobs and homes – the subject of politics itself has become the focus of our politics.'

Gordon Brown concludes that the steps already taken to sort out the expenses crisis are necessary but not sufficient: 'At its first meeting yesterday, the government's Democratic Council decided to bring forward new legislative proposals, before the summer adjournment . . . that the House of Commons – and then subsequently the House of Lords – move from the old system of self-regulation to independent, statutory regulation . . . No more can Westminster operate in ways reminiscent of the last century, where the members make up the rules and operate them among themselves.'

But in the latter part of the statement, the Prime Minister proposes further significant changes – House of Lords reform; considering how to establish a written constitution for the UK; the devolution of power and engagement of people themselves in their local communities; reviewing the electoral system;

and increasing public engagement in politics, including whether to give further consideration to the voting age.

STATEMENT ON CONSTITUTIONAL RENEWAL
House of Commons, London, 10 June 2009

With permission, Mr Speaker, I should like to make a statement about the government's proposal to invite the House to agree further democratic reform, including legislation – before the House rises for the summer – on the conduct of MPs.

The last few months have shown us that the public require, as an urgent imperative, higher standards of financial conduct from all people in public life and an end to any abuses of the past. There is no more pressing task for this Parliament than to respond immediately to this public demand.

I believe that most Members of Parliament enter public life so they can service the public interest. I believe also that the vast majority of MPs work hard for their constituents and demonstrate by their service that they are in politics not for what they can get but for what they can give. But all of us have to have the humility to accept that public confidence has been shaken and the battered reputation of this institution cannot be repaired without fundamental change.

At precisely the moment when the public need their politicians to be focused on the issues which affect their lives – on fighting back against recession and keeping people in their jobs and homes – the subject of politics itself has become the focus of our politics.

Mr Speaker, we cannot move our country forward unless we break with these old practices and the old ways. Each of us has a part to play in the hard task of regaining the country's trust – not for the sake of our different parties but for the sake of our common democracy.

Without this trust there can be no legitimacy, and without legitimacy none of us can do the job our constituents have sent us here to do.

Mr Speaker, we must reflect on what has happened, redress the abuses, make sure that nothing like this can ever happen again and make sure the public see us as individual MPs accountable to our constituents. It will be what we now do, not just what we say, that will prove we have learned and that we have changed.

First, Mr Speaker, all MPs' past and future expenses should and will be published on the Internet in the next few days. Second-home claims submitted by MPs from all sides of the House over the last four years must be scrutinised by the independently led panel. This will ensure repayment where it is necessary and lead to discipline where there have been inappropriate claims.

And, Mr Speaker, I know that you are working to conclude the reassessment process urgently. We must now publish the past four years' receipts and start and conclude the scrutiny process as quickly as possible.

The House has already agreed to restrict expenses further to those needed for parliamentary duties alone, to cap the costs for housing, to require all spending to be receipted and to ensure that incomes from second jobs are fully accounted for.

All parties have committed themselves to accept the further recommendations of the independent Kelly Committee once they are received later this year – provided these proposals meet the tests of increased transparency, accountability and reduced costs for the taxpayer. But, Mr Speaker, these steps to sort out the expenses crisis are necessary but not sufficient; we need to go further.

At its first meeting yesterday, the government's Democratic Council decided to bring forward new legislative proposals, before the summer adjournment, on two issues which have been the subject of constructive cross-party discussion.

First we propose that the House of Commons – and then subsequently the House of Lords – move from the old system of self-regulation to independent, statutory regulation. This will mean the immediate creation of a new Parliamentary Standards Authority with delegated power to regulate the system of allowances. No more can Westminster operate in ways reminiscent of the last century, where the members make up the rules and operate them among themselves.

The proposed new authority would take over the role of the Fees Office in authorising members' claims; oversee the new allowance system, following proposals from the Committee on Standards in Public Life; maintain the register of Members' interests; and disallow claims, require repayment and apply firm and appropriate sanctions in cases of financial irregularity. Mr Speaker, I welcome the cross-party support for these proposals.

I believe that the whole House will also wish to agree as part of this process that the new regulator should scrutinise efficiency and value for money in Parliament's expenditure and ensure, as suggested to Sir Christopher Kelly, that Parliament costs less.

Second, the House will be asked to agree a statutory code of conduct for all MPs, clarifying their role in relation to their constituents and

Parliament, detailing what the electorate can expect from their MPs and the consequences that will follow for those who fail to deliver. It will codify much more clearly the different potential offences that must be addressed and the options available to sanction.

Mr Speaker, these measures will be included in a short self-standing bill – on the conduct of members in the Commons – which will be introduced and be debated before the summer adjournment. Mr Speaker, this will address the most immediate issues about which we know the public are most upset, but it will only be the first stage of our legislation on the constitution.

The current system of sanctions for misconduct by members is not fit for purpose and does not give the public the confidence they need that wrongdoing will be dealt with in an appropriate way. The last person to be expelled from this House was 55 years ago, in 1954, and it remains the case that members can be sentenced to prison for up to a year without being required to give up their parliamentary seat. The sanctions available against financial misconduct or corruption have not been updated to meet the needs of the times. This is not a modern and accountable system that puts the interests of constituents first. It needs to change.

There will be consultation with all sides of the House to come forward with new proposals for dealing effectively with inappropriate behaviour, including, potentially, the options of effective exclusion and recall for gross financial misconduct identified by the new independent regulator and the House itself.

And the House of Lords needs to be reformed, too. So following a meeting of the House Committee of the House of Lords, and at their request, I have today written to the Senior Salaries Review Body to ask them to review the system of financial support in the House of Lords – to increase its accountability, to enhance its transparency and reduce its costs. For the first time there will also be legislation for new disciplinary sanctions for the misconduct of peers in the House of Lords.

We must also take forward urgent modernisation of the procedures of the House of Commons. So I am happy to give the government's support to a proposal from my Right Honourable friend the Chairman of the Public Administration Select Committee that we will work with a Special Parliamentary Commission comprising members from all sides of this House, convened for a defined period to advise on necessary reforms – including making Select Committee processes more democratic, scheduling more and better time for non-government business in the House and enabling the public to initiate directly some issues for debate.

And given the vital role transparency has played in sweeping aside the discredited system of allowances and holding power to account, I believe we should do more to spread the culture and practice of freedom of information.

So as a next step the Justice Secretary will set out further plans to look at broadening the application of freedom of information to include additional bodies, which also need to be subject to greater transparency and accountability. This is the public's money. They should know how it is spent.

I should also announce that, as part of extending the availability of official information and as our response to the Dacre Review, we will progressively reduce the time taken to release official documents.

As the report recommended, we have considered the need to strengthen protection for particularly sensitive material and there will be protection of royal family and cabinet papers as part of strictly limited exemptions. But we will reduce the time for release of all other official documents below the current 30 years, to 20 years.

And so that government information is accessible and useful for the widest possible group of people, I have asked Sir Tim Berners-Lee, who led the creation of the World Wide Web, to help us drive the opening up of access to government data in the web over the coming month.

Mr Speaker, in the last 12 years we have created the devolved administrations, ended the hereditary principle in the House of Lords and introduced the Freedom of Information Act and the Human Rights Act.

But just as through recent changes we are removing ancient royal prerogatives and making the executive more accountable to Parliament, so, too, we will want to establish and renew the legitimacy and status of Parliament itself, which must now become more accountable to the people.

And Mr Speaker, democratic reform cannot be led in Westminster alone. Rather, it must principally be led by our engagement with the public. That is part of the lesson of the last month. The public want to be, and should be, part of the solution. So we must build a process that engages citizens themselves – people of all parties and none, of all faiths and no faith, from every background and every part of the country.

So over the coming weeks, the government will set out proposals for debate and reform on five major issues.

First, we will move forward with reform of the House of Lords. The government's White Paper, published last July and for which there is backing from other parties, committed us to an 80 per cent or 100 per cent elected House of Lords. We must now take the next steps as we complete this reform. The government will come forward with published proposals for the final stage of House of Lords reform before the summer break – including the next steps we can take to resolve the position of the remaining hereditary peers and other outstanding issues.

Second, setting out the rights that people can expect but also the responsibilities that come with those rights as a British citizen is a fundamental step in balancing power between government, Parliament and the people. Mr Speaker, it is to some people extraordinary that in Britain we still have a largely unwritten constitution. I personally favour a written constitution, but I recognise that changing this would represent a historic shift in our constitutional arrangements. So such proposals will be subject to wide public debate, and ultimately the drafting of such a constitution would be a matter for the widest possible consultation with the British people themselves.

Third is the devolution of power and engagement of people themselves in their local communities. The House will be aware of the proposals for the completion of devolution of policing and justice in Northern Ireland. Next week the Calman Commission will report with recommendations on the future of devolution in Scotland within the UK. The government's 2006 Act permits further devolution in Wales, on which there are discussions.

And my Right Honourable friend the Communities and Local Government Secretary will set out how we will strengthen the engagement of citizens in the democratic life of their own communities as we progress the next stage of devolution in England. So we must consider whether we should offer stronger, clearly defined powers to local government and city regions and strengthen their accountability to local people.

Mr Speaker, last year we published our review of the electoral system, and there is a long-standing debate on this issue. I still believe the link between the MP and constituency is essential and that it is the constituency that is best able to hold MPs to account. We should only be prepared to propose change if there is a broad consensus in the country that it would strengthen our democracy and our politics by improving the effectiveness and legitimacy of both government and Parliament and by enhancing the level and quality of public representation and engagement. Mr Speaker, we will set out proposals for taking this debate forward.

Fifth, we will set out proposals for increasing public engagement in politics. To improve electoral registration, we will consider how we increase the number of people on the register and help to combat fraud. And on receipt of the Youth Citizenship Commission Report – and having heard from young people themselves – we will set out the steps we will take to increase the engagement of young people in politics, including whether to give further consideration to the voting age.

Mr Speaker, as we come forward with proposals, in each case the government will look to consult widely. And all proposed reforms will be underpinned by cross-party discussions. Our proposals will also be informed by leading external figures, including academics and others who command public respect and have a recognised interest or expertise in the different elements of democratic reform. I expect this, in time, to shape the government's forward legislative programme and to feed into the Queen's speech.

Mr Speaker, in the midst of all the rancour and recrimination, let us seize the moment to lift our politics to a higher standard. In the midst of doubt, let us revive confidence. Let us stand together because on this at least I think we all agree – that Britain deserves a political system equal to the hopes and character of our people. Let us differ on policy; that is inevitable. But let us stand together for integrity and democracy; that is now more essential then ever. And I commend this statement to the House.

Although the following speech was given in February 2010, and therefore falls outside the timescale of this book, it is included here because it provides a natural end-point for this important strand of the Prime Minister's thinking on constitutional matters.

The speech sets out the next stages on the government's agenda for constitutional and parliamentary reform. This revolves around two fundamental issues – how we restore the legitimacy, credibility and effectiveness of Parliament through reform of the House of Lords and the House of Commons, clarifying and codifying our constitutional rights and responsibilities and creating a public life that better reflects the dynamism and diversity of Britain; and how we distribute power between individuals, neighbourhoods, regions and the centre.

And the Prime Minister believes that our democracy will be in trouble if people are disenchanted with politics. That means working to create a new kind of politics that re-engages the public, involving the following proposals: a referendum, early in the next Parliament, on whether to change to the alternative vote system for elections to the House of Commons; continuing with proposals in the Constitutional Reform and Governance Bill, including to end the hereditary principle in the House of Lords, providing sanctions for gross misconduct by peers; placing the Civil Service Code on a statutory footing; publishing draft clauses for a bill to produce a democratically accountable House of Lords; legislation to allow for the recall of MPs in situations where gross financial impropriety has been proven and where Parliament itself has failed to act; proposals to reform parliamentary procedure, as proposed by the Wright Committee; codification of the existing unwritten, piecemeal conventions that govern much of the way central government operates; and setting up a cross-party group to identify the principles that should be included in a written constitution.

Although the initial response from the opposition to these proposals was that they were too little too late, there was more than just grudging acceptance that Gordon Brown had raised important issues in this speech – issues that will need to be addressed if trust is to be restored in our democracy, for the good of all.

SPEECH TO THE INSTITUTE FOR PUBLIC POLICY RESEARCH
London, 2 February 2010

It's clear people want to change the way politics is done in this country. People want to get involved in big causes and want to be part of a strong community, as they showed so movingly in the recent Haiti disaster appeal and in campaigns like Make Poverty History before it, but we have to accept we have a lot to do to make politics the focus of their idealism and their hopes.

From young people who have more faith in single-issue campaigns than broad-based party programmes to the people who say they won't vote, to those who are tempted by the fringes and the extremes, it is clear that the way we do politics in the future needs to be different from the past.

And while the vast majority of MPs work around the clock to serve their communities, it is clear that the public have been rightly outraged by the expenses crisis, so trust needs to be restored.

And so the question today is do we make the championing of the renewal of politics and a new constitutional settlement a central cause for this decade, or do we just talk about change without giving it substance? This choice must be faced head-on, so that we arrive at a radical, modern, open and democratic agenda to change the way our country governs itself.

As a constitutional reformer and long-standing supporter of change, I admit that at times I have been frustrated by the slowness of the process of change. But with the Constitutional Reform Bill now going through the House of Commons, it is now time to set out the next stage of reform – and how we can reshape the terms of the debate about our constitutional future and how, over the next few months and beyond, we can accelerate the pace of change.

I believe this agenda can inspire progressives who believe in shifting power back to the people, but we must embrace the right kind of change not the wrong kind of change. And so I believe that the choice before us is clear – whether we advance towards a new politics where individuals have more say and more control over their lives or whether, by doing nothing or by design, we retreat into a discredited old politics, leaving power concentrated in the hands of the old elites.

Let me be specific about the choices. It is a choice between the new politics of ending the hereditary principle in the Lords in a bill before Parliament now or letting it continue for far too long into the future.

It's a choice between agreeing to move ahead with a democratically accountable House of Lords or postponing further change for more than a decade.

It is a choice between the new politics of offering the people the chance to ensure each MP has a majority mandate from the voters and the old politics of 'no change'.

It is a choice between the new politics of giving the people a right to recall MPs who break the rules where Parliament itself fails to act or refusing the people a say even if members place their personal greed above their public duty.

It is a choice between putting into people's hands more rights to information and to a say over the work of government or a constitutional stalemate.

And it is a choice which today also goes to the heart of the delivery of our public services – giving people new rights to control the services they depend upon – or simply muddling through in the old ways.

The new politics is, in essence, a choice between parties who want to make the people more powerful and those who talk about change but reject the changes that would genuinely empower people.

My interest in these questions is not new but long-standing. And our government has already helped deliver changes that have given more power to people, with changes that are more profound than any to politics since the war – and where we have been able to achieve it we have sought and won all-party support.

Devolution for Scotland, Wales and Northern Ireland and the creation of a mayor for London is about power redistributed away from the centre and held closer to the people. And I cannot overstate the importance of proceeding with the devolution of policing and justice in Northern Ireland.

The independence of the Bank of England and, more recently, the independence of national statistics is about the executive being prepared to give up long-held powers.

A new Supreme Court establishes a stronger relationship between the legislature, the executive and the judiciary.

Offering people legal rights to public services and entitlements is a way of ensuring fair access to all, while at the same time improving public services for the many.

And guaranteeing individual liberties through the Human Rights Act, making public data available and delivering freedom of information, has started a process of giving more power to the individual and enshrining in our constitution our commitments to liberty – a matter I feel so passionately about that I want to return to it in a later speech.

And one of my first actions on becoming Prime Minister was to propose new powers for Parliament and to set out my thoughts on how we could enshrine our belief in liberty in better policies for the future. Reform of Parliament has included giving to the representatives of the people the final responsibility for the agreement of treaties, agreeing the removal of ancient royal prerogatives, giving select committees the power to hold pre-appointment hearings and, for the first time ever, putting civil service independence on a statutory footing. Indeed, many of these issues are currently contained in the Constitutional Reform and Governance Bill currently going through Parliament.

But while this government's record is one of real change, the changes we have made are not nearly enough to deliver the new politics which I want to see and which we need to secure for the benefit of the British people.

For let us be in no doubt that we are talking today about some fundamental questions about our lives together as citizens – where power is located, how it is distributed, how it can be exercised and how we can make changes when institutions no longer work at their best for the people they should serve.

And there are real choices with real consequences for people's lives. Politics shouldn't be seen just as sport, spectacle or sideshow. For all its shortcomings it is the greatest vehicle mankind has yet devised for lasting peace and shared prosperity.

When politics works, conflicts are resolved, unity is established, cohesion is advanced and nations are prosperous and at peace. And in recent times politics has also become how we are able to determine the care our sick and our old people are entitled to, the help our families receive, the education our children have a right to.

When politics works, health services are delivered, education is of the highest standards, crime and antisocial behaviour are dealt with and we all feel part of something bigger than ourselves. It is not an end in itself but the way that determines the rules of a civilised society.

And if we are to renew the politics of Britain for our times and for the future, the agenda must be about change in how we distribute power between individuals, neighbourhoods, regions and the centre and about change in how we restore the legitimacy, credibility and effectiveness of Parliament through reform of the unelected House of Lords, a referendum on a new voting system for the House of Commons and a public life that starts to reflect the dynamism and diversity of Britain.

And so let me begin with our agenda for change in the House of Lords. There is simply no space for a hereditary principle in a modern legislature, and so in the last few days we have voted to remove the procedures by which new hereditary peers can join the House of Lords. It is for others to explain their opposition to this immediate change, but our proposals for the Lords are based on very simple principles – that the new politics cannot be real without fundamental change of the functioning of our ancient institutions, and we must do away with the unacceptable practices of an earlier age that are redolent of deference and privilege.

Let me put on record my huge admiration for the individual peers of the House of Lords for the professional and dedicated way they have conducted their role.

But I also say today: a modern democracy cannot tolerate power to initiate and revise legislation being held for ever by those without a mandate from the people. So in the next few weeks we will be publishing the key parts of a draft bill for a democratically accountable House of Lords. And my pledge today is that we will take forward these reforms in the next term of a Labour government, completing the work started before the First World War and to which we have been committed since then.

And alongside our moves to bring democracy to the second chamber, we will also bring new politics to the primary seat of power in the land – the House of Commons.

And it was in the search for a new and fairer way of arranging our affairs that we set up the Wright Committee, and in thanking them for their work

I am happy to confirm that we will give Parliament itself more control over its business and the elections of its committees.

So parties should elect their own members of select committees in a secret ballot; select-committee chairs should be elected by a ballot of the whole House; and non-government business should be managed by Members of Parliament, not the executive.

These reforms will increase the ability and the legitimacy of Parliament to hold the government to account – as I believe that the proper role of Parliament is, indeed, to scrutinise the executive, and it should be given all the necessary tools to do so.

On Thursday, Sir Thomas Legg will publish his findings on expenses. It will be a sobering moment for the House of Commons. But transforming Parliament must mean going much further than even our recent root-and-branch changes to the parliamentary allowances system. It was right to take away from MPs their ability to set and police their pay and expenses, and so self-regulation has given way to statutory regulation by people independent of MPs. But we are also determined to do all that is necessary to restore trust and to ensure that all MPs, like the vast majority do already, concentrate on serving the public and not themselves.

And that is why in grave situations where financial impropriety has been proven but where Parliament itself has failed to act, we are proposing the ultimate power of recall by the people.

But, in the new politics, it is also essential that MPs are accountable to their constituents and that their mandate is clear and strong. If the public choose this change as the right way forward, I hope we can move to a situation where every MP is able to say, as they cannot today, that, when it came to the final count, they were the choice of an absolute majority.

The first-past-the-post system maintains a clear link to a Member of Parliament's constituency, and it has usually given governments a clear mandate to govern. But as we seek to re-engage people and enhance public participation, I believe we should ask the people to look afresh at whether the electoral system can enhance the mandate of the constituency MP as well as engaging people further in the choice they have at the ballot box.

The alternative vote system has the advantage of maintaining the benefit of a strong constituency link – allowing MPs to be not simply policy makers but also community leaders, community organisers and the strongest champions for neighbourhoods they know and love.

But if the people decide to back the alternative vote, it also offers voters increased choice with the chance to express preferences for as many of the candidates as they wish. It means that each elected MP will have the chance to be elected with much broader support from their constituency, not just those who picked them as their first choice. In short it offers a system where the British people can, if they so choose, be more confident that their MP truly represents them, while at the same time remaining directly accountable to them.

Any change will not be for the forthcoming election. But we are agreed there should be a referendum at a date in the near future, because any decision on something as fundamental as electoral reform must not be the subject of an executive decision endorsed by Parliament but rather a question for the British people in a referendum. I will argue and campaign for such a change.

And because this is a major change in our democratic arrangements, we are today publishing the key clauses we are tabling as part of the Constitutional Reform and Governance Bill. That bill will have the effect of introducing the primary legislation required to hold a referendum on moving to the alternative vote system, which we intend should be held before the end of October 2011.

And in moving towards a more democratic form of election, I hope too that we can move towards making Parliament itself better reflect the people it serves.

When I entered Parliament in 1983, the House of Commons was an all-white chamber. There were only 23 women. Just think – a chamber where 50 per cent of the population had only 3 per cent of the representation.

And while my party has a proud record of having the first black MP, the first black cabinet minister, the first Asian and the first Muslim MP attending cabinet, and four times more representation of black, Asian and minority ethnic representatives than the other parties put together, there are no grounds for complacency. A black woman did not speak at the Commons despatch box until late last year. That is unacceptable – and it must change.

The Equality Bill is extending all-women shortlists until 2030 – and I'm proud that already three in every five of those candidates selected for the Labour Party in seats we currently hold are women. And we will take measures to improve representation and diversity and remove barriers based on gender or sexuality, disability, race or background.

I am committed to it not just because it is at the heart of my values but because it is also in the interests of the whole country to have the talents and perspectives of all the people of Britain represented in the ways we make decisions. So we will change both the Commons and the Lords, because we are so profoundly committed to the renewal of parliamentary democracy. We will ensure that the new politics will be delivered in the House of Commons, and we will do more to restore the relationship of mutual respect between MPs and those who elect them.

But the test of our commitment to democracy is not merely the changes we make to the institutions at the centre – it is how far we are prepared to give power away, to give citizens themselves greater control over their lives. That is why citizen empowerment must be at the heart of the new politics I want to see. That means opening up government, with much more control and information held by the public and not concentrated in Westminster and Whitehall. Over and above our commitment to transparency through FOI we are committed to progressively reducing the time taken to release official documents – ensuring the public have access to public papers far quicker than ever before.

And we can now open up government in new transformative ways not open to us a decade ago. We have brought public services closer to people in the Internet age through the direct.gov website. And last year I invited Sir Tim Berners-Lee, the inventor of the World Wide Web, and Professor Nigel Shadbolt to work with us on opening up even more government information to all the people of the country.

In a short space of months we have now created data.gov.uk, which already opens over 2,500 data sets to enable people to hold us to account and make decisions about their public services – from monitoring traffic accidents locally to seeing how your local schools are performing.

But this is just the start of creating new, more transparent public services and public sector bodies. Public services will not only be more personal in future but they will be more interactive – with the ability of the citizen enhanced to make their views known directly and influence the way our communities work.

Already as a result of the Berners-Lee–Shadbolt initiative a transformation is at work. A myriad of applications are being developed on the Web, by citizens for citizens – new websites on health, education, crime and local communities – that inform, enrich and enliven our democracy. It is truly direct democracy in action.

Over the next few months we will be releasing more and more information; we will make it easier to link different data sets together so that you can assess the overall picture of public services in your community;

and Nigel Shadbolt is working with local government to extend the same principles there.

To back this up, we must also create a more direct route for the people to make their concerns known to Parliament. And so we will support the case for public petitions to be debated in the House of Commons – a direct means by which the public can influence the political debate and decisions of the country.

Giving people far more say in and power over the services they use is not just about the better provision of public services – it is about new social rights that people can enjoy and see guaranteed.

For too long, until recently, public services have been seen as uniform – as take-it-or-leave-it services without individual control. But now, for the first time, the National Health Service has a constitution setting out individual rights of patients and, rightly too, their responsibilities.

And now we do not rest our case on the delivery of better services to people merely on aspirations or targets – we are offering personal guarantees to citizens about the rights they can expect and enjoy. The right to see a doctor in the evening or at weekends; the right to see a cancer specialist within two weeks; the right to early treatment in hospitals; the right, over time, to free health check-ups for the over-40s.

But we are giving rights not only in health but the right to catch-up tuition in education for those who need it; the right to education or an apprenticeship to 18; and then the right to effective neighbourhood policing.

And not only these rights to services – equally, the rights of many with long-standing conditions to control your own social care or health budgets.

These are lasting innovations which make public services personal services – more tailored to their needs and more subject to people's direct control. And I am sorry that there is not all-party support for this development of these new guarantees.

And as we expand and enhance direct democracy, so too we must let people exercise that power in the places that matter to them most – the towns, cities and local communities where they live. That is why the flowering of local democracy is a key part of our new constitutional settlement.

In 1997 we inherited a situation where local government had been starved of funding and had very little power over decisions taken that affected their communities. Many felt left behind by an over-centralised state in Whitehall which dictated rather than empowered people to shape their own prosperity. No wonder so many people felt that politics wasn't delivering for them; an invisible hand in Whitehall was determining their futures without properly understanding their wishes and concerns.

Our strengthening of local government with more powers and flexibilities – including recent advances such as the Total Place Initiative and John Denham's proposals to enhance scrutiny by communities over local services and public spending – has aimed to meet this legitimate demand for more power. We have also put communities more directly in control over key services that affect their lives – from neighbourhood policing to foundation hospitals.

And I want us to put more power in the hands of local communities and our great cities, ensuring that they are playing a central role in delivering the services, the housing and transport that their communities want and need, as well as generating jobs.

Local government should be free to innovate and to be creative in delivering better public services. And as we move forward with devolution, we can reduce the number of central targets and indicators, relying instead on core national entitlements and guarantees to ensure that increased localism meets the test of equity, so that high standards of public service are met wherever you live.

But make no mistake. Where others see localism as a chance to make cuts out of sight, to put up charges in a cut-price-airline approach to service delivery – a recipe for a postcode lottery – our objective will be local decision-making in a framework of guaranteed standards. So our guiding principle is that wherever possible control over excellent public services will be placed in the hands of the user, and that whenever risk and resources need to be pooled at a higher level than an individual family – whether that is local or national government – they should be responsive and accountable, with decision-making resting at the lowest possible level.

It is true that in the past local government has had too many streams of funding from a multitude of central government sources. Our Total Place reforms are potentially transformative in the better use of resources – they will allow local government and its partners to reach across all the funding coming into an area and enable better choices to be made at a local level about how this money is spent.

So while others may talk about localism, we have been delivering it. Take what is going on in Greater Manchester and Leeds. Out of the glare of publicity and based on the new tools we have provided, we are seeing a quiet but profound revolution starting to emerge as to how England is governed. These great cities have been pioneering new arrangements, and central government is devolving real powers over jobs, skills, transport, housing and low-carbon development so that they can be planned and delivered closer to the communities they serve. These reforms will make a real difference to people's lives – with the city regions and local communities themselves driving their futures, not being dictated to from Whitehall.

And let me add that I see business-led Regional Development Agencies as vital to helping make this work for the city regions and other areas. So while some would abolish RDAs, just when they are needed to help a strong recovery, we will ensure that they play their full role.

Not only do I hope we can finalise the agreements as soon as possible but I also want us to support other city regions to come forward and demonstrate similar innovation and leadership.

There is a wider issue – the question of a written constitution – an issue on which I hope all parties can work together in a spirit of partnership and patriotism. I can announce today that I have asked the Cabinet Secretary to lead work to consolidate the existing unwritten, piecemeal conventions – that govern much of the way central government operates under our existing constitution – into a single written document.

In the summer I announced that we would consult on the question of codifying our constitution as part of the consultation exercise on the British Bill of Rights and Responsibilities. There is, however, no consensus on what a codified constitution would be for, on what it would encompass and on what its status would be.

But if we are to go ahead with a written constitution, we clearly have to debate also what aspects of law and relationships between each part of the state and between the state and the citizen should be deemed 'constitutional'. I can, therefore, also announce today that a group will be set up to identify those principles, and I hereby issue an invitation to all parties to be represented on this group. And if we are to decide to have a written constitution, the time for its completion should be the 800th anniversary of the signing of the Magna Carta in Runnymede in 1215.

I believe the future will belong to those who understand the new politics and the need for change, and respond to the needs and desires of the British people for it. I will work with all parties to build a consensus for change, and I hope that we can all agree to put aside any differences and rivalries to work together for the constitutional renewal this country needs.

Throughout the agenda for constitutional change there is the choice between a progressive, radical approach and one that defends the status quo. And so these, for me, are the key questions to ask any would-be reformer: do they accept the need to remove the hereditary principle now, or do they wish to leave in place the mechanisms for renewing the supply of hereditary peers?; do they want the people to decide in a referendum on an alternative vote system, or do they oppose both change and trusting people with the choice?; do they believe that what really matters is making gestures to diversity or delivering real change?; do they talk about localism, or do they want to join us in giving local government real powers to transform people's lives?

The parliamentary expenses scandal scarred our democracy, battered the reputation of our Parliament and so profoundly breached the bond of trust between the people and those elected to serve them that it called into question the very legitimacy of Parliament and of our political system as a whole.

Politics is, in the end, about public service. So I say that for that reason alone the reputation of politics is worth fighting for; that people's participation in politics is worth fighting for; and building a renewed belief in our political system is worth fighting for.

Because whilst faith in Parliament and political parties has diminished, people have not lost their appetite for politics and for the change it can bring. So the urgent imperative for politicians on all sides is to do everything we can to connect with the people.

The current movement for constitutional change and new politics is of historic importance. It signals the demand for a decisive shift in the balance of power in Britain – a long overdue transfer of sovereignty from those who govern to those who are governed, from the old, outdated sovereignty to a modern popular sovereignty, not just tidying up our constitution but transforming it.

If we, the people, want a politics that is more open, more plural, more local, more democratic and more responsive to our underlying British liberty, then we will need to have the strength to make these changes, because the only way to ensure that politics serves the people's values is to make all those who wield political power genuinely accountable to the people.

That is what the new politics is all about – and that is why today this government pledges a radical programme for change.

17

FIGHTING THE RECESSION

In parallel with mounting a coordinated international effort to steer the global economy through the recession, the Prime Minister has led the effort to make sure that the UK economy weathers the storm effectively and is in the best position to make a strong recovery. His primary concern has, of course, been to protect British jobs, homes and public services, but he has also been concerned to ensure that we plan for the time when the worst of the recession is over and to ensure that the UK gets its share of growth in the world economy that will follow.

In the first speech in this chapter, to the CBI in November 2008, the Prime Minister argues that extraordinary times require extraordinary action: 'If we have learned anything in these last tumultuous and unprecedented months, it is that this is not the time to become prisoners of the old dogmas of the past. All over the world, policy makers are leaving behind the orthodoxies of yesterday, so – just as we set aside conventional thinking to invest directly but temporarily in the banking system – we now face the same challenge in monetary and fiscal policy.'

For the way forward 'is not just one isolated initiative or one individual measure, not even a set of measures for a few months. It is a concerted and comprehensive plan that will give real help to businesses and families while at the same time preparing our economy for the future', using this period of adjustment 'to build both the technological base and human capital to equip us for the opportunities ahead'.

The Prime Minister then explains his strategy going forward, which he says must involve a new approach to macroeconomic management in order to get through the unprecedented global financial recession with minimum damage to our long-term economic prospects – combining 'the use of monetary policy with proactive fiscal policy to support economic activity'. And because of our low public debt, the UK can support demand in the economy 'with all of the instruments at our disposal, while maintaining, not cutting, our programme of investment and reform for long-term benefit'. As Gordon Brown argues, what we need is a 'broadly based economic recovery, combined with prudent tax, spending and asset rationalisation plans over the medium term, that will help us bring the government borrowing back down over the coming years'.

The Prime Minister calls on industry to invest in intangible and knowledge assets, in ideas, brands and research and development – all areas 'dependent on technology and innovation . . . dependent on high-value-added talent and skills. These will be a vital force in building Britain's future high-value-added competitiveness in the global economy.'

And he concludes, 'Simply letting the recession run its course, to say there is no alternative, is not an option . . . To fail to act now would be not only a failure of economic policy but a failure of leadership. Doing "too little too late" would mean more damage, more deterioration, the loss of vital businesses, a weaker economy, lower growth, eventually greater fiscal problems and, in that event, higher interest rates and higher taxes.'

And while the Prime Minister stresses that the transition will be difficult, he also states that 'the prize for Britain is great – provided we can meet and master the challenges we face as we adjust to these new worldwide forces'.

SPEECH TO THE CBI CONFERENCE
London, 24 November 2008

The times we're in make this one of the most important conferences the Confederation of British Industry has convened. So let me first of all thank you for your contribution to British business and the British economy. Your dynamism, your resolution and your resilience – the hallmarks of your success – have never been needed more. Together we can take the British economy through difficult times and equip ourselves for our global future.

Let's just remind ourselves of the scale and speed of what's been happening – $25 trillion erased from global share values, world oil prices, having peaked at nearly $150 a barrel, sinking by two-thirds and, reflecting big forces at work, the rise of Asia, a global capital market, the global sourcing of goods and services. Quite simply, we are making the transition from the old world of sheltered national economies to the new world of a fully open global economy.

And the challenge is for each of us, in the spheres of influence we have, to surmount the risks and insecurities and manage the teething troubles of this new global age, while not losing sight of the vastly increased opportunities it brings.

Let's name one of the great challenges – the global financial system. Even if there had been no systemic banking crisis, we have come to a time when the global flows of capital need to be complemented by a global, not just a nationally based, framework of supervision.

Challenge number two is that of finite global resources – even if there had been no oil spike, our overdependence on oil, the problem of climate change and, indeed, global food shortages would have to be addressed by new policies.

Challenge number three is global restructuring and global inequalities – even if there had been no cyclical rise in unemployment, all of us would have to deal with the consequences of a more specialist international division of labour and the resulting restructuring of jobs, and for Britain that means investing in the new talents and skills required for the technological and creative industries.

Some might want to take a narrow and insular view of today's global crisis; some would say that the best we can do is to let the recession take its course and that there is no alternative but to muddle through.

But there is another way of looking at it. Whatever the troubles of this year and next, we are in the midst of a transition to a truly global economy which in 20 years is likely to double in size. With one billion or so new skilled jobs being created, we want to attract our share of that flow of new jobs. Together we must ensure that British companies will benefit from the new opportunities, as Asia becomes a market not just of millions of producers but of millions of consumers too.

Whatever else we do, as everyone here will know, we have to prepare and equip ourselves for what the world is becoming, investing in our talent and skills, in our technological infrastructure and in our capacity for innovation – the high-value-added products and services that are Britain's best guarantee of a successful global future.

And yes, the transition is difficult, but the prize for Britain is great – provided we can meet and master the challenges we face as we adjust to these new worldwide forces.

And I believe we are well-placed – we are a free-trade country; we have the most open economy in the world; we have a global reach greater than any other country on earth. We understand that protectionism does not work for economies or for workers – that better than simply protecting people in their last job is helping people into their next job.

And so to all those who try to prove, by pointing to this crisis, that globalisation and global markets do not work, our answer is very clear – the route to prosperity is not protectionism but an open, free-trading, flexible globalisation which must also be inclusive and sustainable.

So I am here to speak up for open economies. Our task is not to reject global markets but to repair and strengthen them for the future; not to condone excessive and irresponsible behaviour but to reward hard work, enterprise and responsible risk-taking.

But extraordinary times require extraordinary action. If we have learned anything in these last tumultuous and unprecedented months, it is that this is not the time to become prisoners of the old dogmas of the past. All over the world, policy makers are leaving behind the orthodoxies of yesterday, so – just as we set aside conventional thinking to invest directly but temporarily in the banking system – we now face the same challenge in monetary and fiscal policy, and for two reasons.

Worldwide, the orthodoxy of the last few decades has been that monetary policy is the only effective instrument for economic management. But the financial system that is a key channel of monetary policy has been damaged. So monetary policy cannot be our only tool. Monetary policy must play its essential role, but it would be a mistake to rely entirely upon it to pull the economy quickly out of this downturn.

And there is a second reason for the urgent action we propose. Ever since the Second World War, one of our greatest problems – and our greatest constraint on policy – has been the risk or reality of high inflation. Every framework for British economic policy has had to be focused on the containment of inflation.

But now after many years of inflationary pressures, this last year with sharp rises in global commodity prices, we face today the opposite threat – the prospect of rapidly declining inflation.

So, as the Chancellor will set out later today, and, indeed, as the leaders of the G20 countries agreed last weekend in America, a new approach to macroeconomic management is now needed if we are to get through this unprecedented global financial recession with minimum damage to our long-term economic prospects – an approach which combines the use of monetary policy with proactive fiscal policy to support economic activity; an approach which, because of our low public debt, supports demand in the economy with all of the instruments at our disposal, while maintaining, not cutting, our programme of investment and reform for long-term benefit.

Richard, in your letter you argue – rightly in my view – for a substantial time limited fiscal injection into the economy. And as you say in your pre-budget report submission, it is right to promote action now that can prevent permanent damage tomorrow. Simply letting the recession run its course, to say there is no alternative, is not an option.

We have seen in previous recessions how a failure to take action at the start of the downturn has increased both the length and depth of the recession. That was the mistake made in the recessions of the '80s and early '90s, the mistake made by the Japanese and the mistake made in the Asian crisis.

To fail to act now would be not only a failure of economic policy but a failure of leadership. Doing 'too little too late' would mean more damage, more deterioration, the loss of vital businesses, a weaker economy, lower growth, eventually greater fiscal problems and, in that event, higher interest rates and higher taxes.

The best way for taxes to be low in the long term is for us to ensure that the downturn is as limited in length and scope as possible. And that means help when help is needed, not when it is too late; a boost to the economy to sustain growth that will help to keep businesses open and protect people's jobs and homes; and a temporary fiscal stimulus is just that – temporary.

But to act now means we also have a duty to set out what we will do later. By showing we will take the necessary decisions in the medium term to guarantee stability, we can act today in a strong, decisive way.

And we must ensure that we get the greatest value for every pound we spend. I would like to thank four senior business leaders – Gerry Grimstone, Patrick Carter, Martin Read and Martin Jay – who have in the last five months used all their business expertise and experience to leave no stone in Whitehall unturned as we demand further ambitious improvements in government efficiency. The Chancellor said in the Budget that we must go beyond the £30 billion of efficiency savings already budgeted, and that is why we will be announcing further improvements in efficiency. For it is a broadly based economic recovery, combined with prudent tax, spending and asset rationalisation plans over the medium term, that will help us bring the government borrowing back down over the coming years.

Other countries, too, have agreed or are preparing to agree a fiscal stimulus, including America, where debt is already higher than ours and where the deficit is already rising to levels unprecedented in peacetime.

And just as coordinated international action is necessary to address climate change, energy security and global poverty, so too it is essential to coordinate interest-rate cuts and fiscal policy – magnifying their impact, as called for by the G20 leaders.

So coordinated action on economic recovery will benefit Britain. And a coordinated approach in Europe, our largest trading partner, would be of most benefit. That is why I have been discussing with other European leaders how we can best work together.

But I also believe that – while the downturn may be difficult and especially difficult for countries which have large financial sectors, like ourselves – our economy today is better equipped to weather any global economic storm than it was in the 1970s, '80s or early '90s, because, with your productivity growth, your resilience and your success, British business has achieved the fastest growth in average productivity in the past decade across the whole of the G7. And we will continue to make the changes in regulation and laws necessary to have the best environment to do business.

And we are better equipped today also because of Bank of England independence and now falling interest rates; because of the most flexible labour market in Europe and because we are now making further changes to make it a condition for people on benefits to seek not just work but the skills for work; and because, vital to our ability to invest publicly now, our national debt is considerably lower than a decade ago and lower than all the G7 countries except Canada – so there is scope for the government to increase borrowing at the right time to support the economy.

And I believe we are also making the right long-term decisions for our economy – not shirking the difficult decisions in planning, skills, flexibility, infrastructure and transport. For the way forward is not just one isolated initiative or one individual measure, not even a set of measures for a few months. It is a concerted and comprehensive plan that will give real help to businesses and families while at the same time preparing our economy for the future.

We now have a unique opportunity to do, in a twenty-first-century way, what was done in the twentieth century by the New Deal. As they built roads and bridges to create the infrastructure for the years ahead, we can use this period of adjustment to build both the technological base and human capital to equip us for the opportunities ahead.

So let me assure you that we will continue our programme of investment in the technological revolution ahead, in the talent revolution and in the environmental revolution.

Now, at the very moment of an economic downturn, is precisely when we need to step up our welfare reform and invest in our human capital – as many of you who recently put your names to the statement in the newspapers would agree.

Investment in intangible and knowledge assets, in ideas, brands and research and development – all areas dependent on technology and innovation, all areas dependent on high-value-added talent and skills.

These will be a vital force in building Britain's future high-value-added competitiveness in the global economy.

And to ensure Britain can make the most of the opportunities in the environmental revolution, we will support investment in the low-carbon economy – a worldwide market that could by 2050 be worth as much as $3 trillion per year and which could employ more than 25 million people. Because I want Britain to benefit from these new jobs – with at least 1 million jobs in the green economy by 2030.

So we are taking action to respond to the immediate financial crisis, and we are putting in place reforms and investment to benefit from the longer-term opportunities – so we are optimistic about the future of Britain. For this is a time for resolution and for solidity in responding to a unique financial crisis; a time for powerful action to equip us for globalisation's challenges and, in due course, to reap its rewards; and a time for confidence that, as real incomes pick up again next year and national and international policies work through the economy, so we in Britain have the strength, and everything it takes, to face the global storm and emerge stronger.

The Prime Minister also spoke to union members, and in this next speech to the TUC Congress he reflects on the actions taken by the government over the economic crisis and focuses on the lessons to be learned from the 1930s – particularly the need to maintain and enhance employment.

The Prime Minister starts by comparing what a difference a year makes. Referring to the recession and then Depression of the 1930s, he says, 'if I'd been addressing you a few years ago, that would have been of historical interest, a reflection of the crises of a distant age. But today these lessons, that when people need help you cannot walk away, are profoundly relevant, because the fears of depression have been precisely the worries workers, homeowners, savers and businesses have faced in the last 12 months'.

After covering the choices made by the government, Gordon Brown stresses that this is a long haul: 'But I tell you that we still have a choice to make; the recovery is not automatic, and the road to recovery is still fragile. It is being hard won by government making the right choices and could be quickly wrecked by government making the wrong choices. People's livelihoods and homes and savings are still hanging in the balance, and so today I say to the British people: don't allow anyone to put the recovery at risk.'

His message to the country as well as to union delegates is that growth is the best antidote to debt. 'And so I say to you today: don't allow anyone to derail the recovery and threaten tens of thousands of jobs by calling on councils to stop building the houses our people need. And I say to workers and businesses across our country: don't risk the recovery by abandoning what we know is now working – a modern industrial policy, a laser focus on tackling unemployment and worldwide support for coordinated global action.'

And the Prime Minister concludes on the theme of jobs, particularly for young people entering the labour market: 'And the first thing we must do is to ensure a generation of young people have the best chance of employment. In the 1980s we marched for jobs, we rallied for jobs, we petitioned for jobs, but because we were not in power we couldn't create jobs without a government committed to jobs. And so I ask you, the people who remember, to campaign with us as government to say that we will not allow a new generation of young people to become a lost generation. We won't let that happen – never again. Never again should their potential be lost even before their adult lives have begun. Never again should their talent be wasted or their contribution to the country spurned.'

SPEECH TO THE TUC CONGRESS
Liverpool, 15 September 2009

And it is hard to believe that we meet today in Liverpool, his home city, without the presence of our friend, the giant of the labour movement, Jack Jones. Jack Jones had ideals that were forged in the harsh and bitter experiences of the 1930s. Jack was always there for the people who needed him.

The '30s were, as Jack saw, a time when recession became depression because of the inaction of governments and the failure of the world to come together. And if I'd been addressing you a few years ago, that would have been of historical interest, a reflection of the crises of a distant age. But today these lessons, that when people need help you cannot walk away, are profoundly relevant, because the fears of depression have been precisely the worries workers, homeowners, savers and businesses have faced in the last 12 months.

Like the 1920s and 1930s, banks that should have been stewards of people's money had become speculators with people's money. But unlike the 1930s, and having learned the lessons Jack learned from them, we have not stood aside and left people on their own.

The lesson of the 1930s is that whenever banks collapse and markets fail, governments cannot stand aside; they must ensure that the savings of people, their mortgages, their credit are all protected, and they must intervene to save jobs. For many of you will remember that it was around this time last year that a financial crisis was rolling over the Atlantic towards us – a crisis so great that if we did not act there was every possibility of a great, new depression.

A year ago today, the 160-year history of Lehman Brothers Bank came to an end. A bank that had survived the Great Depression and survived two world wars collapsed and could not survive the global storm, and 25,000 people lost their jobs overnight. But that was only the beginning; Lehman's was so entangled with the rest of the banking system, and we saw what was the equivalent of a power cut right across the banking system of the world and trust collapsing. It was clear we were facing a crisis of such speed and scope that, left unchecked, there was every chance that the whole system could totally freeze up – with people on high streets across our country unable to get any money from the hole in the wall, families' life savings being swallowed up and companies unable to process their payrolls.

The reports I was looking at were as stark as they were serious – we were facing a situation that could have been worse than 1929. And I knew then that it was going to have to be us, the government, that was going to have to step in directly and ensure whatever happened to the banks did not put at risk the savings of the British people, the mortgages households depended on, the credit that businesses need to maintain jobs, and thousands of jobs themselves.

And it was here in Britain that we took the first steps to recovery. We had to make a big choice – whether to trust the banks when many said they simply had a cash-flow problem or whether there were structural failures that had to be addressed.

We had another big choice – to leave the markets to sort it out for themselves or to intervene with radical and unprecedented action to sort them out. And we made our choice – taking majority shares of two of the biggest banks in the world, restructuring the banking system and, to prevent savers losing out, putting in place the biggest insurance policy that Britain has ever had. Fortunately, that is what other countries started to do also.

But then we had another big choice to make – to let the recession run its course, as happened in the recession of the 1980s and '90s, or to intervene to support the economy with fiscal action. Our Conservative opponents said not to intervene, to let the recession run its course. But we made the decision to offer financial support to businesses and to help homeowners and the unemployed.

And I'll tell you why we did so – because for me every redundancy is a personal tragedy. Every mortgage repossession is a hope destroyed. Every business collapse is someone's dream in ruins. And where we can act we will not walk by on the other side. And as a result of taking action I can tell you over 200,000 businesses, employing hundreds of thousands of people, have been able to keep people in work. Not the choice of our opponents but our choice – the choice of the British people. Twenty-two million people have benefited from tax and other changes that have boosted their real income at a critical time. Not the choice of our opponents but our choice – the choice of the British people.

And up to 500,000 jobs will have been saved that might otherwise have been lost without the action that Britain has taken. Not the choices of our opponents but our choice – the choice of the British people.

And by changing the way the courts deal with repossessions and by guaranteeing help to homeowners in difficulty, we have helped 300,000 families with advice with their mortgages and have helped thousands to stay in the homes they've worked so hard for and were in fear of losing. And at no time in our history have we, the British people, done so much to support our homeowners, businesses and the unemployed. This didn't happen by default but by our decisions.

And we had a choice about international cooperation – with Europe and the rest of the world. We had a choice to let global forces, as happened in the 1930s, wash all over us or, unlike the 1930s, to work out a strategy together to deal with global markets.

We had a choice to go our own way, pursue national strategies in isolation and resist EU or G20 coordination – the great mistakes of the 1930s – or to work intensively together to ensure that policies are coordinated and the results of what we each do are magnified and multiplied by what we all do together.

To work with other countries, to have a coordinated attack on the recession, to have joint reductions in interest rates and fiscal action together – these were our choices. Not the choices of our opponents but the choices we made – the choice of the British people.

In each of these decisions the government would have made the wrong choices if we had followed the advice of our opponents and critics. And we know that the better path which we have taken – and not the one our opponents urged – could be worth up to $5 trillion invested in the global economy, and it could make the difference in output of 4 per cent and millions in work who would otherwise have lost their jobs.

We faced the Tories down, and we have been shown to have done the right thing by hard-working British families. But I tell you that we still have a choice to make; the recovery is not automatic, and the road to recovery is still fragile. It is being hard won by government making the right choices and could be quickly wrecked by government making the wrong choices. People's livelihoods and homes and savings are still hanging in the balance, and so today I say to the British people: don't allow anyone to put the recovery at risk.

There is a fundamental difference between the parties as to how to come through this recession and avoid it being deeper, longer and more damaging. And we still have big choices to make – the choice of whether we continue to act to help families and businesses or whether we listen to the Tories and withdraw support from families and businesses, cut public services now and refuse to invest in Britain's future.

So once again the country now has a decision to make about whether we continue the support that is necessary to sustain the recovery or we cut away the support now. And it's a choice that says something about what we believe – not as political parties but as people.

If I were to take the advice of our Conservative opponents, I would stop the school leavers' guarantee that is giving 55,000 young people a chance of work experience or further education. And I say to tell school leavers, after their chances have been destroyed by the failures of the banks, 'I'm sorry, there's nothing we can do', to abandon them to unemployment, is to repeat the Conservative mistakes of the 1980s which led to a generation scarred for ever. It would be callous and cold-hearted, and it's the wrong choice for young people, the wrong choice for Britain.

If we were to take the advice of our Conservative opponents, we would withdraw the support now available to homeowners and do nothing to prevent repossessions rising to the rates of the 1990s. But I say to you to tell a new generation of homeowners who have saved up to buy their first home and now face difficulties because of unemployment, 'we're going to do nothing for you now times are the toughest', is unfair and irresponsible – the wrong choice for homeowners, the wrong choice for Britain.

And I say to tell the business owner we'll wait and see if the strongest will survive but there's nothing government can do to help is the wrong choice for business and the wrong choice for Britain.

This is not the moment to cut apprenticeships; this is the time for government to support them. So I can tell you that we will provide 21,000 additional apprenticeships in the public sector this year. And this is not the moment to withdraw public support for house building but to step it up, and I can tell you that we have set aside £1.5 billion to build 20,000 additional affordable homes over the next two years, including, for the first time in many years, new modern council homes. And this is not the moment to abandon the help that has kept over 200,000 businesses afloat; this is the time to continue it, so I can say that businesses who need deferral of tax will continue to receive it over the coming few months. And we do this because it's right to help people but also because it's right for the economy.

Because the more jobs and homes we lose now, the higher unemployment rises, the lower growth is as a result and the more difficult it will be to secure our recovery, bring our debt down and keep people in their jobs and homes. Growth is the best antidote to debt.

And so I say to you today: don't allow anyone to derail the recovery and threaten tens of thousands of jobs by calling on councils to stop building the houses our people need. And I say to workers and businesses across our country: don't risk the recovery by abandoning what we know is now working – a modern industrial policy, a laser focus on tackling unemployment and worldwide support for coordinated global action.

Just this morning I met with the head of the ILO to discuss the best way of protecting jobs. In two days' time I will be working for British jobs at the EU summit, stressing the need to implement fiscal stimulus packages in full without stopping them prematurely. And next week, when I attend the G20, I will be putting the case for a global compact for growth and stability for now and for the future.

Last April we got an agreement about what we had to do together to move the economy forward through this crisis. Now we need an agreement about what we can do together to maintain the road out of recession.

I will be asking people to contribute to worldwide growth – to the benefit of jobs in all our countries. I will be demanding that banks beyond Britain do what we have done – to isolate their impaired assets and show how they are to be removed. I will be demanding that internationally we look at setting limits on city bonuses. And I will be standing up for what you believe – that there should be no escape from paying your fair share – and that's why I will be arguing that we should implement a blacklist on uncooperative tax havens.

And so be clear – my priorities in the coming weeks and months will be ensuring that jobs are retained, the recovery moves forward and that we offer people our vision of a fairer, more responsible, greener and more democratic Britain.

And I want a new industrial policy to signal the creation of 1.5 million new jobs for the future – jobs in green industries, in making the low-carbon cars that Britain is leading Europe in developing, in new digital services. And let's be clear – yes, jobs in the advanced manufacturing which will be central to Britain's long-term future.

And I believe that the fight for fairness must include agency workers, and so I pledge to you today that, when Parliament returns, our new legislative programme will include equal treatment for agency workers and that in the coming few months the law will be on the statute book.

And when the recovery comes, I want workers on low and modest incomes to benefit from rising prosperity. I want to see their skills rewarded with decent pay. I want them to have more chances to get on at work and get on in life. When people gain new skills, employers should make sure they use them – so that the company goes up the value chain and the workers can go up the pay ladder.

Because we know the pressures many people face as they balance the demands of work with the needs of family life. Since 1997 we have increased paid maternity leave from eighteen weeks to nine months. And we retain our ambition to extend it further. This is not only good for mothers but helps give children the best start in life.

But fathers have responsibilities, too. No Tory government has ever given a single day of paternity leave. This Labour government gave men the right to two weeks' paternity leave. Now from April 2011 we will give fathers the right to take up to three months' additional paid paternity leave during the second six months of a child's life if the mother has returned to work, because Labour believes in giving couples more freedom, dads more rights and children more time with the two people who love them most.

And I want to talk to you about the future of our public services, because in these difficult times people need to know the NHS, our schools, our vital front-line public services will not only always be there for them but, day by day, week by week, always improve the quality of the service they offer.

Take the National Health Service. Let us remember that here in Britain because of the NHS there are not millions of people uninsured. Here in Britain you don't have to check your wealth before they check your pulse. Here in Britain health is a universal right and delivered not on the basis of your ability to pay but your need.

And we are now transforming the Health Service again for this generation. We are now offering personal guarantees to patients about waiting times

– that from the time they go to the doctor to the time they have their operation they will not wait more than 18 weeks. And while the Tories want to abandon these guarantees, we are trying every day to ensure that the vast majority of patients get treatment even earlier. And that we will continue to do.

We have given guarantees to everyone worried about cancer that they will not wait and worry. And while the Tories want to deny that right of no more than a two-week wait to cancer patients, every year we are making it easier and quicker for cancer patients to be treated with speed. And this we will continue to do.

We have given guarantees about GP services – that there will be weekend opening and evening opening to suit you, the patient, to go at the time that is most convenient. And while the Tories want to leave GPs to do exactly as they want, we will ensure that this new right is extended to even more communities in the country.

And we will match those guarantees with the guarantee that every young person will have the right to education not to 16, as before, but to 18. Previously the only way to get personal tuition for children that could not read or write was to pay. Now we are extending the right of young people with learning needs and with special talents to get the personal attention they need. Not through private tuition but free individual tuition in our schools and in our communities.

And we will give a guarantee that every year each and every neighbourhood will have more extensive neighbourhood policing on the beat that communities need to be safe and feel safe.

We will do all these things and more, because we believe that decent education, health and services should be available to not just some but all of our people. But we can only make these improvements within a framework of sustainable finances. And to pay for these improvements and to achieve our budget reduction plan to cut the deficit in half over the next four years, we have to take action like other countries – America, Germany and France. We will have debt levels around 80 per cent of national income, and as the recovery happens we will have to plan to bring that debt down.

And that's why to continue to fund our public services and to cut the deficit we have announced we will raise National Insurance from April 2011 by 0.5 per cent to help pay for our public services. That's why at the same time we will remove unfair tax reliefs on higher-income earners. And why we will raise the top rate of tax to 50p for those on the very highest incomes.

So I must tell you the tough truth about the hard choices. My motivation is always to do the right thing by the British people – investing more during this recession – and others are following our lead.

And we have made the right choice to provide the support that markets and banks failed to offer. And we are doing the right thing to make sure that for the future, as we move into a full recovery, we will invest and grow within sustainable public finances – cutting costs where we can, ensuring efficiency where it's needed, agreeing realistic public sector pay settlements throughout, selling off the unproductive assets we don't need to pay for the services we do need.

Labour will cut costs, cut inefficiencies, cut unnecessary programmes and cut lower priority budgets. But when our plans are published in the coming months people will see that Labour will not support cuts in the vital front-line services on which people depend.

The choice is between Labour – who will not put the recovery at risk, will protect and improve your front-line services first and make the right choices for low- and middle-income families in the country – and a Conservative Party which would reduce public services at the very time they are needed most, make across-the-board public-spending cuts to pay for tax cuts for the wealthiest few and make different choices about public services because they have different values. These would be the wrong choices at the wrong time for the wrong reasons, because they have the wrong priorities for Britain.

We will at all times be guided by our values of fairness and responsibility. We will not cut public services to pay for huge cuts in inheritance tax for the richest few in the country. In contrast, Labour believes that there must be a fair distribution of the risks and the rewards. And so today I tell you we will be saving up to £500 million over the next three years by reforming Whitehall early-exit scheme payouts for early retirement. It's a scheme that's often as much as six times annual pay. These high costs prevent us giving other people jobs, and this is not the best way to spend public money. I am calling on all public authorities to make similar reviews of their terms.

Now I know that some people will say that with all the constraints in the world economy and the problems they have brought, can we still ensure that year by year we will keep advancing towards a fairer, more responsible society? I say when we came in, in 1997, we faced huge constraints to get the debt down and we chose the right priorities; we created the minimum wage, created Sure Start for children, improved schools immediately, ended the neglect of the NHS and created the New Deal that has helped two million people. We did it because we chose the people's priorities – each of us working towards realising the talents of all.

And the first thing we must do is to ensure a generation of young people have the best chance of employment. In the 1980s we marched for jobs, we rallied for jobs, we petitioned for jobs, but because we were not in power we couldn't create jobs without a government committed to jobs. And so I ask you, the people who remember, to campaign with us as government to say that we will not allow a new generation of young people to become a lost generation. We won't let that happen – never again. Never again should their potential be lost even before their adult lives have begun. Never again should their talent be wasted or their contribution to the country spurned.

And so let me tell you what we will now do. For the first time, we will put the apprenticeship programme on a statutory basis and ensure that an apprenticeship place is available for every suitably qualified young person by 2013. And thanks to Labour the minimum apprentice wage rose last month by more than 20 per cent.

And I can also announce today up to 7,000 jobs from the Future Jobs Funding – the next stage as we move to create 100,000 jobs for young people. In total we will spend £5 billion on creating jobs.

And, friends, as I conclude let me pay tribute today to our armed forces, who risk their lives to ensure global security. Their heroism is unsurpassed, and our gratitude to them is boundless.

I want to say just one final thing, because I know that so many of your members were the backbone of the Make Poverty History movement and are anxious about what the recession means for global solidarity and global justice. Let me reassure you today. There are those who would use the excuse of the financial crisis to break their promises to the world's poorest. Well, we will not. We will keep our promises. Let us remember that our beliefs, our conviction, our determination to fight for them has resulted in astonishing path-breaking and life-changing advances – debt relief, 500 million children to be vaccinated, 40 million more children in education, millions more with free health care.

And, friends, our achievements teach us never to believe something is impossible, never to believe a blind fate governs us all, never to believe that justice is beyond our reach. And so this is a moment that calls for the progressive policies we fight for and believe in.

The Prime Minister spoke to the CBI Conference again in November 2009. In this impressive speech, the focus swings towards recovery and growth: Britain's 'investment-led, export-led growth delivering high-value products and services into global markets . . . lifting our eyes to what our future priorities must be'.

The main part of this speech deals with what the Prime Minister calls the new realities of the global market place: 'First, it's clear that international economic cooperation is not now a luxury but a necessity. Put it one way – $1.5 trillion of American consumer spending a year has been taken out of the world economy, threatening growth for years to come. If we are to have balanced and sustainable growth that will keep unemployment low we will have to address together, and my chosen vehicle is the G20, a strategy for global growth – addressing global imbalances in trade, the inefficient use of reserves, the instability in oil prices – and agree together the contribution to higher growth each continent can make.

'Second, in countries like ours, public and private sector – business and government – can no longer engage in a sterile battle for territory with each other. As increasingly is being proposed in America, in France, Germany, China and India, public and private sectors have to work together for the national interest and in particular to promote the common purpose of growth. And more so now than ever before we cannot hold on to old dogmas and walk away from cooperation in Europe and beyond, and from creating an effective partnership between government and business.

'And third, we have learned that the reality is that global financial markets can self-destruct without being able to self-correct. And we must ensure that banks maintain their duties of stewardship, do not overcharge their customers and are held to account when they do so. Not just in Britain but internationally we need to rebuild trust between banks and the societies they serve.'

And the speech then sketches out the efforts the government is making to support the growth that will be required in the UK economy going forward. But the Prime Minister also warns his audience that going for growth requires a consistent and coherent set of policies: 'You cannot say you are going for growth and then in the next breath demand the withdrawal of the very measures essential to lock in the recovery and enable the growth to take place – the maintenance of the fiscal and monetary stimulus until recovery is established; and, within sustainable public finances, a determination to make the long-term decisions I have set out on expanding nuclear power and renewables; swift planning decisions; better transport and airports; investing in skills, science and, with our RDAs, regional economic development; and strengthening our relationships with Europe and the rest of the world. A modern industrial partnership – working with business to deliver support and intervention where it is needed but keeping out of the way when it is not.'

This is an impressive speech, setting out a real partnership for the public and private sectors in Britain to get the growth that is both necessary for deficit reduction and desirable as the engine of prosperity for the long term.

SPEECH TO THE CBI CONFERENCE
London, 23 November 2009

What I want to talk to you about today is growth – Britain's growth in the new global economy. I want to set out the best way forward – investment-led, export-led growth delivering high-value products and services into global markets. And, indeed, it is important that this can be our theme today – lifting our eyes to what our future priorities must be.

It's been a very tough year. These have been the most testing of times for British business – and for businesses right across the world. In less than a year in the United States alone over 120 banks have failed. Banks are expected to record almost $3 trillion in losses. With the collapse in available money, global trade fell in one quarter of this year by almost 20 per cent. And this year global trade is forecast to have its sharpest fall since the 1930s – down 12 per cent in a year. In the second quarter of this year exports from China, Korea, Japan, Germany and Italy were all down by nearly 20 per cent.

Investment flows to the emerging markets have fallen from over $600 billion a year to being negative. And the best estimate for the year 2009 is of 38 million jobs lost worldwide. So the global financial crisis led to a global trade crisis and then a global industry and global jobs crisis. And in the midst of these difficult times, I believe we have seen the true character of British business. Since we last met here, a year ago, you have had to show great resilience, great enterprise, great determination.

In the 1930s J.M. Keynes said we can either fail conventionally or succeed unconventionally. When we met here a year ago – in the face of extraordinary times – I said we were 'leaving behind the orthodoxies of yesterday'. And so with the whole global banking system in danger of collapse, we had a choice – to stand aside or to undertake a wholesale recapitalisation of the banks. We chose to restructure the banks. Thank you for your support in that.

The Bank of England, with our support, had a choice – whether to rest on traditional monetary action or to establish an unorthodox programme of quantitative easing. You supported quantitative easing too. Thank you.

And we had a choice – to let the recession simply take its course or to match monetary action with a fiscal stimulus. You supported us in initiating, through the new G20, coordinated fiscal action – in fact, $5 trillion of stimulus across the world.

Having already taken this unprecedented global action, there is another choice – the timing of withdrawal from that fiscal stimulus. And you agree with the G20, the European Union, the IMF, the OECD and every major economy and every respected economic body that we should be careful not to abandon the stimulus too rapidly. Choking off recovery by turning off the life support prematurely would be fatal to world growth. And it would be fatal to British jobs, British prosperity and British growth, and to our capacity to grow not just for now but for years.

So that's why we will, like other countries, continue with our plans to support our economy until the private sector recovery is established, and we will ensure that nothing we do will jeopardise that recovery. And now as we focus on coming out of recession we recognise that – not just Britain but across the whole world we are looking at new realities.

First, it's clear that international economic cooperation is not now a luxury but a necessity. Put it one way – $1.5 trillion of American consumer spending a year has been taken out of the world economy, threatening growth for years to come. If we are to have balanced and sustainable growth that will keep unemployment low we will have to address together, and my chosen vehicle is the G20, a strategy for global growth – addressing global imbalances in trade, the inefficient use of reserves, the instability in oil prices – and agree together the contribution to higher growth each continent can make.

Second, in countries like ours, public and private sector – business and government – can no longer engage in a sterile battle for territory with each other. As increasingly is being proposed in America, in France, Germany, China and India, public and private sectors have to work together for the national interest and in particular to promote the common purpose of growth. And more so now than ever before we cannot hold on to old dogmas and walk away from cooperation in Europe and beyond, and from creating an effective partnership between government and business.

And third, we have learned that the reality is that global financial markets can self-destruct without being able to self-correct. And we must ensure that banks maintain their duties of stewardship, do not overcharge their customers and are held to account when they do so. Not just in Britain but internationally we need to rebuild trust between banks and the societies they serve.

But whether it be protection against failure or changing the balance of risk and reward between the financial sector and the public, and whether it be the protection of the public through contingent capital or resolution arrangements or insurance or a global financial levy, the only action that will work is global action – action taken together by all the major economies.

But we must not, in the name of clearing up the mistakes made by some banks, do anything other than support and encourage the hard-working, entrepreneurial and responsible many. The agreements we put in place with RBS and Lloyds, in return for our support, will mean £27 billion of new lending for businesses this year and next. Other banks soon followed this commitment to lend so that, despite well-known problems for small business and high-technology companies, gross lending is now up and access to finance is improving. And we will always do whatever it takes to make sure creditworthy businesses can get the finance they need to invest, expand and grow.

And this last year has brought home to people all over the country the reality that Britain has to be competitive in the global economy. The global financial crisis is itself but one of the big changes that reflect the speed, scope and scale of globalisation. To highlight the changes that are happening, we are publishing a series of case studies of cities around the country (the first of which are available at this conference) called 'FutureStory', which illustrate how globalisation is changing the cities we live in, the jobs we do and the industries we are building – and how we are showing dynamism and initiative in responding. It shows how real people and real businesses are stepping up to be successful in the new global economy and should give us confidence that already we can see in our country – and in this room today – the building blocks which will make a success of our own future story.

The inevitable consequence of the events of the last year, and the extraordinary action we have had to take, has been rising fiscal deficits and debt – not just in Britain but in every major economy in the world. We are one of the first governments in the world to announce a time-specific deficit-reduction plan – including measures we have set out in detail on taxation and spending – that will, over four years, cut the deficit in half. And our Fiscal Responsibility Bill will enshrine this commitment in legislation.

Of course, the vast majority of the increased public borrowing has been caused by a lack of growth. And the most important driver of deficit reduction over the period ahead will be the growth performance of the economy and the speed with which we can get unemployment down. So our strategy for growth is not at the expense of necessary deficit reduction; it is absolutely central to that objective. So as we take measures to halve the deficit over the next four years, we will continue to make the investments in growth and skills that I know everyone here would expect this pro-business, pro-enterprise government to make.

You know in your own businesses what it takes to create worldwide operations – how important it is to take the opportunities offered by the new digital technologies; to develop infrastructure and governance that works across the world; to reduce deficits through a focus on growth and to attract investment. Just as these are the priorities for businesses so they are for Alistair Darling and Peter Mandelson and his business team; so the plans I am laying out today are to back up and unleash the entrepreneurial, innovative and dynamic talents of British business leaders and employees, and to enable us as a nation to keep corporation and capital gains tax low and meet these global challenges.

First, our commitment to build the first modern digital infrastructure, with the Digital Economy Bill and our incentives to stimulate private-sector investment, Britain will by 2012 lead the world in fast broadband services. And we are already working with Sir Tim Berners-Lee and Martha Lane Fox so that Britain can lead the next stage of the online revolution – through digital access to create new business opportunities and new jobs and to revolutionise the way government services work and cut their costs.

Second, our commitment to prepare for, and meet, our future energy needs with a shift to low carbon. To lead the world we have to invest now in renewables, in carbon capture and storage, and in new nuclear power stations. And we will now build not 12 gigawatts of nuclear capacity but 16 gigawatts – a total for new building that is bigger than all our current nuclear capacity and represents significant progress towards a low-carbon future.

Third, speeding up planning decisions. Against the opposition of every other political party – and because we believe it is right for the long-term future of our country – we have put in place a streamlined system for key national infrastructure decisions. The new independent body, charged with acting fairly and without delay, is up and running. Alongside our first plan on nuclear energy have come our ambitious plans for swift decisions on the development of our ports – with other plans soon to follow.

Fourth, a modern infrastructure. Going for growth means we are investing £20 billion this year in transport, double that of ten years ago – £1.1 billion to electrify two major rail lines; a decision to go ahead with Heathrow's expansion; and, over a number of years, £16 billion committed to Crossrail. And we are also investing heavily – £800 million by next year – in flood defences. By immediate careful inspection and then re-inspection of all Highways Agency bridges we are determined to keep safe and secure this vital part of our national infrastructure. I am conscious of people's worries about this, and I can say this morning that additional emergency funding will be made available from the Department for Transport to local authorities to support the necessary repair work for bridges and roads.

Fifth, investing in skills and science. Despite the recession – a quarter of a million apprenticeships this year; 100,000 more young people training to higher qualifications; new support for a new class of highly trained professional technicians, with our longer-term aim being 75 per cent of young people in higher education, in advanced apprenticeships or in equivalent technician courses.

And I ask each and every one of you for your support in helping to create and promote internships, apprenticeships and new opportunities for the long-term unemployed – as many of you are already doing – through our Backing Young Britain campaign and to join Lord Sugar as he encourages new enterprise and talent round the country.

Our home-grown talent and skills must provide our businesses with the pipeline of skilled workers they need to compete in the global economy. But today I can assure you that alongside that, while controlling migration, we reject a blanket cap on immigration. Where we as a country need to bring in highly skilled people we will continue to do so. And so you as businesses will have the flexibility to recruit the highly skilled people you need when you need them.

The results of doubling British investment in science speak for themselves – increasing numbers of university spin-outs; knowledge transfers; more private research and development. But as the Rowlands Report published today shows, we know that many small and high-growth companies need capital to grow and, therefore, better access to finance. Where there has been market failure in the past, our new innovation fund will provide support to high-tech start-up businesses, growing to £1 billion over coming years. And where there is a gap also in finance for companies looking to expand, we propose a Growth Capital Fund – a credible channel for private capital to invest in these established and growing SMEs.

So, from new planning laws to airports and nuclear power, at all times we are making and will continue to make the critical long-term decisions for Britain.

Going for growth is possible because, unlike in previous recoveries, inflation is low. But it cannot be a sound bite without substance; it requires a consistent and coherent set of policies. You cannot say you are going for growth and then in the next breath demand the withdrawal of the very measures essential to lock in the recovery and enable the growth to take place – the maintenance of the fiscal and monetary stimulus until recovery is established; and, within sustainable public finances, a determination to make the long-term decisions I have set out on expanding nuclear power and renewables; swift planning decisions; better transport and airports; investing in skills, science and, with our RDAs, regional economic development; and strengthening our relationships with Europe and the rest of the world. A modern industrial partnership – working with business to deliver support and intervention where it is needed but keeping out of the way when it is not.

To succeed in that future, we also need an outward-facing Britain, attracting inward investment and sustaining high-value-added jobs.

Over a very short time, more than 400 Chinese companies have come to Britain. In our new growth strategy, I want not just hundreds but thousands of Chinese companies in Britain and British companies in China. I know that we will soon sign new strategic partnerships with India. Trade relations with the US are strong. And to go for growth in Britain we must also go for growth in Europe.

We must never forget that Europe accounts for 60 per cent of our trade; more than three million British jobs depend on Europe. The European Union is the biggest exporter in the world and the second biggest importer. And it accounts for almost a third of the world's GDP.

So in a global economy we need strong sustainable growth across Europe and beyond. Over recent weeks the discussion around Europe has been mostly about personalities, not policies, institutions, not the real issue of public concern which, for me and the British people, is what the European Union does for the citizens of our countries. Europe needs to think about how we create the growth for the ten million new jobs the continent needs. And higher levels of European growth would mean thousands of new jobs in Britain.

Just 1 percentage point higher European GDP growth for a decade means £15 billion a year net benefit to UK businesses. Which is why I am calling on European leaders for a renewed focus on delivering European growth. And I am pleased to report that under Prime Minister Zapatero of Spain's leadership growth and jobs will be the priority for the next Spanish presidency of the European Council. And I will publish our British proposals for a new European growth strategy.

Now that the European Central Bank, like the Bank of England, has indicated they expect interest rates will remain low for the foreseeable future, I want to see – in this low-inflation environment in Europe – a push for growth which could involve incentives for new private investment, perhaps through new lending from the European Investment Bank; a stronger push on European-wide research and development; and further action to break down the barriers preventing the single market functioning well, including in banking and financial services.

And I also value the progress being made under Andrew Adonis' leadership in transport. So with the new high-speed Channel Tunnel link and the new company we have set up, making recommendations next month for a north–south high-speed line in the UK, let me tell you what we could ultimately achieve – a European network of train services that takes us quickly not just to Paris and Brussels but quickly to Cologne and to Amsterdam. And one that starts not just in London but in the north of our country. So from journey times today from Scotland to London of four hours twenty minutes, to three and a half hours, then three hours and potentially even to under three hours. So faster rail travel not only within Britain but to and from the mainland of Europe is within our grasp.

It is by putting Britain not on the fringes of Europe but at its heart that Britain can protect its interests within Europe and shape the future of Europe from a position of strength that can deliver growth and jobs for the British people. To walk away from this would be to deal a devastating blow to the future of British business, and it's my belief that we must never allow this to happen.

When I consider our prospects I'm optimistic about the high-value-added products and services we are ready to offer the world – and the leading positions we have in industries which are relevant to the future, such as business and financial services, advanced manufacturing, biotechnology and pharmaceuticals, aviation, our creative industries and our higher education. These are exactly the exports that a global economy set to double in the next 20 years will want to buy.

As an outward-looking nation seeking sustainable growth in a world where trade is set to increase rapidly, a priority must be to attract inward investment – and we should be proud to show our strengths in these industries to the world. So finally today I want to tell you about the British international investment conference which I will host in London early next year – with invitations from our Trade Minister, Mervyn Davies, to British and foreign investors to come and see the great opportunities that Britain can offer the world.

It is well said that those who build the present in the image of the past will miss out entirely on the challenges of the future. We are now in a new age of global change. And we should have confidence that, together, we can and will establish Britain's place at the centre of this global economy.

18

Liberty and Citizenship

One of the recurring themes in the speeches given by Gordon Brown while he was Chancellor of the Exchequer is Britishness – and the underlying principles, values and ideas, which, filtered though our history, are central to our national consciousness. The focus of many of these speeches is the nation state and the constitutional implications arising from the successful devolution settlements of 1998.

As Prime Minister, Gordon Brown has given further thought to this issue and, in the process, extended his arguments to the relationship between British liberty and our British identity and in particular what it means in the twenty-first century for the relationship between the private individual and the public realm. As he points out, 'A passion for liberty has determined the decisive political debates of our history, inspired many of our defining political moments, and those debates, conducted in the crucible of great events, have, in my view, forged over time a distinctly British interpretation of liberty – one that asserts the importance of freedom from prejudice, of rights to privacy and of limits to the scope of arbitrary state power but one that also rejects the selfishness of extreme libertarianism and demands that the realm of individual freedom encompasses not just some but all of us.'

While acknowledging that a concern for privacy is central in our tradition, the Prime Minister argues that the British conception of liberty that runs through and defines much of our national experience 'has not led, at least for most of our history, to notions of the isolated individual left on his own – it is privacy not loneliness that British people seem to value'. Nor has it led to selfish individualism: 'Instead, throughout the last 300 years in Britain, as Chief Rabbi Jonathan Sacks has eloquently described, the progress of the idea of liberty has gone hand in hand with notions of social responsibility – "the active citizen", the "good neighbour" and civic pride emphasising that people are not just self-interested but members of a wider community sustained by the mutual obligation we all feel to each other.'

And the Prime Minister goes on: 'So in this modern view, freedom comes to mean not just freedom from interference but also freedom to aspire – the opportunity and the chance to live a rounded life in which for everyone there is a place for choice and talent to flourish.'

The two speeches included in this chapter bring together the Prime Minister's latest thinking on Britishness, with a new take on the relationship between liberty and citizenship. His analysis of these topics is powerful, and the policy implications are rich in nuance and full of concern for the core principles of our liberal and social democratic traditions.

In the first speech, the Prime Minister focuses on what he describes as 'a more rounded and realistic conception of liberty'. And he suggests that, 'In a world of increasingly rapid change and multiplying challenges – facing, for example, a terrorist threat or a challenge to our tolerance – democracies must be able to bring people together, mark out common ground and energise the will and the resources of all.' And he asserts, 'I am in no doubt that our freedoms, our openness and tolerance and our very enterprise and creativity which flow from these qualities – what we value about being British – emerge from this rich and historic tradition.' And he concludes, 'The components of our liberty are the building blocks for such a society. Our belief in the freedom of speech and expression and conscience and dissent helps create the open society. Our determination to subject the state to greater scrutiny and accountability sustains such openness. The reinforcement of civic responsibility and the empowerment of the individual gives our country the underlying strength we need to succeed in the years ahead.'

SPEECH ON LIBERTY
London, 25 October 2007

I want to talk today about liberty – what it means for Britain, for our British identity and in particular what it means in the twenty-first century for the relationship between the private individual and the public realm.

I want to explore how together we can write a new chapter in our country's story of liberty and do so in a world where, as in each generation, traditional questions about the freedoms and responsibilities of the individual re-emerge but also where new issues of terrorism and security, the Internet and modern technology are opening new frontiers in both our lives and our liberties.

Addressing these issues is a challenge for all who believe in liberty, regardless of political party. Men and women are Conservative or Labour,

Liberal Democrat or of some other party or of no political allegiance. But we are first of all citizens of our country with a shared history and a common destiny.

And I believe that together we can chart a better way forward. In particular, I believe that by applying our enduring ideals to new challenges we can start immediately to make changes in our constitution and laws to safeguard and extend the liberties of our citizens – respecting and extending freedom of assembly, new rights for the public expression of dissent; respecting freedom to organise and petition, new freedoms that guarantee the independence of non-governmental organisations; respecting freedoms for our press, the removal of barriers to investigative journalism; respecting the public right to know, new rights to access public information where previously it has been withheld; respecting privacy in the home, new rights against arbitrary intrusion; in a world of new technology, new rights to protect your private information; and respecting the need for freedom from arbitrary treatment, new provision for independent judicial scrutiny and open parliamentary oversight. Renewing for our time our commitment to freedom and contributing to a new British constitutional settlement for our generation.

And my starting point is that from the time of Magna Carta to the civil wars and revolutions of the seventeenth century, through to the liberalism of Victorian Britain and the widening and deepening of democracy and fundamental rights throughout the last century, there has been a British tradition of liberty – what one writer has called our 'gift to the world'.

Of course liberty – with roots that go back to antiquity – is not and cannot be solely a British idea. In one sense, liberty is rooted in the human spirit and does not have a nationality. But, first with the Magna Carta and then through Milton and Locke to more recent writers, as diverse as Orwell and Churchill, philosophers and politicians have extolled the virtues of a Britain that, in the words of the American revolutionary Patrick Henry, 'made liberty the foundation of everything' and became 'a great, mighty and splendid nation . . . because liberty is its direct end and foundation'.

At that time few doubted that modern ideas of liberty originated from our country. Britain 'hath been the temple as it were of liberty,' said Bolingbroke as early as 1730, 'whilst her sacred fires have been extinguished in so many countries, here they have been religiously kept alive'.

'The civil wars of Rome ended in slavery and those of the English in liberty,' Voltaire wrote. 'The English are the only people upon earth who have been able to regulate the power of kings by resisting them . . . The

English are jealous not only of their own liberty but even of that of other nations.'

So powerful did this British idea of liberty become that the American War of Independence was fought on both sides 'in the name of British liberty' and the first great student of American democracy, de Tocqueville, acknowledged its roots across the Atlantic. 'I enjoyed, too, in England', he said, 'what I have long been deprived of – a union between the religious and the political world, between public and private virtue, between Christianity and liberty.'

A century and more later, facing fascism on the right and Stalinism on the left, Orwell wrote that the totalitarian idea that there is no such thing as law, there is only power, has never taken root in England, where 'such concepts as justice, liberty and objective truth are still believed in'.

And while we should not overstate it, the anthems that today celebrate our country have at their heart a call to liberty. In 1902, A.C. Benson wrote 'Land of Hope and Glory' to define Britain as 'the mother of the free', and, two centuries before, 'Rule Britannia', written in England by a Scot, resounded with the resolve: 'Britons never, never, never shall be slaves.'

Of course the cause has been hard fought – won and lost and won again. But if you draw a line through all the peaks and valleys, the direction over time is upward.

A passion for liberty has determined the decisive political debates of our history, inspired many of our defining political moments, and those debates, conducted in the crucible of great events, have, in my view, forged over time a distinctly British interpretation of liberty – one that asserts the importance of freedom from prejudice, of rights to privacy and of limits to the scope of arbitrary state power but one that also rejects the selfishness of extreme libertarianism and demands that the realm of individual freedom encompasses not just some but all of us.

And I believe that to each generation falls the task of expanding the idea of British liberty and to each generation also the task of rediscovering liberty's central importance as a founding value of our country and its animating force.

Indeed, I am concerned that too often in recent years the public dialogue in our country has undervalued the importance of liberty. Too often the political debate has become polarised between a new Right that has emphasised laissez-faire more than liberty and an old Left that has mistakenly marginalised liberty by seeing it as the enemy of equality.

Now is the time to reaffirm our distinctive British story of liberty, to show it is as rich, powerful and as relevant to the life of the nation today as ever, to apply its lessons to the new tests of our time. So instead of invoking the unique nature of the threats we face today as a reason for relinquishing our historical attachment to British liberty, we meet these tests not by abandoning principles of liberty but by giving them new life.

We all approach the history of these islands in our own way. But for me certain key themes emerge over and over again through the centuries to characterise the British conception of liberty.

First, I trace the historical roots of liberty in Britain to a struggle for tolerance, by which I mean also a gradual acceptance of pluralism – a notion of political liberty that would allow those of different denominations and beliefs to coexist peacefully together.

The commitment in Britain to basic freedoms of worship, assembly, speech and press began to emerge in the sixteenth and seventeenth centuries alongside a rejection of religious persecution. 'If not equal all yet free, equally free,' wrote Milton in *Paradise Lost*. This did not happen all at once or without setbacks and struggle. The flames of religious intolerance burned across this land, too, but never as strongly as in continental Europe.

And down the centuries the British people have come to demonstrate a shared belief that respect for the dignity and value of every human being demands that all be given the freedom and space to live their lives by their own choices, free from the control and unjustified interference of others.

There is, of course, always the danger that villains of history become redeemed by the passage of time. There is a human instinct to recast the past as a lost golden age. I do not wish to fall into that trap. Nor should we succumb to an excessively Whig-like interpretation of history that assumes an inevitable, stage-by-stage progress. In particular we should neither glorify nor distort what has gone before – and the struggles, both the ups and downs, of empire are not long behind us – to uphold a particular view of where we are now or what we can become.

So we need to recognise, for example, that it took until 1829 for Catholic emancipation, even later for legislation ending discrimination against the Jewish community. It is true that in 1914 our franchise was more narrowly restricted than nearly all other countries in Europe. It was only in the second half of the twentieth century that Parliament took action to combat discrimination against women and ethnic minorities, and there is still much work to do in these areas and against discrimination on the grounds of sexuality, disability and religion.

But the single most powerful thread that runs though our history is a succession of chapters in the defence of liberty and toleration. We gave refuge to Huguenots fleeing persecution in the 1600s. By the eighteenth century, London was arguably already the world's most diverse city – a situation which we can remain proud of in Britain to this day. The abolition of slavery was an act that led the world in the defence of human dignity, and today our abhorrence of torture is and must be unequivocal.

And as the chapters have unfolded and the battles have been won, tolerance in Britain has evolved from a passive defence of free speech and freedoms of press and assembly into a positive assertion of their place in our progress. Indeed, today one of the qualities British people say they admire most about our country is our tolerance, and the characteristic that makes them most ashamed is any intolerance.

And this British idea of liberty evolved into something even more remarkable in the early modern era – the right to dissent, fought for by the Civil War dissenters and embodied in the campaigns of the Chartists and, later, the suffragettes.

Now, tolerance may have been instrumental in shaping modern British beliefs in liberty, but liberty for Britain steadily became not just about mutual acceptance but also about due process against arbitrary power.

While this great tradition can be traced back to the Magna Carta, it was the rise of the modern state with all the new powers at its disposal that made the seventeenth century the pivotal period in the struggle against arbitrary and unaccountable government – as Britain led the way in the battle for freedom from hierarchical rule, for human rights and for the rule of law.

And tracing Coke's defence of common law, the work of John Locke and the Bill of Rights of 1689, right through to the first of the Reform Acts, Macaulay concluded that 'the authority of law and the security of property were found to be compatible with a liberty of discussion and of individual action never before known'.

And in the mid to late twentieth century, this idea of liberty increasingly became the foundation of a new international order where the right of every one – human rights – should be respected by every one. On an island off Newfoundland in 1941, Churchill and Roosevelt together drew up the Atlantic Charter, and, by beginning the system of international law based on the fundamental rights of all human beings, Britain led the way in asserting the inviolability of individual rights, irrespective of race or nationality, and made the freedoms so dear to Britain the cornerstone of a new international order. And a few years later Britain led the way in the European Convention on Human Rights so that the same insistence on tolerance, the same defence against the arbitrary power of governments, the same fundamental rights and implicit mutual obligations between all human beings could provide protection to all individuals wherever they were.

One view of the American tradition of liberty manifests itself in the 'leave me alone' state. But while concern for privacy is central in our tradition, the British conception of liberty which runs through and defines much of our national experience has not led, at least for most of our history, to notions of the isolated individual left on his own – it is privacy not loneliness that British people seem to value. Nor did it lead to selfish individualism.

Instead, throughout the last 300 years in Britain, as Chief Rabbi Jonathan Sacks has eloquently described, the progress of the idea of liberty has gone hand in hand with notions of social responsibility – 'the active citizen', the 'good neighbour' and civic pride emphasising that people are not just self-interested but members of a wider community sustained by the mutual obligation we all feel to each other.

As Gertrude Himmelfarb puts it, in Britain the Enlightenment's focus on asserting the rights of individuals was accompanied by a cluster of 'social virtues' – benevolence, improvement, civic society and the moral sense underlying shared purpose. Thus John Stuart Mill did not, in the end, call for unfettered freedoms but argued that 'there are many positive acts for the benefit of others, which he may rightfully be compelled to perform'.

So I recall a British story of liberty rooted in tolerance – the liberty that is necessary to uphold the dignity of each and all, reinforced by due process against the exercise of arbitrary power; best advanced in the modern world when we recognise the responsibilities we owe to each other; and now, as a new generation expands the frontiers of liberty, also increasingly about empowering the individual to make the most of their potential. As T.H. Green put it, 'when we speak of freedom as something to be so highly prized, we mean a positive power or capacity of doing or enjoying something worth doing or enjoying and that, too, something that we do or enjoy in common with others'.

Indeed, from more than a century ago, in the view of British thinkers – not just Green but Hobson, Hobhouse and Tawney – freedom could only be fully realised when society was prepared to overcome the barriers that prevented people from realising their true potential. Hobson put it as a question when he asked: 'is a man free who has not equal opportunity with his fellows of such access to all material and moral means of personal development and work as shall contribute to his own welfare and that of his society?'

So in this modern view, freedom comes to mean not just freedom from interference but also freedom to aspire – the opportunity and the chance to live a rounded life in which for everyone there is a place for choice and talent to flourish. So I am in no doubt that our freedoms, our openness and tolerance and our very enterprise and creativity which flow from these qualities – what we value about being British – emerge from this rich and historic tradition.

Yet all too often on the political Right, liberty has been reduced to a simplistic libertarianism in which freedom and licence assumed a rough equivalence and the absence of government from public life was seen as essential to maximise liberty – such as in the nineteenth century with the continued acceptance of child labour.

And some politicians of the Left have mistakenly seen liberty at odds with equality and were too often prepared to compromise or even ignore the sanctity of freedoms of the individual. But these simplistic caricatures are unacceptable; we need a more rounded and realistic conception of liberty.

In a world of increasingly rapid change and multiplying challenges – facing, for example, a terrorist threat or a challenge to our tolerance – democracies must be able to bring people together, mark out common ground and energise the will and the resources of all. It is the open society that responds best to new challenges, and we are fortunate in being able to do so by drawing on that British story of liberty.

Indeed, the components of our liberty are the building blocks for such a society. Our belief in the freedom of speech and expression and conscience and dissent helps create the open society. Our determination to subject the state to greater scrutiny and accountability sustains such openness. The reinforcement of civic responsibility and the empowerment of the individual gives our country the underlying strength we need to succeed in the years ahead.

And while some people argue that in this changing world the concern for liberty has to take its place behind other commitments, I am convinced that, both to rebuild our constitution for the modern age and to unify the country to meet and master every challenge, we need to consciously and with determination found the next stage of constitutional development firmly on the story of British liberty.

This will only be possible if we face up to the hard choices that have to be made in government. Precious as it is, liberty is not the only value we prize and not the only priority for government. The test for any government will be how it makes those hard choices, how it strikes the balance. To claim that we should ignore the claims of liberty when faced with the needs of security would be to embark down an authoritarian path that I believe would be unacceptable to the British people. But to ignore the duty of government to protect its people – and to be unwilling to face up to hard choices – is the politics of gesture and irresponsibility.

In my view, the key to making these hard choices in a way that is compatible with our traditions of liberty is to, at all times, apply the liberty test, respecting fundamental rights and freedoms. And wherever action is needed by government, it never subjects the citizen to arbitrary treatment, is transparent and proportionate in its measures and at all times also requires proper scrutiny by, and accountability to, Parliament and the people.

At all times in our history we have had to debate how the need for strong and effective government can be combined with the pursuit and preservation of liberty. Such debates are both inevitable and desirable. The challenge for each generation is to conduct an open debate without ever losing sight of the value of our liberties.

Indeed the character of our country will be defined by how we write the next chapter of British liberty – by whether we do so responsibly and in a way that respects and builds on our traditions and progressively adds to and enlarges, rather than reduces, the sphere of freedom.

And as we make these decisions, we must never forget that the state and the people are not equivalent. The state is always the servant of the people. We must remember that liberty belongs to the people and not governments.

It is the challenge and the opportunity for our generation to write the next chapter of British liberty in a way that honours the progress of the past and promises a wider and more secure freedom to our children.

At present, around one in ten of the UK population is foreign-born (compared, for example, to around one in four in Australia and Switzerland, and around one in eight in Sweden and Germany). As the Prime Minister has made clear, we need to ensure that we attract the skilled workers from overseas that our businesses need. And he commits us at all times to maintaining our tradition of giving refuge to those fleeing persecution – and of having an unyielding resolution to tackle racism and discrimination.

In the following speech, the Prime Minister deals squarely with the question of immigration, which he asserts is not just an issue for fringe parties, nor a taboo subject, but 'a question to be dealt with at the heart of our politics – a question about what it means to be British; about what are the values we hold dear, the responsibilities we expect of those coming into our country; about how we secure the skills we need to compete in the global economy; about how, out of diversity, we preserve and strengthen the richness of our communities'.

At the time this speech was given, the new points-based system for immigration had been introduced successfully and the UK Border Agency (with substantially increased staff numbers, many of whom are based overseas) had begun to make significant improvements to the control of immigration.

While the Prime Minister argues that attracting highly skilled migrants with rare or specialist skills is essential to our continued success and influence as Britain in the global economy, he accepts 'that doesn't mean there aren't risks or costs to immigration or that we shouldn't acknowledge them and do our best to minimise them. The top line about the benefits of immigration disguises significant variation in how those benefits and costs are felt across the country or across different parts of the economy and society.' But he feels strongly that 'we must set these issues in their proper context, and we must never stop pointing out the facts – that British society has gained immeasurable benefit from its diversity; from being continually refreshed by new talent and new perspectives; from the confidence that comes from defining ourselves positively by our values, rather than negatively by any hostility to others'.

On the question of newcomers who want to stay in our country for any length of time, the Prime Minister announces that 'because we believe those who look to build a new life in Britain should earn the right to do so . . . [we will be] introducing a points-based test not just for entry but also for permanent residence and citizenship. And this will enable us to control the numbers of people staying here permanently, just as we are controlling the numbers coming in.'

SPEECH ON IMMIGRATION
London, 12 November 2009

> We meet this morning in this great hall in a capital city where over 300 languages are spoken – a city that is one of the most culturally rich places in our world, a city that epitomises the strong values and the diversity that has helped to make Britain one of the most dynamic countries in human history.
>
> Today I want to celebrate with you – Members of Parliament, Councillors, representatives of a large range of different organisations from all over our communities – that diversity, and I want to also address head-on the issue

of immigration. The case for managed and controlled migration where it is in the national interest – economically, socially and culturally – is a case that I have constantly made. I have never agreed with the lazy elitism that dismisses immigration as an 'issue' or portrays anyone who has concerns and questions about immigration as a racist.

Immigration is not an issue for fringe parties, nor a taboo subject. It is a question to be dealt with at the heart of our politics – a question about what it means to be British; about what are the values we hold dear, the responsibilities we expect of those coming into our country; about how we secure the skills we need to compete in the global economy; about how, out of diversity, we preserve and strengthen the richness of our communities.

And it's a question which must be seen in its proper context. People who come to this country have made and continue to make an enormous contribution – across the decades, in every walk of life – from business to sport, from the social fabric of our communities to our culture, from our public services to our public life. Right here in Ealing, Virendra Sharma's own story – first coming to better himself on a scholarship, today representing the people of Ealing Southall as their MP – epitomises the contribution that one person can make to our country and the benefits of welcoming talented people to our shores who join in with British society, who pull their weight and contribute to our economy, as seen in thousands, indeed hundreds of thousands, of examples of Great British citizens.

And I believe also that attracting highly skilled migrants with scarce or specialist skills is essential to our continued success and influence as Britain in the global economy. Now, that doesn't mean there aren't risks or costs to immigration or that we shouldn't acknowledge them and do our best to minimise them. The top line about the benefits of immigration disguises significant variation in how those benefits and costs are felt across the country or across different parts of the economy and society.

You see, if you are working for a multinational company in a growing sector in a big city, then a more diverse workforce from across the world is likely to seem like an exciting source of new ideas – and it is. If you work in a sector where wages are falling or an area where jobs are scarce, immigration will feel very different for you, even if you believe that immigration is good for overall employment and growth.

If the main effect of immigration on your life is to make it easier to find a plumber or when you see doctors and nurses from overseas in your local hospital, you are likely to think more about the benefits of migration than the possible costs. But if you're living in a town which hasn't seen much migration before, you may worry about whether immigration will undermine wages and the job prospects of your children – and whether they will be able to get housing anywhere near you. And everyone wants to be assured that newcomers will accept the responsibilities as well as the rights that come with living here – that they'll accept the responsibilities to obey the law, to speak English, to make a contribution.

So if people ask me, 'Do you get it?' Yes, I get it. I have been listening, I understand and I am now announcing some new changes to our policies. You see, ours is a 'something for something', 'nothing for nothing' society. In an older world we could perhaps assume that people would accept all their responsibilities as well as their rights. In a fast-moving world it is vital for cohesion that all people in Britain explicitly sign up to the direct responsibilities that come from being part of a community. So, in the interests of fairness, a condition for entry to our home – our British family – must be that you will commit to maintaining all that is best about the country we love. British values are not an add-on for us – an option or an extra to take or leave. Those who wish to come to our country must embrace them wholeheartedly and proudly, as we do.

And we must set these issues in their proper context, and we must never stop pointing out the facts – that British society has gained immeasurable benefit from its diversity; from being continually refreshed by new talent and new perspectives; from the confidence that comes from defining ourselves positively by our values, rather than negatively by any hostility to others. And we must continually remind ourselves also that net inward migration, from both within and outside the EU, is not rising, but it is falling – with the annual figures showing that overall net immigration is down 44 per cent on last year and with independent migration experts like Oxford Economics predicting further sustained falls. And we must also point out the fact that, over the past decades, people who have come from abroad to our country have boosted employment and growth, have filled key skills gaps in both our public and private sector.

I want to ensure, as I will explain later, that we give British people looking for jobs the best chance of filling vacancies that arise as we come out of the downturn. But where there are vacancies that have been advertised here and are unfilled, it is necessary for businesses and for the economy to be able to recruit more widely. So we reject the views of those who argue for an inflexible, arbitrary quota or cap on immigration. It would deny British businesses flexibility, it would prevent them from getting the skills that they need, it would prevent employers from filling vacancies, it would overturn our obligations to our neighbours in the European Union, it would damage our economy, it would hurt our public services.

To understand the damage a quota system would do to our economy, we should look back to the American system during the early part of this decade. There was an annual quota for skilled IT workers; seven times that quota was exhausted before the end of the year. It is this that has led President Obama to say that he will now reform the difficulties in the system. The chairman of Intel, Craig Barrett, said when the quota ran out with most of the year still to go, 'These arbitrary caps undercut businesses' ability to hire and retain highly educated people in the fields where we need to maintain our leading position. Instead of arbitrary caps,' he said, 'a market-based approach that responds to demand is needed. Only then will the US be competitive and have the ability to hire the best and the brightest.'

So we favour a tough but fair approach rooted in a points system under which we decide what categories of skills are to be allowed into this country. This combines the flexibility and control that is right with a continued commitment to strong borders and the rigorous enforcement of the laws against illegal immigration.

So it's a system which is positive about managed and controlled migration while ensuring that it serves the national interest; it recognises what we, as a country, need for a successful economy, but it also strengthens our society and our communities. So under this system we must continue our efforts, as I will explain today, to equip our people with the skills they need to compete in the global economy. As a result we will, as I can announce today, tighten our successful points system, and I will detail our measures in a minute.

Second, we must understand and manage the impact of immigration at a local as well as a national level – with mainstream funding responding more quickly to changes in population and the new Migration Impact Fund ensuring that newcomers pay an additional contribution to help ease the pressures that happen to some communities.

And then, third, our new proposals for earned citizenship will now ensure more explicitly that people from outside the European Union who want to stay here permanently must earn the right to do so – not just through their economic contribution but also by their respect for our values and our language and by their wider contribution to society.

And then fourth, and finally, the measures to strengthen our borders are now more coordinated than ever: our new Border Agency, biometric visas, electronic border controls counting people in and out, ID cards for foreign nationals – ID cards that are designed to prevent illegal working and protect our national security.

Now let me just address the policy points in turn. First, using the points-based system to target immigration on skills gaps, while at the same time improving the skills of British men and women to fill those gaps for the future. Two years ago there were 80 different immigration categories which had developed in piecemeal fashion over many decades. Now there is a simple, easy-to-control five-tier system with one of the tiers, for low-skilled migrants, currently closed.

We are continually working to improve the management of the system, but we believe it is, above all, the flexibility of the points system which has allowed us to help British workers through difficult times, when it is right to be more selective about the skills levels we need from migrants. In March this year we raised the minimum salary level and the qualification level for Tier One. We required Jobcentre Plus to apply the resident labour-market test for Tier Two, so that no job can go to a migrant unless it has first been advertised to jobseekers in the UK for two weeks. The changes we have made mean that from this autumn local workers will get a better chance – with jobs advertised now for four weeks in local jobcentres before they are offered more widely.

We set up the expert Migration Advisory Committee to advise on the effects of the points-based system on the labour market. And, while their latest report suggests that there remain skills we need to recruit from abroad, it confirms that we no longer need to recruit civil engineers, hospital consultants, aircraft engineers, ship's officers, and so these and other jobs are being taken off the list. And the report shows that we are able to target the list on narrower, more specific vacancies, including certain types of scientist, geologists, critical-care nurses, highly specialist trade workers. But as growth returns I want to see rising levels of skills, wages and employment among those resident here, rather than employers having to resort to recruiting people from abroad.

So I have talked with the chairman of the Migration Advisory Committee, Professor David Metcalf, about how government and the skills agencies and the sectors can respond faster in training the existing labour force for the new skills we need. To date this year we have been taking a further 30,000 posts off the list, and over the coming months we will remove more occupations and thousands more posts from the list of those eligible for entry under the points-based system. So we are building on the Skills Strategy, which set out the new, more tailored programme yesterday to invest in reducing these skills gaps by training up workers here.

And I have asked the UK Commission for Employment and Skills to provide advice in January about national priorities for the skills system. I have asked the Commission to work with the Migration Advisory Committee to consider removing certain occupations on the shortage list – for example, engineering roles, skilled chefs, care workers – and to link that to the priorities of our future investment in the skills of the future. As part of this review I have asked the two expert bodies to consult employers, training providers and other agencies to develop realistic timescales during 2010 for when these occupations will be taken off the list.

As the economy recovers, we need to do more to ensure that people with low skills and poor job prospects are helped into work and to secure decent living standards for them and their families. More investment in skills, more help for families with childcare, tougher welfare reform – all will ensure that British people can meet the responsibility to take up work whenever they can but in return ensure their right to be properly rewarded for doing so.

Now our second priority is to understand and manage the impact of immigration at local as well as national level. Whenever there are short-term increases in the numbers of children at your local school or patients using local GP services, extra resources should, of course, be provided. The new Migration Impact Fund, launched earlier this year, requires every non-EU migrant who comes to Britain to pay – on top of the visa – an additional charge into the £70 million fund. And this fund is already paying out to provide more teaching assistants and to increase GP cover in the areas most affected by immigration. And I believe it is entirely fair that newcomers themselves should be asked to make an additional contribution, over and above tax, to help the communities that they are joining.

There are concerns in some areas about how social housing is allocated. And I want to emphasise the importance of local councils following the new guidance we have just issued, which asks and encourages them to give more priority to local people and those who have spent a long time on the waiting list – and of engaging more closely with their communities in setting allocation policies.

Now this comes on top of a pledge to create more housing opportunities all round – a £1.5 billion investment in housing which shows we are committed to investing through the downturn to continue to build the new housing our communities need, helping to deliver over 100,000 new, affordable and, in this case, energy-efficient homes for young families to rent or buy over the next two years.

And then, third, we must set out clearer expectations of newcomers who plan to stay in our country for any length of time. It is because we believe those who look to build a new life in Britain should earn the right to do so that we will now push forward the points-based system to the next stage, by introducing a points-based test not just for entry but also for permanent residence and citizenship. And this will enable us to control the numbers of people staying here permanently, just as we are controlling the numbers coming in.

So the right to stay permanently will no longer follow automatically after living here for a certain number of years. Instead, as we have said, after living here for five years, migrants will have to apply to become probationary citizens, and at that point they will pass a points-based test with evidence of continuing economic contribution, of skills, of progress in English and knowledge of life in Britain.

And of course everyone must show a clean criminal record. The most basic but also most fundamental principle is that anybody who comes here – whether to work, to study or to live – should obey our laws and pay the price if they don't. Now, our position since August 2008 is that those coming from outside the EU who commit any crime resulting in a sentence of over one year will be considered for deportation. But since April this year our position is that those from inside the EU who are convicted of sex, drug or violent offences resulting in a sentence of 12 months or more will be considered for deportation.

And we are deporting an increasing proportion of foreign criminals. For when a mother or father is grieving for a son who has been killed or caring for a daughter who has been assaulted, it cannot possibly be right for that grief to be compounded by the knowledge that the perpetrator had no right to be here in the first place. In total we remove 68,000 people from the UK each year – double the level in 1997 – and this includes more than 500 European nationals who have committed crimes. Let me be clear – all newcomers to Britain have a responsibility to obey British law. There are no exceptions. Serious offences will be met by deportation, but even less serious offences will count heavily against progress towards citizenship – delaying or even ending the process.

The second requirement of earned citizenship is that, as well as obeying our laws, we expect newcomers to be able to speak English. This applies to workers coming under the points-based system who wish to stay permanently and settle their family in the UK. In 2004 we introduced language requirements for citizenship. Now there are requirements for those coming under the points-based system. And we have set out plans to introduce a new language requirement for spouses.

And we expect that newcomers should not be a burden on the country which has offered them the opportunity to come and make a new life. Those who applied to come here to work and who want to stay must show they are continuing to make the economic contribution. Those who came to settle with their family must show that their family has made every reasonable effort to support them. This message will be clear – if you cannot achieve the points necessary for probationary citizenship, you will not acquire it. And, unlike the current categories, probationary status will be just that – probationary. If after a number of years as a probationary citizen – a minimum of one year but a maximum of five – someone wants to stay in this country, they will have to meet the test of full citizenship or permanent residence – or go home.

Because we believe in a 'something for something' society, under this new system many of the rights and access to public services which are currently available to migrants early in their stay will not be available to probationary citizens. They will follow only when newcomers move to full citizenship or permanent residence. That's the right to post-18 education at the 'home rate', the right to permanent social-housing tenancies, the right to some social-security benefits – saving hundreds of millions of pounds.

But, at the same time, we will encourage probationary citizens to demonstrate their commitment to this country and their local areas through volunteering and community service. This will be reflected in the new points system so people will be able to move more quickly towards citizenship when they have made a difference in their community.

This new pathway to probationary citizenship and then to full citizenship shows the clear expectations we have, as a society, of people who come to our country. Clear expectations at every stage of their journey because living and working here, becoming a British citizen, is, of course, a set of obligations as well as a guarantee of rights, and it's a prized asset to be aspired to, earned and cherished.

Now the final area I want to talk about today is that our systems for managing migration are matched by our continuing work to strengthen our borders – new investment, innovative approaches to meeting the changing demands of what everybody knows is a fast-moving world. More UK immigration staff and equipment are now based abroad, helping, of course, to stop suspect or dangerous travellers before they travel – for example, turning back 240,000 individuals from flights in the last five years. Increasingly, we require visas from most countries – even just for a holiday – and all our visas are now biometric, not just a piece of paper with a stamp on it but fingerprint records which allow us to detect those who try to violate the rules and so prevent those who have abused our system from coming to Britain again.

We are also using the new requirement under the points-based system for all employers and colleges to obtain a licence to act as a sponsor for each migrant and in return accept certain responsibilities to check on their progress and whether they are following the rules. This year, for example, we have inspected colleges approved to sponsor student applications, and we've cut the list of approved colleges by more than half – from 4,000 to 1,800 – as well as temporarily shutting down applications for student visas from parts of China where there was evidence of abuse. And I want to thank Phil Woolas, our immigration minister, who's done so much to make this a far better system.

Where visa abuses arise, we will deal with them. The risk of abuse is higher in relation to shorter courses at lower qualification levels, below degree level. Our universities continue to offer high-quality degree and postgraduate courses to foreign students; they contribute greatly to universities and to our research base and to our economy.

I am announcing today a review of student visas to be conducted jointly by the Home Office and the Department for Business. It will involve key stakeholders and will report in December. We will look at the case for raising the minimum level of course for which foreign students can get a visa. The review will also examine the case for introducing mandatory English-language testing for student visas other than for English courses. And it will review the rules under which students on lower qualification courses work part-time – especially those on short courses – to look at whether temporary students are filling jobs that would be better filled by young British workers.

To enforce these tougher rules, we have more than doubled the number of immigration officers at the border. Last year we set up the UK Border Agency. It is a single force bringing together immigration, customs and visa powers and checks, and last year the agency stopped and turned back almost 28,000 people crossing the Channel illegally. We have toughened the rules on exclusions and deportations. Since November last year we have issued 100,000 identity cards to foreign nationals.

And the next stage of reform is the electronic border controls which are already counting people in and out – not the pointless bureaucratic process which was withdrawn in the 1990s but effective, realtime checks of identities against passports or visas, which are then matched against the warning indexes for crime, terrorism and immigration. It's already led to 4,000 arrests; it's ensured that those who have been properly removed or deported from Britain, or who have committed a serious crime in their own country, will not be able to enter.

One of the greatest obstacles to dealing with illegal immigration is the refusal of foreign governments to accept back their citizens after they have deliberately destroyed their identity documents. Now, where there is a problem of nationals from certain countries overstaying their visas or working illegally, we will require those countries to accept evidence of the travel document scanned at the border as sufficient for them to accept back their citizens.

And, as you know, we are stepping up our action against employers who hire illegal workers – sometimes abusing them shamefully in a way that is completely unacceptable, as well as undercutting people here. And it has caused resentment, as you know, in some areas. So we have raised the penalties for employing illegal workers up to £10,000 or two years in prison and also the penalties for employers who undercut the minimum wage or risk health and safety, and have provided additional money for enforcing these new rules from the Migration Impact Fund.

Many people also feel it's not fair if agency workers can be used to undercut their pay, and most agree it is not fair that, even after months in a job, agency workers can be paid less than staff they work alongside. That is why we are changing the law. Last year Britain took a leading role in negotiating an agreement across Europe that will see agency workers in Britain get equal treatment after 12 weeks in post. And we intend that this law will be on the statute book soon.

So we live in a fast-changing world. Government must change to meet the new challenges. Our immigration system is a very clear example. In 1997 we inherited an immigration system with 80 different categories, a small and old-fashioned immigration service, a paper-based system for recording entry and exit which the previous government had accepted was unworkable but had no plans to change.

This was a system which was clearly not ready to respond to the new global trends that were already evident. As these new trends continued in our first few years in government, our first priority became to reform our asylum system to deal with the worldwide increase in asylum applications. And, as those reforms succeeded and numbers came down, our priority in the last two years, as I have set out, has been to reform our system of entry for working migrants.

The changes I have set out today – the new points-based system on entry, the proposed points-based system for citizenship – amount to far more than a different mechanism for handling these difficult issues. Together they constitute a fundamental reform of a decades-old system – a reform founded on the British values of personal responsibility and our civic duties. They are aimed at ensuring our economy continues to attract and retain the highly skilled workers we need, whilst reinforcing the rights and responsibilities of newcomers as part of our community and the expectations society has of them at every stage. They amount to a fundamental restatement of what we expect of those who aspire to British citizenship and how we intend to strengthen the idea of what it means to be British.

I am proud of my country; I am proud to be British. Everybody here is proud to be British. This is a country of diversity and yet solidarity, of different cultures and yet universal values. And we will always be a country that, whatever the challenges we face, can never be broken by anyone or anything. For we will never compromise on that enduring British ideal – that rights and opportunities will always be matched by clear responsibilities for everyone. That is what a Britain of fairness and a Britain of responsibility means to me.

19

HEALTH

When Gordon Brown speaks of the NHS, he speaks with a passion born of personal experience. For him, the NHS has been witness to the greatest of triumphs – the saving of his sight – and the deepest of tragedies – the loss of his cherished daughter. It is precisely because of this shared past with the health service that Gordon cares so deeply about its future. Each day, those of us working in the health service are profoundly privileged to share in the most important moments in people's lives – delight and rejoicing, suffering and mourning, together.

Our health service is stitched into the fabric of British life. It stands as an enduring commitment to social solidarity, the institution that gives the greatest definition to our values – compassion, fairness, equality. In a sometimes fractured world, it shows what we can accomplish when we come together in pursuit of the common good.

For Gordon, improving our NHS is a noble task of clear moral purpose. I joined with him in this quest for a better NHS in June 2007. I had gathered a group of London clinicians together to share the findings of our review of the capital's health services. At the back of the room, Gordon Brown had slipped in to watch and to listen and to learn. A few weeks later, I was called to a meeting with the man who was soon to be Prime Minister. As I walked the few steps from the entrance of HM Treasury to the then Chancellor's private study, I imagined the reasons I might have been summoned. I stood prepared to be challenged and to defend my recent proposals to improve London's health care.

I was welcomed in and soon found myself and Gordon alone, discussing the future of health care. It was a captivating discussion, but I was not clear why it was taking place. Then he asked the question: would I join his government as a health minister? 'Surprised' does not capture how I felt; I was absolutely shocked, equally elated and terrified. And a few weeks later, I found myself standing at the despatch box of the House of Lords.

It took great courage to appoint a front-line doctor as a minister; I felt that at the time. I was untried and untested in politics, unfamiliar and unsure of the workings of Whitehall. Yet at every stage of the review I knew that I could rely on the Prime Minister's support to complete my task of defining the future of the NHS for the decade ahead. With his leadership, we have helped transform the process of policy making, embracing 2,000 of my fellow front-line clinicians to harness their energy, their creativity, in fashioning great plans to improve the health service.

Perhaps what surprised me most was the intellectual freedom I enjoyed. In an atmosphere of simple trust, ideas were debated on their merits alone and tough choices were made. It took enormous resolve to acknowledge that quality of care can vary too much in our health service, with too little explanation.

When Gordon and I visited NHS patients and staff, I saw a man humbled by those that bring comfort by holding the hands of those that are afraid of what the night might bring and who share in the joy of the morning. I saw a man gentle and kind. As the health service celebrated its 60th birthday, Gordon welcomed long-serving NHS staff to Downing Street to recognise their service. 'Please treat this as your home', he began, 'stay as long as you wish; you are here so we can celebrate what you have done for this country'. And so he stayed long into the evening, listening to the tales that were told of 60 years of service.

I know Gordon asks what balm he can bring to those who are suffering and the contribution he can make as a leader and as a man. And I know that everything mankind has accomplished in this world has been in answer to the question: What can I do? It is because of his answer that I admire Gordon Brown.

The Prime Minister used this important speech, given at the start of the year that saw the 60th anniversary of the founding of the National Health Service, to set out his thoughts on how the service should be renewed to meet the challenges of the future. As he says, the fact is that the health service of the next decades will need to recognise and respond to very different challenges from those that faced the NHS 60 years ago, 'as advances in medical knowledge and technology have made it possible for us to do more than ever before; as rising aspirations and expectations challenge the traditional ways of delivering NHS care; and as demographic change and changing lifestyles create new health care needs'.

Paying tribute to the service and to those who work in it, the Prime Minister points out that, over the last six decades, the NHS has cared for tens of millions of people and saved many hundreds of thousands of lives – and with its unique offer of health care free for all at the point of need, it has liberated all of us from the fears of unaffordable treatment and untreated illness. Gordon Brown goes on to argue that, in today's world, families more than ever need a system of funding like the NHS that insures everyone as comprehensively as possible against the risks of huge medical bills. And this is as true for the most comfortably off members of our society as it is for the poorest, because charges for treating illnesses such as cancer or living with the long-term effects of heart disease or strokes could otherwise impoverish individuals, households and families far up the income scale. He also makes the point that 'Such a system is also efficient because it is comprehensive, and for the same reason it is cost-effective too. And the care we get is the care we need, not just the care we can afford or the care our own insurance coverage will allow. And that, to put it bluntly, may make the difference not just between solvency and bankruptcy but between life and death.'

In the main section of the speech, the Prime Minister anticipates some of the findings of the forthcoming Darzi Review, the third stage of reform of the NHS since 1997, which will see 'matching increased diversity of supply with an ability to respond to the new diversity of demand in preventative and curative medicine, tackling the underlying causes of health inequalities as well as providing the best care'. And he suggests that 'we also need a new articulation of the rights and responsibilities of a modern, twenty-first-century health service. So this year we will, for the first time, set out the "NHS offer" to patients as part of an "NHS constitution" – what you can expect to get from the NHS and what we expect to give you in return.'

SPEECH ON THE NATIONAL HEALTH SERVICE
London, 7 January 2008

Almost 150 years old, the Florence Nightingale School of Nursing is one of the oldest colleges of nursing and midwifery in Britain, with a modern reputation for outstanding professionalism, excellence in research and world leadership in the training of nurses, and there is nowhere more appropriate for me to talk about how we can work together to renew Britain's NHS for the future.

This July we celebrate the 60th anniversary of the National Health Service, which is not just a great institution but a great, unique and very British expression of an ideal – that health care is not a privilege to be purchased but a moral right secured for all.

Over the last six decades, the NHS has cared for tens of millions of people and saved many hundreds of thousands of lives. It has been at the forefront of innovation in health care, too, pioneering advances in medical treatment such as triple therapy for TB; in surgery, such as artificial hip replacement; in imaging, with the development of MRI scanning.

And with its unique offer of health care free for all at the point of need, it has liberated all of us from the fears of unaffordable treatment and untreated illness.

But as we begin to celebrate the achievements of the NHS over the last 60 years, it is also right that – as new technologies emerge, as expectations rise and as health care needs change – we look ahead and continue to reform and renew the NHS for the future.

Ten years ago people questioned whether the British NHS could survive. And it is a testimony to the extraordinary work done by nurses, doctors and all NHS staff, backed up by the extra investment which has seen the health budget treble to almost £100 billion a year, that ten years on the NHS is now, more firmly than ever, part of the fabric of British national life – an achievement that in itself should give us the confidence to look forward with ambition to an even greater future for the NHS.

It is because the NHS has been a central priority since June last year that we have made immediate changes to improve safety and cleanliness in every hospital – beginning the deep-cleaning of our wards, making provision for MRSA screening for all patients entering hospital and giving matrons new powers to report safety concerns direct to the Care Quality Commission.

And we have also taken practical steps to give patients access to treatment and advice at times that are more convenient to them, with our plans for greater access to GP services in the evenings and at weekends in every area of the country. It may be controversial, but we will see it through as part of our modernisation of public services to meet the rising expectations of the British people.

But these immediate actions are just a start; our ambitions for the future of the NHS can and should go much further. We can build on its strengths and make it stronger. The NHS of the future will do more than just provide the best technologies to cure; it will also – as our population ages and long-term conditions become more prevalent – be an NHS that emphasises care too. The NHS of the future will do more than just treat patients who are ill; it will be an NHS offering prevention as well.

The NHS of the future will be more than a universal service; it will be a personal service too. It will not be the NHS of the passive patient; the NHS of the future will be one of patient power, patients engaged and taking greater control over their own health and their health care too.

And so if the NHS is to change like this – to meet the challenges of twenty-first-century health care and our twenty-first-century lives – we will have to embrace even deeper and wider reform.

For the fact is that the health service of the next decades will need to recognise and respond to very different challenges than those that faced the NHS 60 years ago – as advances in medical knowledge and technology have made it possible for us to do more than ever before; as rising aspirations and expectations challenge the traditional ways of delivering NHS care; and as demographic change and changing lifestyles create new health care needs.

Changing the NHS to address these twenty-first-century challenges is precisely why we have asked the eminent surgeon Professor Ara Darzi to conduct a fundamental review of how the NHS must continue to reform, talking to patients and staff across the country about what should be done.

And during the course of 2008 the Secretary for Health, Alan Johnson, will set out the steps we can take to begin to make this transformation a reality. New access to check-ups that empower patients and their clinicians; new access to screening and preventative vaccines; millions – especially older people – making choices to become part of active patient programmes; primary care far more open and convenient, with new providers and more weekend and evening access; new and decisive action against failing services, whether in hospitals or primary care; a new statement – through an NHS constitution – of rights and responsibilities in health care; and new help for individuals and families as they strive to lead healthier lives.

This is the third stage in our reform of the NHS since 1997. Stage one of reform was to set minimum standards – a success story in ensuring improved access to key treatments and renewing the physical infrastructure through hospital building.

Stage two was to widen diversity of supply to create new incentives for better local performance and more choice for patients – a success story in achieving the shortest ever waiting times, including meeting our commitment to less than 18 weeks from doctor's appointment to hospital treatment and improving the management of NHS resources through foundation hospitals and the use of the private sector.

Stage three will see us continuing the work of stage two and matching increased diversity of supply with an ability to respond to the new diversity of demand in preventative and curative medicine, tackling the underlying causes of health inequalities as well as providing the best care. And it is about taking new and decisive action against failing services – establishing a new Care Quality Commission with tougher powers to impose fines and close down wards in the case of poor standards; removing underperforming hospital management; foundation hospitals able to take over failing hospitals to turn around their performance; and, as primary care plays an ever greater part in our health care, greater diversity of supply and strengthening the power of our commissioners so that weak GP or community health care services can be improved or replaced. And the changes are necessary because of the new challenges facing the health service today.

First, the NHS has to respond to technological change. When the NHS was created in 1948, much of what could be offered was a standard and, in practice, rather modest service, and the scientific and technological limitations of medicine were such that high-cost interventions were rare or very rare. But over the last half-century technology has opened up vast new areas of diagnosis and treatment and the potential of further scientific advance is colossal.

With cutting-edge techniques from genetics to stem-cell therapy and life-saving drugs to prevent, alleviate or cure conditions like Alzheimer's likely to be developed in the years ahead, what seem medical miracles today will be medically routine tomorrow.

So, if we are to prevent as much suffering and save as many lives as possible, it is clear that utilising these new technologies must continue to be at the heart of any progressive health policy. And I am delighted to support Europe's largest medical science centre here in London, developed under Nobel Prize winner Sir Paul Nurse – public and private sectors working together to pioneer new technologies and new treatments.

At the same time, new technologies are giving clinicians the ability to diagnose and intervene earlier than ever before. With new tests to identify women who are at heightened risk of breast cancer, new drugs aimed at preventing allergies and the discovery of new genes that are key to the progression of conditions like Alzheimer's – to give just three examples – we are at the dawn of a whole new era, with growing understanding of individual risk factors; the possibility of anticipating the development of future illness; and perhaps even that of pre-empting such illness with specific advance interventions.

And already the effectiveness of early intervention – as soon as symptoms develop – has been demonstrated. Many people suffering heart attacks now receive life-saving drugs on the doorstep and in some areas of the country are being delivered directly to specialist units for treatment. If – as the NHS is working to do – we extend this nationwide, we could save another 500 lives a year.

Some stroke patients are also now getting immediate treatment with the latest clot-busting drugs in specialist centres. Extending that across the country could allow 1,000 more stroke survivors every year to avoid disability and lead independent lives.

And, where the evidence and advice from local clinicians and the independent clinicians on the National Review Panel shows that specialist units can offer life-saving access to the latest treatments, we must not be afraid to support them.

To be true to its principles, the NHS must continue to change. So we will reject the views of those who say the NHS must put a moratorium on change and reject those who oppose further reform. This would be a massive failure of leadership. If, for example, reconfigurations of services into specialist units proposed by the consultants were postponed or abandoned, this would lead to lives lost as nurses and doctors are denied the use of new technologies, treatments and cures. And we must be prepared to listen to the clinicians and the public and take the tough decisions, which will save lives. Indeed, now more than ever the NHS must adapt to take advantage of our world-class medical research and support the genius of British scientists and doctors by making reforms to support their endeavours to combat disease.

There is also a second challenge for the twenty-first-century NHS which goes beyond technology – a rise in expectations about the care people want to receive.

Growing expectations about choice, access and convenience in health care are a fact of modern life. Our increasing freedom to make individual choices as consumers we rightly take for granted. And people want health care services which meet their needs and busy lifestyles. People tell me of the truly excellent experiences of care when they get into the NHS – of the nurses and doctors dedicated to their care – but at the same time of their frustrations with access to services, with a service too often centred on the needs of the providers rather than those of patients.

That is why giving patients choices through reforms to encourage plurality of provision, create a genuine level playing field between competing local providers and allow money to follow the patient is so important in building a more responsive and more accessible health care system.

The third challenge facing the NHS is a transformation in the patterns of need the NHS must provide for. In the last century the main concerns were infectious diseases, acute medical and surgical illness and the long struggle against cancer. Much of what the NHS delivered consisted of brief episodes of increasingly successful acute care. But today, with the ageing population and a rise in so-called 'lifestyle diseases', the NHS finds itself with new challenges in supporting and caring for patients with long-term conditions.

In 1948, when the NHS was founded, 11 per cent of the UK population was 65 or over. In 2008 that figure is 16 per cent. In 2028 it will be over 20 per cent. More and more of us can now expect to survive into our eighth, ninth and tenth decades – our 70s, 80s and 90s. And, because much of ill health is age-related, health care costs rise with age, with the average annual cost to the NHS of a person aged over eighty-five approximately six times the cost for those aged between sixteen and forty-four.

At the same time, advances in medical science are enabling people with debilitating conditions to live longer and more active lives. There are now more than 15 million people in England with a chronic or long-term disease, ranging from asthma to heart failure to the 900,000 living with the after-effects of a stroke. This could mean even greater costs for all health systems as they adjust to providing ongoing care, particularly for older people.

So, one of the main challenges that the NHS faces in the coming decades is that of providing high-quality, cost-effective care for increasing numbers of older people. And it won't just be the NHS that has to respond to this challenge but our social care system as well. That is why, through personal budgets, we are pursuing the reform of our care services; we will be consulting on a Green Paper on the long-term funding issues for care and for carers; and in the coming months I will say more about the reforms needed in both the NHS and our social care system in order to meet this challenge.

Alongside these demographic trends, increasing numbers of people suffer from what are often called 'lifestyle diseases' – with smoking and drinking, but most of all obesity, increasingly the main threats to the health of ourselves and our children.

On current trends nearly 60 per cent of the UK population will be obese by 2050 – that is two out of three in the population defined as severely overweight.

If we do not reverse this, millions of adults and children will inevitably face deteriorating health and a lower quality of life. Hundreds of thousands more will suffer diabetes and hypertension; thousands more will die from cardiovascular disease, strokes and cancers.

It has been estimated that 42,000 lives could be lost each year because we do not eat enough fruit and vegetables, 20,000 because of eating too much salt and that, overall by 2050, the direct health care costs of obesity will have risen seven-fold, with the wider costs to society and business reaching almost £50 billion a year.

So these lifestyle diseases now pose as great a threat to the future of a world-class NHS as underinvestment posed ten years ago. And our response and the response of our NHS to these changes will be one of the defining elements in our lives over the next 20 years – one of the most powerful influences on the kind of society in which we live.

Already more and more of us are taking our own health seriously, but I believe we could go further in finding new ways of expressing the idealism of the NHS, to do more to help patients feel engaged and empowered by managing their own conditions; taking advantage of support offered by GPs and nurses in the home or on the high street; exercising more control over their lives and care; becoming more focused on what they eat and whether they participate in sports and exercise, more conscious of their own choices and encouraged and better supported in making them.

And as more of us live longer, we need to put support in place to help us all stay active into old age, and thus to stay healthy – adding life to years, not just years to life.

So all the changes that I have outlined this morning – the impact of new medical technologies, of rising expectations and the changing nature of the medical problems facing us due to demography, long-term conditions, lifestyle choices – are putting pressure on the NHS. But I also believe that these challenges themselves mean that the NHS – with its central commitment to health care free for all at the point of need – is today even more relevant, more essential, than ever. Let me explain why.

In too many countries around the world new technological breakthroughs become available only to a select few with the ability to pay. Even those systems which offer protections to disadvantaged groups very rarely offer them the same quality of care as the well-off. But because we provide a universal service, not a minimum service – and by prioritising the adoption of medical advances across the NHS – we can make sure that the very best care is offered to all British people based on the need they have, not the money they have.

And, whereas in many other countries this scientific revolution could become a profound social injustice as those with a predisposition to specific conditions face exorbitant private insurance costs or even exclusion from cover altogether, in Britain health care will be provided to everyone free of charge, regardless of medical conditions. Indeed, as the cost of ever more effective technology intervention rises and there is little advance knowledge of upon whom those costs will fall, it is more important than ever to pool the risk and share the cost of those interventions fairly across our whole population.

In today's world, families more than ever need a system of funding like the NHS that insures everyone as comprehensively as possible against the risks of huge medical bills. And this is as true for the most comfortably off members of our society as it is for the poorest, because charges for treating illnesses such as cancer or living with the long-term effects of heart disease or strokes could otherwise impoverish individuals, households and families far up the income scale.

As individuals in Britain we know that, should serious illness strike, we will be cared for and the cost of that care will be absorbed not by us as individuals but by all of us together – in a comprehensive health care system publicly funded by taxation. And we know that our doctors will never ask us, 'Who's paying for this?' We leave hospital and are not followed by a bill or by complex negotiations with an insurance company – even when we have had care the costs of which might run to thousands, indeed, many thousands, of pounds.

Such a system is also efficient because it is comprehensive, and for the same reason it is cost-effective too. And the care we get is the care we need, not just the care we can afford or the care our own insurance coverage will allow. And that, to put it bluntly, may make the difference not just between solvency and bankruptcy but between life and death.

So I believe the NHS is the best insurance system for the long term and even more relevant to Britain's needs today than it was in 1948. But for too long in this country the pressures on the hospital system meant funding for prevention and a personal service took second place. But the record levels of investment since 1997 have opened up the potential for us both to provide an excellent hospital and GP service and to fund new preventative programmes and care more tailored to need.

This means an NHS which is personal to the patient not just because it's available at a time to suit you, with the clinician of your choice, in the setting and environment which meets your needs, but also because it works directly for your needs and wishes. It identifies your clinical needs earlier than before, is targeted to keeping you healthy and fit and puts you far more in control of your own health and your own life. And in the long run a preventative service personal to your needs is beneficial not just to individuals but to all of us as we reduce the costs of disease.

Choice between providers has been among the forces for change that have meant hospitals, GPs and others have been thinking about how they offer the kind of personal service we all expect. But real empowerment of patients will come from going further. The driving force – higher patient aspirations, more patient expertise, more trust between clinicians and patient, patients becoming fuller participants and partners in health and health care.

In this way the nature of NHS provision will and must change to be based not just on what it can do for you but what, empowered with new advice, support and information, you can do for yourself and your family. So, if in the last generation the big medical advance was the doctor administering antibiotics, in the coming generation it will be patients working with doctors and NHS staff to improve our own health and manage our own conditions. And this means health professionals building on the plethora of good evidence-based practice that exists already and becoming champions and advocates of more empowered patients. The doctor not just physician but adviser; the nurse not just carer but trainer; patients more than consumers – partners.

Professor Darzi's report later this year will deepen and broaden this process of reform. But today I want to briefly describe some of the changes we will seek to make in this 60th year of the NHS to establish this new direction.

First, a more personal and preventative service will be one that intervenes earlier, with more information and control put more quickly into the hands of patient and clinician. Over time everyone in England will have access to the right preventative health check-up.

The next stage is offering men over 65 a simple ultrasound test to detect early abdominal aortic aneurysm, or 'triple A' – the weakening of the main artery from heart to abdomen which kills over 3,000 men a year – eventually saving more than 1,600 lives each year. And in the next few months Alan Johnson will also set out plans to go even further – to introduce on the NHS a series of tests to identify vulnerability to heart and circulation problems.

So there will soon be check-ups on offer to monitor for heart disease, strokes, diabetes and kidney disease – conditions which affect the lives of 6.2 million people, cause 200,000 deaths each year and account for a fifth of all hospital admissions.

And we will extend the availability of diagnostic procedures in the GP surgery, making blood tests, ECGs and, in some cases, ultrasounds available and on offer not only when you are acutely unwell or if you can pay but when you want and need them, where you need them – at the local surgery.

Second, we will do more to extend screening, for example for colon cancer and for breast cancer. The National Screening Committee, an independent clinical body, will look at the evidence and advise on what additional screening procedures would be genuinely useful in detecting other conditions. And I can commit today that wherever they recommend a new form of screening on clinical grounds we will make it available to everyone, not – as happens too often now – just for those who can pay.

Last month we made available the cervical cancer vaccine, which will prevent over 1,000 cases of cervical cancer each year. And we will go further, offering, wherever they are needed – and there is the clinical case for doing so – new preventative vaccines currently being developed.

The third change necessary to create a more personal and preventative health service is to give people the choice of taking a more active role in managing their own care. Patients benefit from being treated as informed users, and choice will help deliver this, so we will continue to make it more widely available.

But this third stage of reform involves moving beyond people being seen as simply consumers and empowering them to become genuine partners in care – not just making choices but knowing more about their condition and taking more responsibility for their health and their lives. This is not about shifting costs but about enhancing care and in doing so making it more cost-effective too.

So even when we are healthy we should have access to information about our risks and advice on how we can maintain our health. That is the kind of real control the NHS must give us all if we are to have a service fit to meet the challenges of the twenty-first century.

There are 15 million people in England with long-term conditions ranging from asthma to heart disease. Many are already taking more active roles in their own care, for example by using new technologies that allow remote monitoring of their condition via the Internet or on the telephone. And earlier this year on a visit to Southampton hospital I met Robbie, who was managing his treatment for a heart condition from home, monitoring his own blood pressure and weight and feeding his results back to his doctor.

This gave him far greater freedom, with the security of knowing his condition was still being checked. And he spent far less time in hospital – reducing the cost of his care to the NHS. What worked for Robbie could also work for more patients, many of whom rightly want a greater say over their care, including in later life. With the right kind of NHS care and support, an active, fulfilled life should be possible for far more of us in our later years.

So over the next few years we will give 100,000 people with long-term conditions the opportunity to manage their care in this way as 'expert patients'. And during 2008 we will bring forward a patients' prospectus that sets out how we will extend, to all 15 million patients with a chronic or long-term condition, access to a choice of 'active patient' or 'care at home' options clinically appropriate to them and supported by the NHS.

Real control and power for patients – supported by clinicians and carers. More than today's new choice of where and when you are treated, a new choice tomorrow, in partnership with your clinician, about your treatment itself – something made even more accessible by using NHS Direct, the Internet and digital TV, as well as the telephone, to improve support for patients who want an active part in their care. And where it is appropriate – just as with personal care budgets for the 1.5 million social care users – it could include the offer of a personal health budget, giving patients spending power and thus a real choice of services.

Empowering patients also means giving them a greater say in their care in the later years of their lives. Our ambition must be to give everyone a choice, and we can expect this will mean more and more people choosing to be cared for at home. This will depend on a new flexibility and responsiveness in primary care and new partnerships with the voluntary and private sectors where they can contribute and innovate. And it means a more seamless integration of services between acute and primary care and between health and social care, reflecting far better the needs and wishes of patients and of their carers – a subject I will return to in depth later.

The fourth area I want to highlight is the importance of being clear what a focus on prevention means for our hospitals and primary care services and how they are run. The reforms of recent years have undoubtedly created a better-managed, more flexible, more accountable and transparent NHS. They have reduced waiting times and they have led to crucial improvements in health outcomes.

But we must do far more to make sure that NHS organisations and incentives are truly responsive to patients while supporting clinicians in keeping people healthy and that funding not only follows the patient through an illness but prevents illness too.

So we will strengthen commissioning, give more responsibility to primary care professionals and open up primary care – with more providers, new primary care services and more weekend and evening access. And we will continue to open up acute care with, from the spring, the choice of hospitals trusts across private and public sectors in England extending to over 300 – including more than 150 private sector hospitals working as part of the NHS and at NHS cost and standards of quality.

We will use all mechanisms available to us to improve our NHS. Public, private and voluntary providers can all play their part, and there will be no 'no-go areas' for reform as we seek to deliver the preventative and personal services which will renew and secure the health service for the future.

And to drive up performance we will not just increase the freedoms and autonomy of our local NHS – giving hospital clinicians and GPs stronger incentives to work together and allowing foundation trusts the freedom to provide primary care services where this is in the interests of patients – but we will also increase accountability of local services to local people.

Patient involvement is vital to local accountability. I want to see three million foundation trust members by 2012, up from one million today, and give them an even greater say in the workings of their trust – that's two million more staff, patients and members of the public playing a direct part in running their local NHS.

And as we seek to devolve more responsibilities to the local level, we will also explore the ways of improving the legitimacy and accountability of primary care trusts and of the commissioning decisions they make on behalf of their local communities. As part of this change in relationship between patient and clinician, between the NHS and us all, we also need a new articulation of the rights and responsibilities of a modern, twenty-first-century health service. So this year we will, for the first time, set out the 'NHS offer' to patients as part of an 'NHS constitution' – what you can expect to get from the NHS and what we expect to give you in return.

As patients we will know the guarantees of service we can expect – for example, the maximum time from GP referral to the commencement of treatment or the right to screening and advice at certain points in our lives. But we will also set out the responsibilities that come with this – our responsibility to make good use of NHS resources by turning up for booked appointments. So patients who do not turn up for appointments, for example, should not have the same entitlement to waiting-time guarantees.

And, with these changes in the NHS, we also want a wider debate on how society as a whole should face up to the new health care challenge. There can be no doubt that the influences on all of us – from advertising to peer pressure – affect our decisions and choices, particularly so for our children. We cannot remove from individuals and families their responsibility for their own health and that of their children. But we can and must do more to be on people's side, helping them live a healthier life. In the coming months we will be looking at what more government should be doing to help tackle these problems – by information, education and through the very latest advice from clinicians.

As we look forward to London 2012, our ambition is to have all children offered at least five hours of sport each week. We will increase the availability of physical activity prescriptions on the NHS. We will improve the accessibility of gyms and other sporting facilities. And Alan Johnson will bring forward proposals to enhance the role of employers in helping their staff lead healthy lives, extending to many the kind of employment benefits currently only available to the few.

We will also look again at the responsibility of food producers, caterers and retailers in helping tackle ill health, especially obesity. Parents tell me of their frustrations with the different food labelling they find on shelves when trying to make decisions on what their family eats. We are reviewing the multiple labelling systems currently in use, and I want to see consensus on a single labelling system, easily understood by consumers, which will deliver real improvements in the health of the country.

And because we know parents are concerned about excessive food advertising online or via mobile phones, the Culture Secretary, James Purnell, will be working with the industry to make sure the codes of practice are as tough as parents want them to be.

These are all measures in line with our vision of a renewed and reformed NHS – handing power and control to individuals and ensuring they have the information and support they need to make their own choices about their and their family's health.

Reform means not a new unelected quango, which would be about ducking responsibility for the tough decisions, but greater operational independence for local NHS organisations and NHS clinicians, and I want this to be established through the constitution. Reforming the system itself requires real leadership, real accountability and the strength to see through real change.

So my guarantee to you today is that our vision for change will be based on clinical evidence and the new drive for a more preventative health service. It will be founded on greater local control and greater freedom for staff, within the context of the right incentives and minimum standards. And above all it will seek a new relationship in which the patient and clinician are both active and responsible – a vision for a healthier and more empowered population.

Amongst global health care systems, the NHS is almost uniquely well placed to deliver this transformation in the relationship between patients and clinicians – one of the most trusted organisations in British society, its doctors, nurses and staff recognised by everyone as a force for good in our country. And let me thank everyone who is working so hard to make these changes possible.

The renewal of the NHS will be our highest priority. Our goal – deeper and wider reform, building on the values, principles and idealism of the NHS to create for the next decade an NHS that is here for all of us but personal to each of us; focused on prevention as much as cure; and strong and confident enough to put real control into the hands of individuals and their clinicians.

This is a worthy mission for an institution as great and as significant in our lives as the National Health Service, and it is a transformation I ask you all to be a part of.

20

EDUCATION

In this speech, the Prime Minister sets out the next stage of improvement in the school-education sector. As he says, what we need to do is to realise 'our shared ambition to raise school standards for all and to guarantee a place at a good school for every child in Britain'.

The speech starts with praise for the teachers and school leaders in the audience: 'No one ever forgets their teacher, and each and every day you do what people remember and are grateful for decades later – you nurture minds, develop characters, instil ambition, offer friendship and build confidence. In short, you change lives, and, as it has been said, if you change one life you're changing the world. You should be very, very proud. And we are proud of you.'

The context for this speech is the global economic crisis and the role that schools can play in this. The Prime Minister is clear that, in his view, 'The countries that will succeed in this increasingly skilled global economy are those that are investing heavily, as we are, in education and training, developing support for the all-important early years of a child's life and ensuring that more of their young people take up the opportunities that higher education offers.' And, as he explains, 'Once, developing a skill was something ambitious people did to get on. Now, skills are essential for us all just to get by. And the skills people need are changing fast too. Today's teenagers aspire to jobs – such as in software engineering and graphic design – that our parents' generation hadn't even heard of.'

In the main section of the speech, Gordon Brown sets out the next stage of reform of the school system: 'First, that we should extend the reach of the leaders within our public services, allowing government to play a more strategic role focused on clear priorities, not hundreds of initiatives. We must be unapologetically hard-edged to intervene when schools consistently underperform but not afraid to stand back and allow greater freedom to innovate when there is success.

'Second, that public services are only ever as good as the professionals who deliver them. So we must invest in, and build trust in, our public service professionals.

'And third, that modern public services must be accountable and responsive to the people who use them. Every parent – as every patient in the health service and, indeed, everyone who uses our public services – must have the ability to influence and shape those services. For we will only achieve true excellence when we have not just universal services but also personal services.'

EDUCATION FOR THE NEW GLOBAL AGE
Prendergast School, London, 5 May 2009

Everyone remembers their teachers. When Sarah, my wife, was writing a book for charity and asked people around the country who, apart from their parents, had inspired them the most, the answer was invariably the same whether from Sir David Frost, Andrew Motion or Lord Bill Morris – their inspirational heroes were their teachers and often their head teachers.

No one ever forgets their teacher, and each and every day you do what people remember and are grateful for decades later – you nurture minds, develop characters, instil ambition, offer friendship and build confidence. In short, you change lives, and, as it has been said, if you change one life you're changing the world. You should be very, very proud. And we are proud of you.

I'm proud, too, that today we're here at a school which is one of the great success stories of our country's education system – a tribute to great teaching and leadership, not just providing outstanding opportunities for its pupils, with a specialist status in languages and music, but, through federation and partnership arrangements within Lewisham, working with the local authority to drive up standards in schools across the area.

Prendergast School's success is a direct result of the tireless dedication and commitment of everyone involved in running it. But especially of its executive head teacher, Erica, whose outstanding vision and drive exemplify the power of great school leadership – something I know Steve Munby and all those at the National College for School Leadership have been working to develop and extend right across our education system.

And I know, too, that Erica is in good company today. The National College for School Leadership has brought together this afternoon some of our finest teachers and head teachers and many others who dedicate their lives to making our schools the best they can be. And not just head teachers but system leaders – people who have given outstanding leadership, not only to our schools but to the education service at every level across Britain. So let me first thank you all and pay tribute to each of you here today.

As I will suggest, in the new global age a good teacher matters more than ever, leadership matters more than ever and the pursuit of excellence matters more than ever, and we owe you a debt of gratitude.

And this afternoon I want to discuss with you how we can build on the Children's Plan – and what you are already achieving – and take the next steps, in a new world of global competition, to realising our shared ambition to raise school standards for all and to guarantee a place at a good school for every child in Britain.

Historians will look back and see the events of the last few months – the first global financial crisis – and the forces of change that lie behind them, like the rise of Asia, as defining a new global age.

People today are understandably worried about their jobs now and their jobs for the future. Things that they took for granted a few years ago, or even a year ago, they cannot take for granted any more. We've all realised that globalisation creates risks as well as opportunities. And we have to be ready to respond more rapidly, more flexibly and more creatively than ever before.

But while we are taking action to deal with the global downturn, we must also build a better Britain for the future. And the key to that future is education, for we will start building for the new world not in our financial system but in our education system, not at bank counters but in school classrooms.

Last year, through our new Global Fellowship scheme, we sent 100 enterprising 18 and 19 year olds from diverse backgrounds and from all over the country to get first-hand experience of the major countries driving the new global economy – China, India and Brazil. They came back with clear messages. With the directness that comes from seeing it for the first time, they said, 'We've just met young people who want our jobs and are studying to get them. But in Britain we're not producing much now really, other than our people. But we shouldn't be afraid of global competition, because we've got the most important thing to offer – talent.'

They understood that if Britain is second in education and skills we can never be first in business and that if we come second in business our young people will not have the opportunities and chances in life we wish for them.

The countries that will succeed in this increasingly skilled global economy are those that are investing heavily, as we are, in education and training, developing support for the all-important early years of a child's life and ensuring that more of their young people take up the opportunities that higher education offers.

Last month, Barack Obama set out his plans for investing in and reforming American schools. As he said, 'Education is no longer just a pathway to opportunity and success; it's a pre-requisite for success.' And Obama is not alone. Prime Minister Rudd in Australia is taking similar steps to raise education standards. India and China – great nations that are already transforming the world we live in – today produce more graduates than the USA and Japan.

But it is not enough for us simply to learn from the best practice of other countries or to build on our own successes in recent years. No. The upheavals of the last two years mean we must completely re-chart our approach to education.

Once, developing a skill was something ambitious people did to get on. Now, skills are essential for us all just to get by. And the skills people need are changing fast too. Today's teenagers aspire to jobs – such as in software engineering and graphic design – that our parents' generation hadn't even heard of.

A good education for every child is no longer just desirable; it is indispensable. Everyone needs to develop a skill and everything we do in government must be directed towards equipping people for these jobs of tomorrow. Put simply, if we don't invest in the future, we have no future.

Until last year people assumed that their children would have a better life than they did. But the traumatic events around the world have shaken that assumption as never before. Some in politics are so pessimistic about Britain's prospects that they talk of the next decade only in terms of the politics of austerity and defeatism – and if their message is one of cutting back on our investment in the future, of course people feel our prospects will be worse.

But if we invest in people, and if we modernise education, the prospects for the next generation can be much better than for the last. Over the next 20 years the world economy will double as Asian producers become consumers of our goods. That means more jobs and more opportunities that could come Britain's way. This is the foundation for a new decade of growth and opportunity.

But we will only take advantage of these opportunities if we invest in the skills, the technologies and the industries of the future. So we must build on some of our country's many strengths, including hi-tech manufacturing, the creative industries and a thriving low-carbon sector. For there are thousands of new jobs to be found in green technologies, information technology, digital technologies and advanced manufacturing and in a range of services from teaching to social care.

The onus, therefore, is on opening up the new horizons in education for all who can benefit, not for the few, and giving anyone who can benefit the qualifications for these jobs both now and in the future.

So let me be clear – this is a banking recession that needs banking action, but you cannot cut your way out of the recession bad banking has caused. We cannot allow the failure of the financial system to leave us ill-equipped for the economic and educational future. So you can only invest and grow your way out, because high skills and good-quality education are the key to succeeding in the global economy in the twenty-first century. So the downturn is no time to slow down our investment in education but rather to build more vigorously for the future.

Under this government, education will not become a victim of the recession but rather the focus of our path to recovery and long-term growth – which is also the key to sustainable public finances. So now is the time to build on our record investment in education – to invest in raising school standards for all our children so that every child in Britain has the opportunity, indeed the entitlement, to make the most of their talents.

And now we have made the first big decision – with education to 18. This will cost money, but it is the right thing to do, and by making educational maintenance allowances available more will be able to stay on in school itself. This autumn the first 11 year olds who will all go right through from 16 to 18 will enter secondary school.

Investment for the global age means also that we are stepping up our investment during the downturn – including creating an additional 35,000 apprenticeships – with a further £1 billion for apprenticeships in 2009–2010 and, from 2013, an entitlement to an apprenticeship place for all suitably qualified young people. And we are fully funding our September guarantee so all 16 and 17 year olds who want it can have a place in education or training.

Investment for the global age also means expanding second-chance education, including nearly one million people now being helped by Train to Gain. One of the reasons I'm so passionate about second chances is because I've met people who have seized them with both hands. Take Dave Gustave. He grew up in a tough estate and had an abusive relationship with his dad. He left school and home at 16 and spent nearly 15 years having run-ins with people and with the law. Then he ended up doing A levels at 30, when he was spotted by an Oxford tutor who saw an extraordinary mind at work. He got a place, got a brilliant degree and then got a scholarship to the Bar.

But he's given all that up to go back to Peckham as a youth worker, because he didn't want to be well-educated to get away from his community but in order to help it. So don't let anybody tell you education doesn't make a difference; often it's the only thing that can.

And that's why we have made the next big decision of this global age to make our core aim the realisation of everyone's potential. And why we must now take the next steps to realise this aim and support the children of the new global age, who have new needs, new opportunities to seize and new risks to confront. In short, we must adopt the politics of opportunity and growth and reject the politics of austerity and defeatism.

And my guiding belief is that the countries that will succeed in this new century – the ones that will shape the destiny of humanity – will be those that put power in the hands of their citizens; that liberate the talents, creativity, enterprise and ingenuity of their people; and forge a common national purpose from the values, beliefs, aspirations and ambitions of their people.

It arises from a simple but profound point – that the defining question of the twenty-first century will not be whether power is held by the state or by the market but whether it is in the hands of the many, not the few. So the defining test for any political party will be not whether it can take power but whether it can give it away. What does this mean for education?

My argument is that neither a free-market, voucher-style reform of education – where some are helped while others are left to fall behind – nor top-down, centralised government control can provide the innovation and leadership needed to take the next steps on the road to world-class schools for our children.

We must always be restless in our ambition and relentless in our determination to improve. But instead of the free-market or the heavy-handed state, we should put our trust in you and look to great schools and great head teachers, working with local parents, to lead the next stage of reform.

It will mean the best heads moving into positions of system leadership – as Erica has done here – becoming executive heads working with a group of schools. It will mean more devolution and freedom to innovate in all our schools. And it will mean giving parents new rights and responsibilities.

As Ed Balls will set out in a White Paper next month, the drive for world-class schools will require a more strategic role for government – intervening when schools consistently underperform but standing back and allowing teachers and school leaders greater freedom to innovate; more freedom for the professionals working in our schools, with those professionals taking responsibility for consistently improving classroom practice and demonstrating their success to parents and the public; more involvement for parents in their child's education – with the responsibilities that brings for parents – and also the need to ensure that our system responds to parental views on the quality of education and the availability of good school places; and, above all, investment in excellence – in resourcing a system that can unleash the talents and potential of every child.

It is not elitist to strive for excellence, quite the opposite. I believe there is limitless potential in every child. For each is precious and unique, born endowed with a contribution only they can make. So schools must promote a culture of innovation and excellence, supporting the unique abilities of every child to reach their potential and defending not just the right of the struggling to get support to catch up but also the right of the very able to travel as far and as fast as their talents will take them.

And by 'talents' I don't just mean academic – the core skills of English and Maths – as central as they are to the education of every child. Talent takes many forms – practical, creative, communicative and enterprising abilities, as well as analytical intelligence. We must step up our commitment to recognise and discover them all in our children and young people.

And we must build resilience, determination and grit – the strengths of character and mind, the ability to plan, to think ahead, to work with others and stay the course – the invaluable skills which apply whatever you do and increasingly determine how well we do in life.

Two teenage boys from a special school summed it up for me. Let me read you what they said. 'All students have some talent which may be hard to find or encourage. In my school we have students who cannot walk any more and now manage in wheelchairs. That's talent. Many of my friends find reading really hard and feel really good when they read a little bit and somebody notices. Please notice all achievements.'

His friend said, 'I have heard lots about students getting A* to C grades. In my school nobody will get any of these grades. Does that mean none of us has any talent? Please look hard for talent. We love it when we spot it.'

Those words challenge us all, and I believe they should inspire us, too. Indeed, for many teachers it's the reason they went into the profession. That's why we commit to supporting the unique abilities of every child.

There can be no ceiling to the aspiration of our children; there can be no child we overlook.

When it works, the power of education is truly inspiring. Last month I hosted a reception for the Every Child A Reader programme, and I met some of the pupils who had improved the fastest. I met Immanuel who had just written his first letter and decided that when he grew up he wanted to write books for others to read. And I met two boys who both had parents in prison and who had never before left their council estate but who felt, that day, standing in Downing Street, that learning to read really had opened a whole new world for them. This opportunity – for every child to succeed and to have the chance to develop their talents – is, and must always be, a right for all and not a privilege for a few.

Yes, it's economic, because the future of our economy and the prosperity of our nation will be determined more than anything else by the skills and contributions of our young people today. But it's more than economic – it's personal.

This is a very personal mission for me because I grew up in an ordinary industrial town and went to the local school. I saw at first hand the power of opportunity to change lives, but I also saw how the devastating denial of that opportunity can crush potential. I benefited from great and dedicated teachers, and I was fortunate enough to get to university, but as a teenager I also saw close friends of mine who might have gone to college, become an apprentice or studied at university but who never did.

University or college was, they thought, or their parents thought, not for people like them. Often invisible barriers – the background they came from, the assumptions they made, the encouragement they never had – held them back, to their permanent disadvantage.

So I don't just celebrate the potential of education because I understand it in some abstract sense. No. My commitment is greater than that. It is the frustration, the anger, that such opportunities were not there for my friends when I was growing up that drives me to say that we have to find a way to give every child in Britain the opportunity to discover and develop their own talents, fulfil their potential and improve their chances in life. So let me sum up where I think we can advance.

I believe the next phase of innovation and reform in our schools will be crucial. And for me it must begin – as with all our public service reform – with three fundamental propositions.

First, that we should extend the reach of the leaders within our public services, allowing government to play a more strategic role focused on clear priorities, not hundreds of initiatives. We must be unapologetically hard-edged to intervene when schools consistently underperform but not afraid to stand back and allow greater freedom to innovate when there is success.

Second, that public services are only ever as good as the professionals who deliver them. So we must invest in, and build trust in, our public service professionals.

And third, that modern public services must be accountable and responsive to the people who use them. Every parent – as every patient in the health service and, indeed, everyone who uses our public services – must have the ability to influence and shape those services. For we will only achieve true excellence when we have not just universal services but also personal services. So let me turn first to strategic leadership of the school system.

A decade ago so many of Britain's public services were of such poor quality that it was right for central government to act as an effective proxy for the interests of those users, challenging providers on their behalf and demanding improvement. This approach has led to major improvements in standards and proved particularly successful in tackling failure, including in our schools. But it has not led to consistently world-class provision in every school and in every classroom. And although individual school autonomy has increased, it has also led to an increasingly large role for central government.

Now there are some who argue that we should tackle school failure by relying on market forces – that we should allow a market to develop in education with voucher-style approaches for parents to buy school places for their children.

What would this achieve? Consider the implications of new schools and surplus places springing up unplanned wherever a group of parents or sponsor came forward. Realistically, these new schools would not be targeted at areas of greatest need. Instead they would pick off the children with the most educated and aspirational parents from existing schools at the expense of the majority who would be left behind. And they would not raise standards for all. Instead they would divert some £4.5 billion of capital spending from the refurbishment and improvement programme of around 360 existing schools across the country. And, unlike our academies, these schools would not replace existing ones, or at least not until the education of a generation of children had been damaged.

A market free-for-all would fail because, as some schools go under slowly as competitors overtake them, children in those weaker schools would be left behind – a whole generation failed, waiting for the market to work;

power for a few parents, not for the many; opportunity for some children, not excellence for all. So I reject this approach.

An alternative approach would be a significantly increased top-down role for government in the education system, with a return to local authorities running every school to meet centrally set targets and regulations. I reject this approach too. It would stifle innovation, deny teachers and school leaders the freedom they need to drive change, and it would cut parents out of any role in improving education standards.

Instead our approach must be to look to great schools and great heads to lead the next stage of reform – with parents given new powers and government, both local and national, exercising a strategic, not directive, role.

I believe that all of you in this hall today – your talents and your expertise – are the vital ingredients to success in taking our education system to the next level. Outstanding head teachers are showing what can be achieved by extending their sphere of leadership. As well as this federation here in Lewisham, there are now many notable examples of federations. The Ark chain of schools is raising standards across London. And Outwood Grange – in federation with North Doncaster Technology College and Harrogate High, led by Mike Wilkins – is demonstrating what can happen when a high-performing school federates with schools in need of support.

We must make this the norm rather than exception. So we will bring forward proposals in our White Paper for a radical expansion of the role of federations, chains and executive heads in our school system.

And as local professional leadership of the system strengthens, government can and must play a more strategic role, overcoming the temptation to try to control too much. This means local government being a commissioner of services, for example for children with additional needs, and being responsible for the provision of sufficient good school places.

And it means central government being clear about its priorities. It should focus on setting overall direction and the most important objectives. So the new school report card will set out, with greater clarity than ever before, what we expect of schools – a single point of focus in the place of a multiplicity of targets. And where the school is successful, we will back that leadership.

Of course, central government must continue to intervene to enforce minimum standards both where schools are consistently underperforming or where they are coasting along. I make no apology for that.

National Challenge has raised the bar and, backed by £400 million of resources, will make a real difference in hundreds of secondary schools. And in the forthcoming schools White Paper we will set out how we will make more use of the best leadership to drive improvement across the whole school system in the coming years. In the primary school arena, for example, for too long persistently poor schools have been allowed to continue. So before the summer a primary school improvement strategy will set out how – starting in the next year and true to our approach of building on the professionalism in the system – we will ensure that the best leadership in primary schools is engaged to drive up standards across the board.

But government also needs to know where to step back. Academies and trusts have additional freedoms. But we must look harder at how we can rationalise the statutory duties, correspondence and guidance that schools receive. Learning the lessons from our recent progress with other services like the NHS, the White Paper will come forward with proposals to reduce the burden on schools.

And in doing so we will free up schools to push forward the frontier of innovation – like the Leigh Academy, which has organised into a series of small schools within the school so that every pupil knows and is known by every teacher within their small school, with vertical tutoring of groups of students with ages ranging from year seven to sixth form; or the Young Foundation, which is currently developing studio schools with seven local authorities, engaging young people by offering a range of qualifications through an enterprise-based curriculum and working in partnership with local businesses to help pupils develop employability skills.

So as government steps back and offers greater freedoms, we must support the leadership of our schools to step forward.

The second belief I set out earlier is that public services are only ever as good as the professionals who deliver them. Today teaching is becoming a profession of choice once again for the best graduates – in fact the number one career choice for this year's graduates. The success of Teach First means it is now one of the top recruiters of Oxbridge graduates.

In this economic downturn, we are investing to attract more graduates and talented career-changers into teaching. We are transforming the training of teachers through the introduction of a new master's qualification. And from this September schools in the most challenging circumstances will be able to offer a £10,000 incentive to attract the best teachers.

What is being demonstrated again and again in our programme of public service reform – and what excites me about the potential we have to go for – is that real excellence depends upon liberating the imagination, creativity and commitment of the public service workforce. This does not mean giving up on reform, as some would encourage us to do. But instead it requires us to create new opportunities for professionals to control the process of change, with less top-down control and a greater say for front-line staff.

We have already acted to free up the curriculum in secondary education, and the Rose Review will do the same for primary. We must make the leap to a 'high trust' approach to reform, not one where driving up standards is always seen as something which government does to schools.

That is why in next month's White Paper we will set out plans increasingly to move towards a system in which schools decide for themselves their priorities for improvement and buy in tailored support for their needs, including from other schools.

We already have over 200 training schools, leading on the delivery of high-quality continued professional development. And the Teacher Development Agency and the National College of School Leadership are working together to ensure that it will become the norm for groups of schools to drive improvements in practice – teachers learning from other teachers in local clusters.

We must build on these partnerships. Already, as part of our Academies Programme, schools are partnering with universities, and I know that many of you here today share the desire to make the most of these links. For example, where schools partner with our best teacher-training providers, they could become leading innovators in teacher training and classroom practice.

And we will take forward with our social partners the idea of a guaranteed entitlement to professional development for all teachers – a guarantee which for many teachers will mean more ongoing investment in their skills and professionalism. So our approach to professionalism is clear. We know that increasingly it is professionals themselves who will be the engines of innovation and improvement in our schools. And we know that it is only by empowering you that we will achieve our shared goal of truly world-class standards.

Finally, we all know that the greatest influence on a child's life is parents. The evidence is clear that the most important role for parents in their child's education is talking to them, reading with them and taking an interest in their progress. So most crucially of all in our approach to extending opportunity in education will be maximising parent power and improving services for parents that involve them in their child's education in the years ahead.

Fundamentally, of course, public accountability has to be based on clear information about performance in schools, as in other public services. That is why we make no apology for continuing external assessment of pupil attainment at the end of primary school, as there is in secondary education. And that is why we are looking to introduce a new school report card, which can provide comprehensive but clear information for parents on the performance of the school their child attends.

But we need more than intelligent public accountability for schools to be more responsive. In the last few years, education has become increasingly personalised to the specific needs, aptitudes and aspirations of individual children. This personalisation has been driven by powerful new forms of teaching, learning and assessment in our schools. We've seen greater use of information technologies to enhance learning and track pupil progress; access to wider services that parents need to support them, for example when their child has a disability; new methods of organising the curriculum; and innovative classroom teaching practice. Positive changes led by innovators in our education system.

And personalising education for every child must lead us on to find new ways of involving parents in the education of their children. Parents have important responsibilities. Whether it's simply ensuring that their children arrive at school ready to learn or helping teachers address persistent behaviour problems, good parenting is crucial for children's success.

But, to match these responsibilities, we need to do more to make sure that our education system responds to parental views on the quality of education and the availability of good school places. Just as we put more trust in our front-line professionals, we need also to empower parents.

For parents to influence the education of their children they need rich, varied and easily accessible information on the progress, behaviour and attendance of their children. Many of our schools and best leaders are already using the latest technology to do this, but it should be a right for all parents.

So from 2010 all secondary schools, and from 2012 all primary schools, will report online to parents – something that has been made possible because of our investment in universal home Internet access for all families with children. So the mother who's worried about her son struggling with his reading can find out more about how she can help, or the dad who works long hours and can't make a parents' evening can keep in touch with his daughter's progress at whatever time of the day or night that he's free.

And because we know that sometimes talking face to face to a teacher who knows their child well is what parents really want, we will build on the good practice that already exists in schools and ensure that, by September next year, every secondary pupil has the opportunity of a personal tutor.

For me, like all parents, school discipline matters. A school that has 'satisfactory' behaviour is simply not good enough. We know what works – as many of you here today have shown, clear rules, consistently enforced, can turn around poor discipline. It is simply unacceptable that a minority of pupils can disrupt the learning of the majority.

But as well as being directly engaged in their children's learning and knowing that their school is tackling their concerns about behaviour, parents most want to know that they will have a good offer of secondary school places and, crucially, that if the offer is not good enough they can demand action. Now there are some who argue that the solution is for parents who aren't happy with the choice available to break away and create their own schools. I believe that there is a role for parents running schools where they wish to. Indeed, that is why it is this government that has made it possible, with the first parent-promoted school already opened in Lambeth. And it is why we will go further in improving the support we give to parents' groups who want to take this route.

But the vast majority of parents don't want the burden of running their own school. They don't want to be expected to do it themselves. They want world-class teachers and school providers to do it for them. So if parents are dissatisfied with the availability of good school places in their local area or with the mix of provision on offer, then we have an obligation to respond to their concerns.

We have made significant progress on providing all parents with a good choice of school. This year 83 per cent of parents got their first choice school and 94.6 per cent got one of their first three choices. And through policies like the National Challenge we will continue to drive up the quality of school places and so improve the options for parents. But I want to go further still.

So we will look at how local authorities can improve their knowledge of what parents want and how satisfied they are with their local schools. And where there is significant dissatisfaction with the pattern of secondary school provision and where standards across an area are too low, then the local authority will be required to act. This could mean either the creation of a federation of schools, an expansion of good school places or, in some cases, the establishment of entirely new schools.

Working towards these improvements needs to happen within the context of a system of fair admissions, so that the education of other children in the area will not be undermined. Unlike the free-market free-for-all, this is a policy agenda focused on raising standards for all, not raising standards for some at the expense of others.

Through the steps I have outlined today we will deliver a system that is more accountable to parents, offering them more access to information; emphasising an increasingly personal approach to the teaching and support their child receives; enforcing stronger discipline; and providing testing and assessment with a school report card that informs them about the performance of the school in a well-rounded way, not just in the basic, traditional subjects but across the breadth of the education the school delivers.

We will focus on developing the professionalism and great leadership of our teachers – supporting their development with new opportunities for training, bringing new talent into the profession – and we will back success and offer greater freedoms in return for a continuous and relentless focus on raising the bar for every child.

And through extending the reach of our best leaders as executive heads and in the development of chains and federations, we will improve schools across the country so that, working with you, we raise standards for all, not just standards for some.

With your help we can achieve the goal of a good school place for every child in Britain. With your excellence we can secure the economic future of Britain for generations to come. And with your leadership we can enable every child to say that, truly, their education focused on making the best of their talents and potential and that their destiny will be determined by them and never again determined for them.

21

NORTHERN IRELAND

An important area that has received little coverage during his premiership is the time and effort Gordon Brown has devoted to securing the Good Friday and St Andrews Agreements affecting Northern Ireland. In order to redress this perception, a speech given to the Northern Ireland Assembly, the first given by a British prime minister, is included here.

The Prime Minister uses this powerful and persuasive speech to congratulate the people of Northern Ireland on the way they have adopted the politics of peaceful change. And he commends all those who have helped with this process: 'After decades of conflict, you are on an entirely different path. No longer the ever-present threat of violence; the uncertainties of what might happen at the supermarket, at the petrol station or in the city centre. Together you have transformed this society. And that is a momentous achievement.'

And the Prime Minister concludes that the success is down to the elected politicians choosing the democratic path instead of conflict: 'the reason the Northern Ireland of today commands respect from all round the world is because politicians – and that means all the elected representatives in this Assembly – have shown that the political path to peaceful change, while it can be difficult, is the only way from conflict to a stable and secure future; that however great the divisions, dialogue can move us on from ancient battlegrounds to new common ground'.

SPEECH TO THE NORTHERN IRELAND ASSEMBLY
Stormont, Belfast, 16 September 2008

Mr Speaker, members of the Assembly. It is an honour and a privilege to be in Stormont to address the elected members of this fully representative, power-sharing administration and Assembly – and to be the first prime minister to do so. It is also a humbling experience, because for all the cynicism about politics today, you are living proof that politics can win through and that public service can make a great difference.

So let me say at the outset that the reason the Northern Ireland of today commands respect from all round the world is because politicians – and that means all the elected representatives in this Assembly – have shown that the political path to peaceful change, while it can be difficult, is the only way from conflict to a stable and secure future; that however great the divisions, dialogue can move us on from ancient battlegrounds to new common ground. Because the measure of the strength of our new politics is that in difficult times we renew our efforts, go back to the table and find a way through. That is what you and this Assembly are showing to the world.

After decades of conflict, you are on an entirely different path. No longer the ever-present threat of violence; the uncertainties of what might happen at the supermarket, at the petrol station or in the city centre. Together you have transformed this society. And that is a momentous achievement.

And I acknowledge the historic contributions of Tony Blair, Bertie Ahern and Bill Clinton, the First and Deputy First Ministers, the Former First Minister here and so many others who have worked to make real the ideal of a new Northern Ireland. It's invidious to select any one of you here. All of you have worked for your community. Our government and the governments of the Republic, led by Brian Cowen, and the United States, led by George Bush, continue to be pledged to this. For what you have done here, and what you are still doing and have still to do, is an inspiration for the whole world – showing that the light can come to the darkest places when people are empowered to take control of their destiny and decide to change it for ever.

But for Northern Ireland – once more, and now more than ever – the outcome is in your hands. But what the politics of Northern Ireland has proved is that hope can triumph over fear. Northern Ireland – no longer the byword for endless, corrosive despair but a beacon of promise for the future. Northern Ireland – increasingly at peace with itself. A Northern Ireland of rising prosperity and cohesion.

So what you have done here, and what you are still doing and have still to do, is an inspiration for the whole world – showing that the light can come to the darkest places when people are empowered to take control of their destiny and decide to change it for ever.

All around there is a new sense of confidence and achievement. Over the past decade Northern Ireland has delivered one of the highest rates of growth of any UK region outside London and the South East. We have seen businesses attracted by competitive operating costs, excellent transport links and world-class skills.

Now, as we have seen in recent days, the instability in global financial markets is affecting every major economy in the world. Financial turbulence that started in the US subprime mortgage market has now spread to some of the biggest institutions in Wall Street. This is the first crisis of a truly globalised economy. And these twin shocks of the credit crunch and inflationary pressures that are hitting every country in the world will require new international as well as domestic solutions.

Of course, given the importance of financial services to the UK economy, neither the UK nor any part of the UK can be insulated from these global financial shockwaves. And as we have seen again this morning, like all the major economies we are also being hit by the inflationary impact over the last couple of years of higher global commodity prices, which have a direct effect on family budgets.

But because of the five fundamental strengths of our economy – low inflation and therefore low interest rates; flexible labour markets; the financial strength of our industrial companies; public debt repayments over the last decade meaning we can prudently increase government borrowing at the right time; and the long-term decisions we are taking on planning, energy and our national infrastructure – we are better placed than we have been in the past to weather this global downturn.

At home we have taken action to help households through this difficult period, including tough decisions on public sector pay to keep inflation and interest rates down; support through the New Deal and Jobcentre Plus to help those affected by job losses; £120 family tax cut for 22 million basic-rate taxpayers this year; and targeted support for the housing market, including a stamp duty holiday, to help those affected.

And we will continue to use our credibility and experience to lead international work on those issues that can only be tackled at the global level. This summer we worked with Saudi Arabia to focus urgent global attention on the problems in the world oil market. Since their peak, oil prices are down more than a third, though we continue to work with our international partners to improve the functioning of the market.

Global problems require global action. And in New York next week I will meet with world leaders and press for the reforms the UK has been proposing to the global financial architecture – more transparency of financial institutions to reduce the uncertainty in financial markets; a better early-warning system for global investors, including a stronger role for the IMF; and better coordination between financial regulators, building on the reforms we made to create the Financial Stability Forum in response to the increasing global integration of financial markets.

To build more momentum for these reforms, the government is sending senior representatives to visit all G7 countries in advance of the IMF meetings. So, we will continue to do whatever is necessary to keep our economy moving forward and to maintain the integrity of our financial institutions.

And as the fundamentals of Northern Ireland's economy remain strong, so I believe Northern Ireland has powerful reasons for optimism. Last year you had one of the lowest rates of unemployment of any UK region. And today you have more people in work than ever before. And because you have ensured that the politics of peace has prevailed over violence, you have also made possible a new era of international investment in Northern Ireland.

In the past, because of the violence, because of the conflict, investment here was too often seen as risky. When investment did happen, it was despite the troubles. But today you are able to reap real benefits from international investment. The world's service, financial and manufacturing companies see Northern Ireland as equal to, or even the best of, places to invest.

In May this year I spoke to the Investment Conference the Executive organised here in Belfast. More than a hundred CEOs, chairmen and senior executives from the United States were drawn here by the opportunity of Northern Ireland. We saw companies like Bloomberg vote with their dollars and make their investments. And we're seeing existing investments grow rapidly from Marriott, the New York Stock Exchange and, most recently, Bombardier.

We know the immediate impact of that conference alone – over £80 million of new investment in Northern Ireland. And Invest Northern Ireland has received over 40 expressions of interest from overseas, which they are currently following up.

I remember meeting with the CEO of Bombardier at Hillsborough and talking through with him the work being done to attract huge resources for work on a new passenger jet here in Belfast. And I watched with pride the deal being announced in July at Farnborough – in this, Shorts' centenary year – with over 800 jobs secured and the first orders being placed by Lufthansa. Earlier this afternoon I visited Bombardier and met some of those whose skills will lead Northern Ireland into the future – young and adult apprentices and those who had qualified through the Engineering Skills for Industry Programme, which has helped 130 people into sustainable employment in Belfast. And I met pupils from local schools being introduced to aerospace through Bombardier's educational outreach programme.

Progress like this is possible only because of the skills and enterprise of the people of Northern Ireland and the investment of business here in Northern Ireland. So you are superbly placed to compete and lead in the new global economy set to double in size over the next two decades.

You have a wealth of talent and the capacity to build a strong knowledge-based private sector around your universities. You have a strong business climate and the will to win in the global economy.

The peace dividend in Northern Ireland grows day by day, year after year – every year of peace. So now is not the time for Northern Ireland to rest on its laurels or retreat but rather to redouble its efforts, to invest in what matters most for the future – world-class education and skills. That is a challenge that I know you will meet, because I know what you have done already. And I am confident that, with the strength of leadership we have all witnessed over the past year, the prosperity of Northern Ireland will endure and expand in the years ahead.

But, of course, the economic strength of Northern Ireland depends crucially on its political stability. The IMC report two weeks ago made it crystal clear that the IRA is not the danger; that the army council is redundant; that the military structures have been disbanded and consciously allowed to fall into disuse; that the IRA as an organisation does not pose a terrorist threat.

As all Northern Ireland knows, the end to violence marked the beginning of prosperity. And the continued success in preventing violence is the precondition of continued growth. We have seen in the last nine months a series of attacks on police officers. And there are criminal elements who must be confronted with the utmost determination. And that is exactly what will happen.

So let me say to all those brave men and women, the officers from both communities who form the police family, you have our gratitude for the sacrifices you make, for your strength in the face of danger and your determination to protect the people of Northern Ireland. The criminals who have targeted you have done so because they have much to fear from democracy backed by effective policing.

So let us send an unequivocal message to those who would defy the will of the people – the politics of peaceful change is winning in Northern Ireland and will overcome whatever obstacles are put in its way. And the clearest sign that democracy will triumph is this Assembly and Executive working together, meeting together, fulfilling all its functions, carrying out all its duties on behalf of the people who elected it and completing the process of devolution.

What you have achieved to date is historic, not least in the unique joint and equal leadership of the First and Deputy First Ministers. Some thought that power sharing between the parties would never happen, that the burden of shared government would be too heavy. No one assumed it would be easy. The cynics, with their doubts and misgivings, have at every turn been proved wrong. You have made history, but you have more history to make.

We can see in the research from the past week the extent of the support to complete the transfer of policing and justice powers. Across the community the majority of people want to see this accomplished. And fewer than one in ten say 'never'.

I can only hope that even this small minority will eventually come to see that completing devolution is not only the right thing to do but the only thing to do. I believe it would be wrong to allow this minority to exercise a veto on further progress now. Yes, let's understand their concerns, but let us also agree that they cannot and will not call a halt to progress.

So I urge you to continue your crucial work in this Executive and Assembly, to finish the job and complete a journey not just of a generation but of centuries. I believe we have gone beyond our crossroads in history. And this is no time to turn back or to stall or delay, because the completion of devolution is much more than the final step in a process – it is the creation of a whole new permanent future for Northern Ireland.

To falter now – to lose the will that has defined your progress – would be worse than a setback; it would put at risk everything that has been achieved by the work and sacrifice of the past decade and more. So my message to you today is to have confidence; to stay the course, to continue your work and reach that final settlement; to show the world the peace and prosperity you have achieved is here to stay.

And if you make this commitment, then we in the British government will match your resolve and do everything within our power to support you in it. Because we have not only prepared the ground for the transfer but we stand ready to help you through a smooth transition.

We pledged in the St Andrews Agreement that we would be ready to transfer powers one year after the Assembly was elected. And we have kept that promise. So now leaders here in Northern Ireland must reach agreement between themselves and set the date for the transfer of policing and justice from the Secretary of State to a justice minister, in and of Northern Ireland.

None of us should doubt the importance of this. Because in the agreement you reach here among yourselves, in the transfer of these powers back from Westminster, the world will see you affirm that stability is here to stay, your affirmation that peace is here to stay, your affirmation that prosperity is here to stay.

When President Bush came to Northern Ireland earlier this year, he did so not only because he is a true friend to the people of this country but because he wanted to see the huge inward investments from America continue to flow. And when I spoke to him a few days ago and told him I was coming here again, he talked movingly about his visit. About his commitment to you and all the people of Northern Ireland.

His message to everyone on every side was clear – it's time to complete devolution not just for yourselves but because that's the signal investors need to see. Because it's the best safeguard for the investment which has been made and will be made in the future from America. This is a commitment shared by Senator McCain and Senator Obama. So whoever becomes the next president of the United States is resolved to help. And they are right to do so. But not just because of the economic impact and not just because of the political consequences – as important as they are for the future of your people.

For there is something more vital at stake for your entire society – that only the completion of devolution can deliver. How can you, as an Assembly, address common criminality, low-level crime and youth disorder when you are responsible for only some of the levers for change; when you have responsibility for education, and health and social development but have to rely on Westminster for policing and justice?

The people of Northern Ireland look to you to deal with these matters, because to them they are important. Full devolution is the way to deliver better services tailored to the needs of all communities, regardless of the politics. It is the best way for you to serve them.

And my mission – the British government's mission – is to help you deliver for them and for future generations in Northern Ireland. My job is to be there for you, to refuse to give in or give up, to reach with you your shared destiny and our shared hope.

And as we stand at this point – and as you take those decisions that will shape the future of your nation – I am reminded of the poem by Robert Frost, who wrote:

Two roads diverged in a wood, and I –
I took the one less traveled by,
And that has made all the difference.

Today I say to you have faith that if you take the road less travelled, it will make all the difference; have faith that your hopes will be rewarded; that while the arc of the moral universe may be long – and it has been so long here in Northern Ireland – it bends eternally towards peace and justice. And have faith that the people of Northern Ireland – and indeed the people of the world – are with you and always will be.

Let us show the people of Northern Ireland – and the people of all the world – that the astonishing transformation of Northern Ireland can be completed, that the future of Northern Ireland is in the right hands because it is in your hands.

PART V

FIGHTING FOR BRITAIN

Gordon Brown took office just over two years into the third term of the Labour government originally elected in 1997. He became not only leader of the country but leader of the Labour movement and of the party he had supported passionately since he was a boy. Extracts from two of Gordon Brown's party conference speeches as leader have been selected to end this book.

As anyone close to the political process will tell you, the annual conference speech is rarely far from mind and gradually assumes greater and greater significance from the early summer until it is finally delivered in the autumn conference season. A leader's speech can go through 40 or 50 or more drafts, and it is not unknown for changes to be being made as the text is prepared for press release and the autocue. Why should this be? It is partly the fact that these speeches have to fulfil so many different functions – for the party faithful in the hall they are a rallying call; for the wider TV audience they are a rare glimpse of the leader in full flow, unmediated by the press and not restrained by the artificial trappings of Prime Minister's Questions; and for the media they provide an opportunity to focus in on and interrogate the policies and issues that will be arising in the coming months. But it is also about personalities – who's up and who's down. And in some years it can be a place where new policy is announced and discussed.

Both the speeches selected here are typical of the genre, and both have the added ingredient of occurring at times when the Prime Minister was under attack from within his party and needed to rise to the occasion – as he did. On both occasions he was introduced by his wife, Sarah Brown, whose remarks are reproduced here as well.

22

PARTY CONFERENCE SPEECHES

INTRODUCTION BY SARAH BROWN

'Good afternoon everyone. I asked if I could have a chance today to talk briefly to you, because one of the privileges of my life over recent years has been the opportunity to meet so many different and extraordinary people. These have all been great moments, often private ones, but always meaningful, and I thank you all. I remember the warm welcome you gave me and Gordon at Conference after our wedding. And I'm so proud that every day I see him motivated to work for the best interests of people all around the country. I would like to welcome to the stage, to address us all, my husband, the leader of the Labour Party, your Prime Minister – Gordon Brown.'

Looking again at the recording of that special moment when Sarah Brown appeared, as if from nowhere, at the podium in the hall at the Manchester conference, you can feel the palpable mixture of surprise, delight and approval of the audience. The decision to introduce her husband was her idea and a closely guarded secret, known to only a very few people, and it did not leak. So the press and broadcasters were as amazed as the delegates and the wider audience watching on television, and the effect was astonishing. Though she said only a few words, she reminded everyone that they were ordinary people in extraordinary circumstances and that Gordon Brown is first and foremost a loving family man who understands that people want the best for themselves and their children.

There is rarely a leader's speech at any party conference that is not billed in some way as the most important speech he or she has ever given. There are some grounds for conceding that in September 2008 this speech by Gordon Brown was of that ilk. The early months after his appointment had gone well, but in the year that followed, Labour had suffered in the polls and the papers were full of rumours of plots and intrigues. During the late summer and early autumn, the global financial crisis was gathering pace and the Prime Minister had been playing the central role in the rescuing of the British banking system and organising international action to ensure that the world financial system did not go into meltdown. This speech, then, was an opportunity both to talk openly about the financial crisis and to show how the government's decisive actions were leading the way for the world; a chance to reaffirm what the Labour Party stands for in a time of recession; and an opportunity to convince the public that Gordon Brown was the right man to be leading the country now and in the future because of his strength and character and his experience in government.

The headlines the day after the speech rightly highlighted the role played by Sarah Brown in introducing the Prime Minister. They also seized on one line: 'Everyone knows that I'm all in favour of apprenticeships, but let me tell you this is no time for a novice' – an effective demolition of the inexperienced shadow chancellor and the lack of solutions to the recession coming from the Tory front bench. Unfortunately, the focus on this section took attention away from what was a tour de force of political speechmaking. The speech comprehensively rose to the challenge of the times, giving full answers to the questions posed about the policies to be adopted in addressing the financial crisis. It also put across the Prime Minister's personal beliefs about fairness and the need to use the financial crisis to press even harder to develop all the talents of all the people by 'helping those who are working their way up from very little and lifting up those in the middle who want to get on. It means supporting what really matters – hard work and effort and enterprise. This is not just the new economic necessity; it is the modern test of social justice and the radical centre ground we occupy and will expand.'

SPEECH TO THE LABOUR PARTY CONFERENCE
Manchester, 23 September 2008

I want to talk with you today about who I am, what I believe, what I am determined to lead this party and this great country to achieve.

As we gather here today, I know people have real concerns about the future of the country, the future of the economy, and people in this hall have concerns about the future of our party too. And so I want to answer your questions directly, to talk with you about how, amidst all the present difficulties, we should be more confident than ever that we can build what I want to talk to you about today – a new settlement for new times, a fair Britain for the new age.

But let me start with something I hope you know already. I didn't come into politics to be a celebrity or thinking I'd always be popular. Perhaps that's just as well. No, 25 years ago I asked the people of Fife to send me to Parliament to serve the country I love. And I didn't come to London because I wanted to join the establishment but because I wanted, and want to, change it.

So I'm not going to try to be something I'm not. And if people say I'm too serious – quite honestly, there's a lot to be serious about. I'm serious about doing a serious job for all the people of this country.

What angers me and inspires me to act is when people are treated unfairly. So when people share with me stories about the hard time they're having with bills, I want to help, because I was brought up seeing my parents having to juggle their budget like the rest of us.

And when I talk to parents about schools, I'm determined that every child should have a good school because, while I got my break in a great local secondary, not all my friends got the chance to get on. And when I speak to victims of crime, I get angry because, like them, I know the difference between right and wrong.

And so here I am, working for this incredible country while trying as far as possible to give my children an ordinary childhood. Some people have been asking why I haven't served my children up for spreads in the papers. And my answer is simple – my children aren't props; they're people.

And where I've made mistakes I'll put my hand up and try to put them right. So what happened with 10p stung me, because it really hurt that suddenly people felt I wasn't on the side of people on middle and modest incomes – because on the side of hard-working families is the only place I've ever wanted to be. And from now on it's the only place I ever will be.

And so I want to give the people of this country an unconditional assurance. No 'ifs', no 'buts', no small print – my unwavering focus is taking this country through the challenging economic circumstances we face and building the fair society of the future.

The British people would not forgive us if at this time we looked inwards to the affairs of just our party when our duty is to the interests of our country. The people of Britain would never forget if we failed to put them first – and, friends, they'd be right.

And because this is a time of greater-than-ever change around us, it must be a time of higher ambition from us. And because the world of 2008 is now so different from the world of 1997, I want to talk about the new settlement we must build for these new times.

You know, each generation believes it is living through changes their parents could never have imagined, but after the collapse of banks, the credit crunch, the trebling of oil prices, the speed of technology and the rise of Asia, nobody now can be in any doubt that we are in a different world and it's now a global age.

In truth, we haven't seen anything this big since the industrial revolution. This last week will be studied by our children as the week the world was spun on its axis and old certainties were turned on their heads. And in these uncertain times we must be, we will be, the rock of stability and fairness upon which people stand.

And, friends, it's a calling that summons us because in every time of profound change those with great wealth and privilege have always been able to look after themselves. But our duty, what gives us moral purpose, is serving the people who need us most – Britain's vast majority, people on middle and modest incomes who need to know that they are not on their own amidst this change. We are on their side.

Where there are new risks and new pressures our duty is, and will be, security for all. And where there are new opportunities our duty is, and will be, fair chances for everyone matched by fair rules applied to everyone.

And insuring people against the new risks and empowering people with new opportunities is the mission of the hour. And those who say that governments should walk away when people face these risks and need these opportunities will be judged to be on the wrong side of history.

And when the country is asking their government to meet these new challenges, I say to our opponents – those who don't believe in the potential of government shouldn't be trusted to form one. So this is a defining moment for us – a test not just of our judgement but of our values. Today, once again, we are called to apply our enduring beliefs to completely new conditions.

New Labour has always been at its best when we have applied our values to changing times. In the 1990s, Tony and I asked you to change policy to meet new challenges.

We are, and will always be, a pro-enterprise, pro-business and pro-competition government. And we believe the dynamism of our five million businesses, large and small, is vital to the success of our country. But the continuing market turbulence shows why we now need a new settlement for these times; a settlement that we as a pro-market party must pursue; a settlement where the rewards are for what really matters – hard work, effort and enterprise; a settlement where both markets and government are seen to be the servants of the people, and never their masters; where what counts is not the pursuit of any sectional interest but the advancement of the public interest; and where at all times we put people first.

Let us be clear – the modern role of government is not to provide everything, but it must be to enable everyone. And just as we know that governments cannot and should not do everything, so, too, we know markets cannot deliver it all on their own. And just as those who supported the dogma of big government were proved wrong, so, too, those who argue for the dogma of unbridled free-market forces have been proved wrong.

And so it falls to this party and to this government, with its commitment both to fairness and to business, to propose and deliver what, after recent events, everyone should now be willing to accept – that we do all it takes to stabilise the still turbulent financial markets and then in the months ahead we rebuild the world financial system around clear principles. And, friends, the work begins tomorrow.

I, and then Alistair, will meet financial and government leaders in New York to make these proposals. First, transparency – all transactions need to be transparent and not hidden; second, sound banking – a requirement to demonstrate that risks can be managed and priced for bad times as well as good; third, responsibility – no member of a bank's board should be able to say they did not understand the risks they were running and walk away from them; fourth, integrity – removing conflicts of interest so that bonuses should not be based on short-term speculative deals but on hard work, effort and enterprise (I know that the British people think it's hard work, effort and enterprise we need to reward); and fifth, global standards and supervision, because if the flows of capital are global then supervision can no longer just be national but has to be global.

And if we make these changes, I believe London will retain its rightful place as the financial centre of the world. And we know that the challenges we face in this new global age didn't begin in the last week or in the last months but, in fact, reflect deeper changes in our world. For all its benefits, the global age has revealed not just financial instability but another major pressure – a rising global population demanding more energy.

So the new settlement also requires another great and historic endeavour to end the dictatorship of oil and to avert catastrophic climate change – a transformation in our use of energy, new nuclear power, an unprecedented increase in renewables and investment in clean coal.

And I am asking the climate change committee to report by October on the case for, by 2050, not a 60 per cent reduction in our carbon emissions but an 80 per cent cut. And I want British companies and British workers to seize the opportunity and lead the world in the transformation to a low-carbon economy. And I believe that we can create, in modern green manufacturing and service, one million new jobs.

And it's not just our duty but our basic philosophy that we do everything we can to help families through the world downturn. And while the Conservatives did nothing to help people with their gas and electricity bills in the last world downturn, this winter, millions of people will receive the help with heating bills, insulation, social tariffs – help they never received from the Conservatives.

But, you know, when it comes to public spending you can't just wave a magic wand to conjure up the money – not even with help from Harry Potter. And so there are tough choices, and I have to say that, as a result of the events of recent weeks, there are going to be tougher choices we will have to make and priorities we will have to choose. And just as families have to make economies to make ends meet, so this government must and will ensure that we get value for money out of every single pound of your money that is spent. But I say to you that we will invest it wisely, continuing our record investment in schools, Sure Start centres, transport and hospitals.

And if we make the right decisions to take people through the world downturn fairly, we will find that, despite the current troubles, British firms and British workers can reap the rewards of a world economy set to double in size.

With Britain's great assets – our stability, our openness, our scientific genius, our creative industries and, yes, our English language – I know that this can be a British century, and I'm determined it will be. But my argument today is that the new settlement for the global age must do even more to empower people with new opportunities, insure people against new risks and, as a result, value hard work, effort and enterprise. It's the economy that's been making the headlines, but there are other big changes, too.

People feel their communities are changing before their eyes, and it's increasing their anxiety about crime and antisocial behaviour. And so we will be the party of law and order.

And for the first time ever, we've got more British pensioners than British children, more people living longer on fixed incomes and worried about whether they'll need long-term care. And so we will be the party that will ensure security and dignity for pensioners.

And there are new pressures on parents – worrying about balancing work and family life but also about advertising aimed straight at their children and what their children are watching or downloading from the Internet. And so we will be the party of the family.

And so the new settlement for our times shows how Britain can meet all these challenges too, and it's more than about a fair prosperity; it must be about fair chances and fair rules too.

You know, some people say that there's an inevitable political cycle in this country, as sure as night follows day. I don't agree. The challenge of these new times demands a truly progressive government to help people cope with the new risks and make the most of the new opportunities. That's why I believe that, now more than ever – even more than in 1997 – this country needs a Labour government.

You know, to govern is to choose, and it's what a government chooses to do when it's tested that demonstrates its priorities and reveals its heart. It is not the arithmetic of statistics but the fabric of people's lives.

When we talk about three million more people in work since 1997, that's not just a number – that's a life that's been changed three million times over. That's the young woman laid off in the mid-'90s who's now built a booming business of her own. Three million new jobs – not by accident but by our actions. And in the years to come we will demonstrate again that real power of Labour to change lives.

And when we talk about the one million small and medium-sized businesses set up in the last eleven years, that's not just a number – that's the entrepreneur who can treat her parents to a summer holiday and the local businessman who's taken on two local teenagers as apprentices. One million new businesses demonstrating, yet again, the real power of Labour to change lives.

And when we talk about one million people benefiting from New Labour's minimum wage, that's not just a number – that's a dad doing security shifts who can now afford a birthday party for his child, and it's a mum who doesn't have to go to a loan shark to pay for her kids' Christmas. One million people freed from exploitation, and now the minimum wage rising year on year – that's the real power of Labour to change lives.

And when we talk about the 240,000 lives that are saved by the progress Labour's NHS has made in fighting cancer and heart disease, that's not just a number – that's the dad who lives to walk his daughter up the aisle and the gran who is there to clap and cry at her grandson's graduation. Two hundred and forty thousand families still together and now thousands more with new and better treatments from an expanding NHS. We're changing the world the only way it can ever really change

– one life, one family, one hope at a time. That's the real power of Labour to change lives.

And why do we always strive for fairness? Not because it makes good sound bites. Not because it gives good photo opportunities. Not because it makes for good PR. No. We do it because fairness is in our DNA. It's who we are and what we're for. It's why Labour exists. It's our first instinct, the soul of our party. It's why, when things get tough, we get tougher. We stand up; we fight hard – for fairness. We don't give in, and we never will.

For me, fairness is treating others how we would be treated ourselves. So it isn't levelling down but empowering people to aspire and reach ever higher. And to take advantage of all the opportunities of the global economy, I want to unleash a new wave of rising social mobility across our country.

For too long we've developed only some of the talents of some people, but the modern route to social mobility is developing all the talents of all the people, helping those who are working their way up from very little and lifting up those in the middle who want to get on. It means supporting what really matters – hard work and effort and enterprise. This is not just the new economic necessity; it is the modern test of social justice and the radical centre ground we occupy and will expand.

And fairness is why Harriet is introducing the first ever Equalities Bill. And let me thank her for her tireless work as Deputy Party Leader. Fairness is why Ed Miliband is ensuring that community and third-sector organisations can play their proper part in every neighbourhood. And it is why our whole party is leading the fight against the British National Party. Fairness is why John Denham is extending university access, why Ruth Kelly has introduced, for the first time, free bus travel for pensioners and why John Hutton and our Labour members of the European Parliament are fighting to free agency workers from the scourge of exploitation.

But fairness for the future also means a big change that I want to explain today. We have always stood for public services that are universal, available to all. Now we must stand for public services that are not only available to all but personal to each.

For me, the fairer future starts with putting children first – with the biggest investment in children this country has ever seen. It means delivering the best possible start in life with services tailored to the needs of every single precious child.

In 1997, there were no Sure Start centres, and nursery education was for only the few. Today, thanks to the work of Beverley Hughes, there are children's centres opening in every community – to serve three million children who a few years ago had nothing – and free nursery education for every three and four year old.

But our ambitions must be greater still. I want Britain to take its place among the leading nations in preschool services, and so I pledge here today in Manchester, starting in over thirty communities – and then over sixty – we will, stage by stage, extend free nursery places for two year olds for every parent who wants them in every part of the country, backed by high-quality, affordable childcare for all. That's the fairness parents want, and that's the fairness every Labour Party member will go out and fight for.

And because child poverty demeans Britain, we have committed our party to tackle and to end it. The measures we have taken this year alone will help lift 250,000 children out of poverty. The economic times are tough, of course, and that makes things harder, but we are in this for the long haul – the complete elimination of child poverty by 2020. And so, today, I announce my intention to introduce groundbreaking legislation to enshrine in law Labour's pledge to end child poverty.

And Ed Balls and I will never excuse, explain away or tolerate low standards in education. So we will keep up the pace of reform. More academies, trust and specialist schools; more of the brightest and best graduates becoming teachers; more investment in building schools for the future – state-of-the-art schools for world-class schooling.

Fairness demands nothing less than excellence in every school, for every child. So today I guarantee to parents two fundamental rights. Because every child should leave primary school able to read, write and count, any child who falls behind will not be left behind but will now have a new guaranteed right to personal catch-up tuition; and because all parents should see their children taught in schools which achieve good results at GCSE, our pledge today is that any parents whose local state school falls below the expected standard will have the right to see that school transformed under wholly new leadership or closed and new school places provided.

And we want to enable all families to use the Internet to link back to their children's school, and so Jim Knight is announcing that we will fund over a million extra families to get online, on the way to our ambition of Britain leading the world, with more of our people than any other major economy able to access the Internet and broadband.

And now, as we celebrate the 60th anniversary of the NHS, let me on behalf of all of us here, and all the people of the country, thank all the NHS staff – the cooks and cleaners, the paramedics and porters, the doctors and midwives and nurses. You have served our country and served a great ideal – the principle that in a fair society health care should not be a commodity to be bought by some but a right to be enjoyed by all.

Labour is the party of the NHS – we created it, we saved it, we value it and we always will support it. And you know already that, for me, this isn't a political agenda but a personal mission. Last year in Bournemouth I told you how, when I was 16, I got injured playing rugby and lost the sight for ever in my left eye. I knew I couldn't play football or rugby any more. But I could still read.

But what I didn't tell you last year was that then, one morning, I woke up and realised my sight was going in my good eye. I had another operation and lay in the darkness for days on end. At that point my future was books on tape. But, thanks to the NHS, my sight was saved by care my parents could never have afforded. And so it's precisely because I know, and have heard from others, about the miraculous difference a great surgeon and great nurses and great care can make that I'm so passionate about the values of the NHS and so committed to reforming it to serve these values even better.

That's why, in just one year in the fight against hospital infections, we have doubled the number of matrons and achieved a 36 per cent reduction in MRSA. And let us remember what a Labour government has now achieved – the lowest ever waiting times in the whole history of the NHS.

And now, to respond to new times and higher aspirations, we want to make the National Health Service more personal to people's needs – patients more involved in their own health care, with more choice and more control than ever before. And I've always found it unfair that we cannot offer on the NHS the comprehensive services that private patients can afford to buy. And so, in April, a Labour Britain will become the first country in the whole world to offer free universal check-ups for everyone over 40.

And I say that there is no vested interest, no matter how powerful, that we are not prepared to take on when change is needed for the sake of the nation's health.

We have already made it easier for busy families to go to the doctor. Whilst a year ago only one in ten patients had access to GPs at weekends and in the evening, now almost half of all practices are open and by the end of next year the majority will be open even longer.

And today I want to show how this government will pursue what I believe to be one of the noblest and boldest contributions of this country to our shared human fortunes. Since the war, nearly one third of Britain's Nobel Prizes have been for our genius in medicine. We should now aspire to stretch the boundaries of human knowledge and human health ever further. I want Britain to lead the world in beating the diseases which cause so much heartbreak for families. Over the last few years we've made major breakthroughs in research relevant to cancer, Alzheimer's, Parkinson's and strokes and many more. But these are yet to be turned into treatments from which we can all benefit. And so let me tell you today that the unprecedented £15 billion we are investing in medical research will be directed to turning the major advances of the last few years into actual treatments and cures for NHS patients. Over the next decade we can lead the way in beating cancer and other diseases – a great endeavour worthy of a great country, proud because we have a health service focused on twenty-first-century needs.

An NHS that is available to all and personal to each means meeting another challenge of the future – offering, for the first time, every patient with a long-term condition their own care plan. But alongside new patient responsibilities will be new rights. And because we know that almost every British family has been touched by cancer, Alan Johnson and I know we must do more to relieve the financial worry that so often goes alongside the heartache. And so I can announce today, for those in our nation battling cancer, from next year you will not pay prescription charges.

And this is not the limit of our commitment to a fair NHS in a fair society. As, over the next few years, the NHS generates cash savings in its drugs budget, we will plough savings back into abolishing charges for all patients with long-term conditions. That's the fairness patients want and the fairness every Labour Party member will go out and fight for. And in a fair society the fact that older people are living longer should be a blessing for their families, not a burden. We are committed to linking pensions to earnings. And I am proud that we will now be implementing, for the first time, equality for women in their retirement.

No one should live in fear of their old age because they worry their social care will impose financial burdens they could never afford to face and that, the minute they need care, puts the family home at risk. The generation that rebuilt Britain from the ashes of the war deserves better, and so I can tell you today that Alan Johnson and I will also bring forward new plans to help people to stay longer in their own homes and provide greater protection against the costs of care – dignity and hope for everyone in their later years. That's the fairness older people deserve and the fairness every Labour Party member will go out and fight for.

So when people say in these tough times there's nothing we can do, there's nothing higher to aim for, no great causes left worth fighting for, my reply is: our ideas are the ideas that will realise the hopes of families for a better future. Providing free nursery care for more children who need it is a cause worth fighting for. Providing better social care for older people who need it is a cause worth fighting for. Delivering excellence in every single school is a cause worth fighting for. Universal check-ups and new help to fight cancer – these are all causes worth fighting for. This is the future we're fighting for.

And in this world of vast economic and social change, new opportunity for all must be matched with a new responsibility from all. Our aim is a 'something for something', 'nothing for nothing' Britain – a Britain of fair chances for all and fair rules applied to all. So our policy is that everyone who can work must work. That's why James Purnell has introduced reforms so that, apart from genuine cases of illness, the dole is only for those looking for work or actively preparing for it. That's only fair to the people pulling their weight.

And let me be clear about the new Labour policy on crime – taking action on the causes of crime will never mean indulging those who perpetrate it. Fairness demands that we both punish and prevent. Jacqui Smith and Jack Straw are introducing a landmark reform in our justice system to put victims first. In consultation with victim support we will create an independent commissioner who will stand up for victims, witnesses and families – the people the courts and police exist to serve.

And justice seen is justice done. So you will be seeing more neighbourhood policing on the street, hearing more about the verdicts of the court, able to see the people who offended doing community payback which will be what it says – hard work for the public benefit at the places and times the public can see it. That's only fair to the law-abiding majority. Nobody in Britain should get to take more out of the system than they are willing to put in.

I am proud that Britain will honour our obligations to provide refuge from persecution. And we recognise the contribution that migrants make to our economy and our society, but the other side of welcoming newcomers who can help Britain is being tough about excluding those adults who won't and can't. That's why we have introduced the Australian-style points-based system, the citizenship test, the English-language test, and we will introduce a migrant charge for public services. That's only fair to the public who play by the rules and to the new citizens who uphold the rules. So, across the board, we will create rules that reward those who play by them and punish those who don't. That's what fairness means to me.

You know, our party, so often in its history, has been home to the big ideas – ideas later taken for granted but revolutionary in their time. Just think – the vote for working men and then for women, the NHS, legal protection from race or sex discrimination. These are no longer just Labour policies; they are established British values – they are the common sense of our age.

And we should never forget one thing – that every single blow we have struck for fairness and for the future has been opposed by the Conservatives. And just think where our country would be if we'd listened to them. No paternity leave, no New Deal, no Bank of England independence, no Sure Start, no devolution, no civil partnerships, no minimum wage, no new investment in the NHS, no new nurses, no new police, no new schools.

And so let's hear no more from the Conservatives; we did fix the roof while the sun was shining.

And just think if we'd taken their advice on the global financial crisis. Their policy was to let Northern Rock fold and imperil the whole financial system; our Labour government saved Northern Rock so not a single UK depositor lost out. Their policy said, in this week of all weeks, that speculative short selling should continue. We acted decisively to end reckless speculation.

And the Conservative policy would mean that, at this very moment, there would be no regulation at all to protect homeowners. We are the party of protecting homeowners' rights.

Do you know what their shadow chancellor really said? In the week that banks were collapsing, the man who wants to run our economy not only said, 'This is not a problem caused by the financial markets,' but went on to say, and I quote, that 'It's a function of financial markets that people make loads of money out of the misery of others.'

Just imagine where we'd be if they'd been in a position to implement their beliefs – no rescue of Northern Rock, no action on speculation, no protection for mortgages, doing nothing to stop banks going under.

What has become clear is that Britain cannot trust the Conservatives to run the economy. Everyone knows that I'm all in favour of apprenticeships, but let me tell you this is no time for a novice. But I believe in giving credit where it's due. The Conservative leader's team are smart; they've got a plan, and they are implementing it ruthlessly.

Their strategy is to change their appearance, to give the appearance of change and to conceal what they really think. And when salesmen won't tell you what they are selling, it's because they are selling something no one should buy.

But I'm a man for detail, and I've discovered some clues about what would be in store in a Conservative Britain. They want us to believe that, like us, they now care about public services. But when Mr Cameron actually talks to his party about their spending plans he says the difference between Labour and Tory levels of public investment will be 'dramatic' and 'fundamental'.

They want to tell us we're all progressives now, but the day that Hazel Blears and Caroline Flint were announcing a £1 billion package to support millions of homeowners, the Conservatives were confirming that their first tax priority is to take that £1 billion from hard-working families and hand it over to the 3,000 richest estates in Britain.

And they want to tell us they now believe in investing in education, but they are committed to slashing £4.5 billion from the schools building programme, axing the educational maintenance allowances that help poorer students stay on and opposing raising the education leaving age to 18 and stopping training programmes. And yes, friends, they would even take away Sure Start from infants and their parents – one of our greatest gifts to the future one of the first priorities for Tory cuts.

The Conservatives may want to represent the future, but whether it's Europe or energy, planning or tax credits, university places or '42 days', whenever they are tested on substance they have nothing to offer to meet the big challenges of tomorrow, because they are prisoners of their past.

If you look beneath the surface, you'll see that the Conservatives might have changed their tune, but they haven't changed their minds. The Conservatives say our country is broken, but this country has never been broken by anyone or anything. This country wasn't broken by fascism, by the cold war, by terrorists.

Of course there are problems, but this is a country being lifted up every day by the people who love it. We've got four million people helping Neighbourhood Watch, six million sports volunteers and over five million people doing amazing work as carers.

And, just as we celebrated our national triumph when we won the 2012 games for London, so too were Andy Burnham, Tessa Jowell and I, along with all of you, filled with pride this summer as our Olympic and Paralympic heroes showed British brilliance at its best.

That's why, for all the challenges, I don't believe Britain is broken; I think it's the best country in the world. I believe in Britain. And, stronger together as England, Wales, Scotland and Northern Ireland, we can make our United Kingdom even better.

And ours is a country full of heroes. And we pay special tribute to the heroism of our armed forces, as Des Browne said yesterday, to their service and sacrifice in Iraq and in Afghanistan and in peacekeeping missions around the globe – quite simply the best armed forces in the world.

The whole lesson of the new world I described earlier is that we must work together to meet the great, shared challenges vital to our future. And unlike the Conservatives, who are extremists and isolationists on Europe, we will work with our partners in the European Union, and we will work with America – not just to deal with the immediate security challenges in Georgia and in Iran.

And I tell you that what we do together for the poor and vulnerable is an act of compassion, but it is more than that. It is what will determine whether this new global society succeeds or fails.

And David Miliband, Douglas Alexander and I will do everything in our power to bring justice and democracy to Burma, to Zimbabwe and to Darfur. And I promise you I will work with other countries to bring a permanent settlement – a secure Israel and a viable Palestine – to deliver peace for the people of the Middle East.

And this week, at Britain's request, the United Nations has summoned the leaders of the world to a special summit on what we know is a global poverty emergency.

You know, in the museum in Rwanda which commemorates the millions who lost their lives as the world looked the other way, there is a picture of a young boy called David – a ten year old who was tortured to death. His last words were 'Don't worry; the United Nations will come for us.'

But we never did. That child believed the best of us only to discover that the pieties repeated so often meant in reality nothing at all. The words 'Never again' became just a slogan and not what they should be – the crucible in which our values are tested. I tell you, this Labour government will not allow the world to stand by as more than 20,000 children die today from diseases we know how to cure. We will not pass by as 100 million men, women and children face a winter of starvation.

So the poor will not go unheard tomorrow at the United Nations, because we the British people will speak up for them and for justice. The fair society, fairness at home, fairness in the world – that's the new settlement for new times.

I know what I believe. I know who I am. I know what I want to do in this job. And I know that the way to deal with tough times is to face them down. Stay true to your beliefs. Understand that all the attacks, all the polls, all the headlines, all the criticism – it's all worth it if, in doing this job, I make life better for one child, one family, one community. Because this job is not about me, it's about you.

And I'll tell you what else I've learned – that tough times don't weaken the determination of people who believe in what they're doing but strengthen our resolve.

You know, when I talk to the people who do the tough jobs – nurses, teachers, police officers, soldiers, carers – about why they do what they do, so often they say to me, 'Because I want to make a difference.'

And doesn't each of us want to say of ourselves that I helped someone in need; that I come to the aid of a neighbour in distress; that I will not pass by on the other side; that I will give of myself for something bigger than myself.

And each of us can make a contribution, but together we are even more than that. United we are a great movement led by hopes, not fears, gathered person by person. One individual and then a few more, then hundreds, then thousands, then finally millions strong – a movement where I want each of us to say to each other, 'This is our country, Britain. We are building it together; together we are making it greater; together we are building the fair society in this place and in this generation.'

The mission of our times – the fair society, the cause that drives us on. And we will win, not for the sake of our party; together we will win for the future of our country.

In Brighton, a year later, Gordon Brown's speech to the party conference was again billed as his 'most important ever'. In some senses the speech had to do much the same job as the previous year – asserting that the Labour government should be allowed to continue its work to ameliorate the effects of the recession caused by the global crisis and drawing the public's attention to the qualities that Gordon Brown possesses, and contrasting them with his opponent. But this speech did much more; it had to respond to the burgeoning crisis for politics itself, caused by the parliamentary expenses scandals over the summer. And it was also the first shot in the forthcoming general election campaign, drawing the boundaries between the parties and setting out the lines of attack to be used in earnest once the election is called.

It was introduced, once again, by an unannounced Sarah Brown, who gave a personal and passionate account of the man she called her husband and hero.

≈≈≈

'Gordon and I have been married for nine years now. We've seen each other through some tough times, had some great times, and we will be together for all time.

'And because we've been together for so long, I know he's not a saint. He's messy, he's noisy, he gets up at a terrible hour. But I know that he wakes up every morning, and goes to bed every evening, thinking about the things that matter. I know he loves our country. And I know he will always, always, put you first.

'The first time I met him I was struck that someone so intense and so intelligent could be so gentle, could ask so many questions, could really care. He will always make the time for people, our family, for his friends and anyone who needs him – that's part of the reason I love him as much as I do.

'And you know, friends, that's what makes him the man for Britain, too. Gordon has got a tough job and I wouldn't want it for the world, but each time I am thankful that he's the one who has it, that he's the one choosing the policies and making the calls, because I've seen what a Prime Minister's day is like, up close. I've seen how Gordon and his ministers have to square up to big choices, huge challenges, serious times.

'And I've seen what can happen as a result of the changes government make. One of the great privileges of being married to Gordon is that so many of you are so generous with your time for us. So many of you have invited us into your homes and workplaces and the hearts of your local communities. Thank you for letting us into your lives, and thank you for giving Gordon the chance to change so many lives.'

This speech begins by listing just some of the ways Labour has been changing lives since 1997 and got a rousing reception and an early standing ovation. The Prime Minister then taunts the Conservative Party, saying they had been 'faced with the economic call of the century, and they called it wrong'. He goes on to say, 'a party that makes the wrong choices on the most critical decisions it would have faced in government should not be given the chance to be in government'.

Then follows an important trope, likely to take a central place in the Labour manifesto, about the Labour Party ethos of fairness and responsibility that, the Prime Minister asserts, stem from its core values, which 'we teach our children, celebrate in our families, observe in our faiths and honour in our communities.

'Call them middle-class values, call them traditional working-class values, call them family values, call them all of these. These are the values of the mainstream majority, the anchor of Britain's families, the best instincts of the British people, the soul of our party and the mission of our government.' He also links these values back to his own upbringing: 'I grew up in a family, a party and a country that believes no obstacle is so great that it can stop the onwards march of fairness and of justice.'

In the main sections of the speech, the Prime Minister introduces two different lines of argument. The first is what he calls the new mission for New Labour, which is to 'realise our passion for fairness and responsibility in these new global times . . . And when people say, faced with the constraints of the recession, can you make progress towards a fairer and more responsible Britain, let us tell them we did, we can and we will . . . Markets need what they cannot generate themselves; they need what the British people alone can bring to them. I say to you today: markets need morals.'

And the second main point, a response to the parliamentary expenses crisis that had erupted over the summer, is to rehearse the action being taken to clean up MPs' allowances and to outline a substantial programme of constitutional reform, with the aim of rebuilding trust in our parliamentary democracy.

While the press and media reports after the speech and on the following day concentrated mainly on the introduction of the Prime Minister by Sarah Brown and on the tone of the speech, this is a well-crafted and important speech, containing much of direct interest for its time and acting as a harbinger of the election to come. As Gordon Brown says, there will be a choice in the 2010 election based on the values he says are to be found 'in the DNA' of each party: 'this is a timeless difference in our approach. It's between those like them whose vision is limited to how things are and those like us who reach for the world that can be.'

SPEECH TO THE LABOUR PARTY CONFERENCE
Brighton, 29 September 2009

You know, friends, it is the fighters and believers who change the world. We've changed the world before, and we're going to change the world again. And, you know, our country faces the biggest choice for a generation. So we need to fight, not bow out, not walk away, not give in, not give up but fight – fight to win for Britain.

Because if anyone says that to fight doesn't get you anywhere, that politics can't make a difference, that all parties are the same, then look what we've achieved together since 1997 – the winter fuel allowance, the shortest waiting times in history, crime down by a third, the creation of Sure Start, the cancer guarantee, record results in schools, more students than ever, the Disability Discrimination Act, devolution, civil partnerships, peace in Northern Ireland, the Social Chapter, half a million children out of poverty, maternity pay, paternity leave, child benefit at record levels, the minimum wage, the ban on cluster bombs, the cancelling of debt, the trebling of aid, the first ever climate change Act. That's the Britain we've been building together; that's the change we choose.

And so, today, in the midst of events that are transforming our world, we meet united and determined to fight for the future. Our country confronts the biggest choice for a generation. It's a choice between two parties, yes, but more importantly a choice between two directions for our country.

In the last 18 months we have had to confront the biggest economic choices the world has faced since the 1930s. It was only a year ago that the world was looking over a precipice and Britain was in danger. I knew that, unless I acted decisively and immediately, the recession could descend into a great depression with millions of people's jobs and homes and savings at risk.

And times of great challenge mean choices of great consequence, so let me share with you a little about the choices we are making. The first choice was this – whether markets left to themselves could sort out the crisis or whether governments had to act. Our choice was clear – we nationalised Northern Rock and took shares in British banks, and as a result not one British saver has lost a single penny. That was the change we chose – the change that benefits the hard-working majority, not the privileged few.

And we faced a second big choice – between letting the recession run its course or stimulating the economy back to growth. And we made our choice – help for small businesses, targeted tax cuts for millions and advancing our investment in roads, rail and education. That was the change we chose – change that benefits the hard-working majority and not just a privileged few.

And then we had a third choice – between accepting unemployment as a price worth paying or saving jobs. And we in Britain made our choice; it's meant half a million jobs saved. And so, Conference, even in today's recession there are 29 million people in work – 2 million more men and women providing for their families than in 1997.

And then we faced the mortgage choice – to do nothing as repossessions rose or save the family homes people have worked so hard to buy. Two hundred thousand homeowners given direct government support to stay in their home. That was the change we chose – change that benefits the mainstream majority and not just a few.

And then we faced another choice – between going our own way or acting with other countries. And everybody knows the choice we made – we picked internationalism over isolationism, leading the G20 to a global deal that will save 15 million jobs.

Every government across Europe made the choice to act. Every government across the G20 chose to act. Almost every major political party across the world chose to act. Only one party thought it was best to do nothing. Only one party with pretensions to government made the wrong choice – the Conservative Party of Britain.

They made the wrong choice on Northern Rock, the wrong choice on jobs and spending, the wrong choice on mortgage support, the wrong choice on working with Europe. The only thing about their policy that is consistent is that they are consistently wrong.

The opposition might think the test of a party is the quality of its marketing, but I say the test for a government is the quality of its judgement. The Conservative Party were faced with the economic call of the century, and they called it wrong. And I say a party that makes the wrong choices on the most critical decisions it would have faced in government should not be given the chance to be in government.

And what of the big choices that this country has to make now – to help young people into work or to see, like the '80s, a wasted generation. And I'll tell you the choice we're making – to reject every piece of Conservative advice. And instead we will ensure school leavers training, guarantee the young unemployed work experience, expand university places and increase, not cut, the apprenticeships we need. I'm sorry to say that, by opposing these measures, Conservative policy would callously and coldly return us to the lost generation and cardboard cities of the 1980s; we say 'Never again.' That's the change we choose – the change that benefits the many, not the few.

Every day we are facing the business choice – to support our companies, from car manufacturers to the self-employed, or simply let great British businesses go to the wall. And we are making our choice. Labour believes in the businesses and enterprise of Britain – more than 200,000 agreements signed to give direct support to small businesses.

That was the change we chose – change that benefits the enterprising backbone of Britain. In opening up planning, in improving transport, in opting for nuclear energy it is Labour that is the party of British business and British enterprise and the Conservative Party whose policy has been to walk away.

And the Conservatives were wrong on all these choices, because they were wrong about something more fundamental still. Because what let the world down last autumn was not just bankrupt institutions but a bankrupt ideology. What failed was the Conservative idea that markets always self-correct but never self-destruct. What failed was the right-wing fundamentalism that says you just leave everything to the market and says that free markets should not just be free but values-free.

One day, last October, the executive of a major bank told us that his bank needed only overnight finance but no long-term support from the government. The next day I found that this bank was going under with debts that were among the biggest of any bank, anywhere, at any time in history. Bankers had lost sight of basic British values – acting responsibly and acting fairly – the values that we, the hard-working majority, live by every day.

Like the small businessman who came to see me when his credit dried up at the bank. He was crying with the shame of missing some payments, but so responsible was he that he was determined that every penny he owed would be paid. Or like the woman who wrote to me and said that when we announced our decision to rescue Icesave, and her family's savings, it was the first night's sleep she'd had since the crisis started.

When markets falter and banks fail it's the jobs and the homes and the security of the squeezed middle that are hit the hardest. It's the hard-pressed, hard-working majority – the person with a trade, the small-business owner, the self-employed. It's the classroom assistant, the worker in the shop, the builder on the site. It's the millions of people who do their best and do their bit and in return simply want their families to get on, not just get by. It's the Britain that works best not by reckless risk-taking but by effort, by merit and by hard work. It's the Britain that works not just by self-interest but by self-discipline, self-improvement and self-reliance. It's the Britain where we don't just care for ourselves, we also care for each other. And these are the values of fairness and responsibility that we teach our children, celebrate in our families, observe in our faiths and honour in our communities.

Call them middle-class values, call them traditional working-class values, call them family values, call them all of these. These are the values of the mainstream majority, the anchor of Britain's families, the best instincts of the British people, the soul of our party and the mission of our government.

And I say this, too: these are my values, the values I grew up with in an ordinary family in an ordinary town. Like most families on middle and modest incomes, we believed in making the most of our talents. But we knew that no matter how hard we worked free education was our only pathway to being the best we could be. Because, like most parents, my parents could not easily afford to put me and my brothers through fee-paying schools. And I come from a family which, independent and self-reliant as it was, could not have kept going without the compassion and caring of the NHS, because my parents could not easily have afforded to pay for operations on my eyes.

So I come from a family for whom the NHS was quite simply the best insurance policy in the world. For us the NHS has not been a 60-year mistake but a 60-year liberation. And it has been those experiences and that background that have taught me that, yes, too much government can make people powerless. But too much government indifference can leave people powerless too.

Government should never try to do what it cannot do, but it should never fail to do what it needs to do. And in a crisis what the British people want to know is that their government will not pass by on the other side but will be on their side. So we will not allow those on middle and modest incomes to be buffeted about in a storm not of their making. And so this is our choice – to toughen the rules on those who break the rules.

Markets need what they cannot generate themselves; they need what the British people alone can bring to them. I say to you today: markets need morals.

So we will pass a new law to intervene on bankers' bonuses whenever they put the economy at risk. And any director of any of our banks who is negligent will be disqualified from holding any such post.

Some people believe that the public will end up subsidising the bankers' mistakes. And so I tell you this about our aims for the rescue of the banks – the British people will not pay for the banks. No. The banks will pay back the British people. That's what we need to do to rectify the problems of the past. Now it's time to make changes that are even more fundamental for a world that is being utterly transformed.

In the uncharted waters we sail, the challenge of change demands nothing less than a new model for our economy, a new model for a more responsible society and a new model for a more accountable politics. Staying with the status quo is not an option. The issue is not whether to change but how.

And always a party of restless and relentless reformers, the new mission for New Labour is to realise our passion for fairness and responsibility in these new global times. And as we rise to the challenge of change, so this coming election will not be a contest for a fourth-term Labour government but for the first Labour government of this new global age.

Our new economic model for a strong economy is founded on three guiding principles – that in future finance must always be the servant of people and industry and not their master, that our future economy must be a green economy and that we must realise all of Britain's talent if we are to lead and succeed.

The best way finance can serve our country now is to help ensure that the inventions and innovations pioneered in Britain are developed and manufactured in Britain. So we will create a new national investment corporation to provide finance for growing manufacturing and other businesses; our £1 billion innovation fund will back the creativity and inventions that are essential to the economy.

And I want the Post Office to play a much bigger role, bringing banking services back to the heart of people's communities. And our economic future must be green. We are already global leaders in wind power, green cars, clean coal and carbon capture. And now we will lead again, with new designated low-carbon zones around the regions of this country. And I say to you today: we will create over a quarter of a million new green British jobs.

And every day we stall on a climate change deal, the people of the world are denied the chance to protect their world. And so I say: I will go to Copenhagen, and I will go with our British plan to secure a climate change deal this year.

And the new model for education in the twenty-first century – the biggest step we can take into the future – is to unlock the talents of all young people. Let the new economy be one where social mobility is not held back, and in this new economy there must be no cap on aspiration, no ceiling on opportunity and no limit on where your talents can take you. And so I can tell you that in the next five years we cannot and will not cut support to our schools. We will not invest less but more. And our guarantee to parents is a ruthless determination to raise standards in every school. We will aggressively turn round underperforming schools so that your child will have a good local school no matter where you live.

Our guarantee to all young people is that with millions of new opportunities – from apprenticeships to internships to a new class of modern technicians – we will discover, coach, develop and showcase the wealth of aspiration and talent that exists in Britain.

And to add to the 100,000 new young people's jobs we are already creating, we can today offer, in partnership with the Federation of Small Businesses, 10,000 skilled internships so that, even in the midst of tough economic times, we are encouraging a whole new generation of young Britons to embrace ambition and British enterprise.

And I can also announce that we will work with the Eden Project and Mayday Network to create the biggest group of green work placements we have ever done – up to 10,000 green job placements so that our young people can make the most of the opportunities the low-carbon economy will open up to them.

And, friends, let me talk bluntly – to pay for our schools, hospitals, police and the change we want to make we have to make choices about taxation and public spending.

Let no one be in any doubt – as a result of Labour's economic management, Britain started the downturn with the second lowest debt of any G7 economy. And just as we have always taken the hard and tough decisions on stability in the past, we will continue to apply the same rigour to our decisions in the future.

Our deficit-reduction plan to cut the deficit in half over four years will be made law in a new Fiscal Responsibility Act. And I can say today that every change we make, every single pledge we make, comes with a price tag attached and a clear plan for how that cost will be met. For there are only two options on tax and spending, and only one of them benefits Britain's hard-working majority. One is reducing the deficit by cutting front-line public services – the Conservative approach. The other is getting the deficit down while maintaining and indeed improving front-line public services – the Labour approach.

So we will raise tax at the very top, cut costs, have realistic public sector pay settlements, make savings we know we can and, in 2011, raise National Insurance by half a per cent, and that will ensure that each and every year we protect and improve Britain's front-line services.

Our opponents would take a different approach. They want to cut spending now; so that means less money now for front-line services. They want to cut inheritance tax for the 3,000 wealthiest estates; so that means even less money for front-line services. And they are against the measures we took to raise taxes, and so that means even less money for front-line services. These are not cuts they would make because they have to; these are spending cuts they are making because they want to. It is not inevitable; it is the change they choose.

And when people say, faced with the constraints of the recession, can you make progress towards a fairer and more responsible Britain, let us tell them we did, we can and we will.

In 1997 we held back spending, and people said there could be no progress, but we introduced the New Deal, Sure Start, the minimum wage and paved the way for tax credits and new hospitals and schools. In the last 12 years we've already given teenagers educational maintenance allowances to help them stay on until 18. And in the next 5 years not just some but all young people will be staying in education or training until 18.

We've already ensured that three-quarters of our GP practices are open out of hours, and in the next five years we will ensure every patient has the right to see a GP in the evening or at the weekend.

We've already lifted 900,000 pensioners out of poverty and in the next five years will restore the earnings link for the basic state pension.

And in the last twelve years we created the first legal national minimum wage. And in every year of the next five years we will increase it. The minimum wage was the dream of Neil Kinnock, and he's with us today. It was the dream of John Smith, whom we remember today. And it was one of the achievements of Tony Blair, and we thank him today. And when the minimum wage rises this month it will be 60 per cent higher than when it started. And I can say today that not just the minimum wage but child benefit and child tax credits for families will continue to rise every year.

And for all those mums and dads who struggle to juggle work and home, I am proud to announce today that by reforming tax relief we will, by the end of the next Parliament, be able to give the parents of a quarter of a million two year olds free childcare for the first time.

And I do think it's time to address a problem that for too long has gone unspoken – the number of children having children. For it cannot be right for a girl of 16 to get pregnant, be given the keys to a council flat and be left on her own. From now on all 16- and 17-year-old parents who get support from the taxpayer will be placed in a network of supervised homes. These shared homes will offer not just a roof over their head but a new start in life where they learn responsibility and how to raise their children properly. That's better for them, better for their babies and better for us all in the long run.

We won't ever shy away from taking difficult decisions on tough social questions. Because we have to be honest – it's not just bankers and politicians that have lost the people's trust. Even though there is so much that is amazing about Britain, if you ask your neighbours or your workmates how they feel right now, in this fast-changing world, they will probably talk about their sense of unease. The decent hard-working majority feel the odds are stacked in favour of a minority who will talk about their rights but never accept their responsibilities.

In a faster-changing, more mobile world of communities – where family breakdown is more common, where children are at risk on the Internet, where elderly people are too often isolated in their communities – the new society must be explicit about the boundaries between right and wrong and about the new responsibilities we demand of people in return for the rights they have. And I stand with the people who are sick and tired of others playing by different rules or no rules at all.

Most mums and dads do a great job, but there are those who let their kids run riot, and I'm not prepared to accept it as simply part of life, because there is also a way of intervening earlier to stop antisocial behaviour, slash welfare dependency and cut crime. Family intervention projects are a tough-love, no-nonsense approach, with help for those who want to change and proper penalties for those who don't or won't.

I first saw this tough approach at work in Dundee, where a young single mother who got into trouble with drugs was at risk of her kids being taken into care. But within months she was going to college to get a decent job to look after the children she loved. Family intervention projects work. They change lives, they make our communities safer and they crack down on those who are going off the rails.

Starting now, and right across the next Parliament, every one of the 50,000 most chaotic families will be part of a family intervention project – with clear rules and clear punishments if they don't stick to them.

And we have said that every time a young person breaches an ASBO there will be an order not just on them but on their parents, and if that is broken they will pay the price. Because whenever and wherever there is antisocial behaviour, we will be there to fight it.

We will never allow teenage tearaways or anybody else to turn our town centres into no-go areas at night-times. No one has yet cracked the whole problem of a youth drinking culture. We thought that extended hours would make our city centres easier to police, and in many areas it has. But it's not working in some places, and so we will give local authorities the power to ban 24-hour drinking throughout a community in the interests of local people.

And let me say this bluntly: when someone is found guilty of a serious crime caused by drinking, the drink banning order which is available to the courts should be imposed. And where there is persistent trouble from binge drinking, we will give local people the right to make pubs and clubs pay for cleaning up their neighbourhood and making it safe.

Neighbourhood policing is now a reality in every council ward in our country. Recent cases have shown it is time for a better service for the citizen. So if it's an emergency, you must get action in minutes, where it's a neighbourhood priority, within the hour and where it's a general but not urgent enquiry, no one will have to wait more than 48 hours for a reply or a visit. That's what I mean by public services personal to people's needs.

And I can tell the British people that, between now and Christmas, neighbourhood policing will focus in a more direct and intensive way on antisocial behaviour. Action squads will crack down in problem estates, protect the public spaces you want safe and hold monthly beat meetings to consult you directly on your priorities for action.

This is a new and more mobile world, and so we have to step up the protection of our borders against terrorism and illegal immigration. And it means we must take a tough approach to who gets to come to our country and who gets to stay.

Tightening our points-based immigration system ensures that those who have the skills that can help Britain will be welcomed and those who do not will be refused. And the ID cards for foreign nationals are working. But in the last two years, we have looked again at how we can give the best security to our British citizens whilst never undermining their liberties. We will reduce the information British citizens have to give for the new biometric passport to no more than that required for today's passport. And so, Conference, I can say to you today: in the next Parliament there will be no compulsory ID cards for British citizens.

So I have been candid about the challenges we face. But we are also proud of our achievements and what makes this country we love so special.

Britain. The four home nations. Each is unique, each with its own great contribution, and we will never allow separatists or narrow nationalists in Scotland or in Wales to sever the common bonds that bring our country together as one. And let me say to the people of Northern Ireland: we will give you every support to complete the last and yet unfinished stage of the peace process which Tony Blair, to his great credit, started and which I want to see complete – the devolution of policing and justice to the people of Northern Ireland, which we want to see happen in the next few months.

I want a Britain that is even more open to new ideas, even more creative, even more dynamic and leading the world, and let me talk today about how we will do more to support the great British institutions that best define this country.

The first is the one I spoke about in detail on Sunday, when I talked about the mission of our brave men and women in Afghanistan. The heroism of our fighting men and women is unsurpassed, and we owe them a debt we can never fully repay. And let us on behalf of the British people pay tribute to them and their courage today.

The British armed forces truly are the finest in the world. And let us say to them: all British forces will always have all the equipment they need and the best support we can give. And, Conference, let me say: Britain will work with President Obama and 40 other countries for peace and stability for the people of Afghanistan and to make sure that terrorism doesn't come to the streets of Britain. And we will work for peace and stability for the peoples of Israel and Palestine.

We will work to end nuclear proliferation and, as I said last week when I talked of the contribution Britain can make, we will work as partners to end the world's nuclear arms race. And I say to Iran as they face a crucial date this week: join the international community now or face isolation.

And let me say: what was once an aspiration – 0.7 per cent of national income spent on international development aid – has become with Labour a promise and will in future become a law. We will pass legislation that the British government is obliged to raise spending on aid to the poorest countries to 0.7 per cent of our national income. Others may break their promises to the poorest – with Labour, Britain never will.

And there is huge debate around the world today about how countries can manage health care. Countries from every continent look to our NHS for inspiration. And this summer didn't we show them we love our NHS? We can sometimes talk about the NHS purely in statistics, purely about the record numbers of doctors and nurses and operations and treatments under Labour, but it isn't about the figures – it's about the individuals who get help.

I got a letter from Diane, a mother from Rugby, who wrote to me saying her life had been saved because the NHS used its extra investment to reduce the age for breast cancer screening. Before, she would have had to wait until 50, and her surgeon told her that if she had, she'd probably be dead. But, thanks to the changes we made, Diane was diagnosed early, treated early and was back at work within three weeks. When she wrote to me about us lowering the screening age, she said, 'This may seem small in comparison to all the other issues you deal with, a small thing to do, but it probably saved my life.'

And so I say to you today: Labour fought for the NHS, you fought to save and invest in the NHS and, because you did, you are saving lives every day. You should be very, very proud. Because if you've changed one life, you've changed the world.

And because we know that our investment in breast cancer screening works and early intervention saves lives, I am proud to announce that we will go much further. We will finance a new right for cancer patients to have diagnostic tests carried out, completed and with results – often same day results – within one week of seeing your GP. That is our early-diagnosis guarantee, building on our current guarantee of only two weeks' wait to see a specialist.

And so with three major steps forward – early diagnosis, early treatment and our historic investment in research for cancer cures – we in Britain can transform cancer care, and our ambition is no less than to beat cancer in this generation.

That is the change we have chosen – change that benefits not just the few who can pay but the mainstream majority. For a few days this summer, Sarah and I worked helping in a local hospice near our home, and I say now that the care and compassion shown by volunteers and staff must be matched by greater support for this work of mercy.

And in our times there is a new challenge that no generation has ever had to face before. We have an ageing society and new rightful demands for dignity and for support in old age. And so we need social care for our elderly which is not subject to a postcode lottery but available to all – to the hard-working majority and not just the few who can pay. And so we will say in Labour's manifesto that social care for all is not a distant dream, that to provide security for pensioners for generations to come we will bring together the National Health Service and local care provision into a new national care service. That is the change we chose.

And we can start straight away. Today more and more people see their parents and grandparents suffering from conditions like Alzheimer's and dementia, and they see their dignity diminish. And for too many families the challenge of coping with the heartbreak is made worse by the costs of getting support. The people who face the greatest burden are too often those on middle incomes who have savings which will last a year or two, but then they will see their savings slip away. And the best starting point for our national care service is to help the elderly get the amenities to do what they most want – to receive care and to stay in their homes as long as possible.

And so for those with the highest needs we will now offer, in their own homes, free personal care. It's a change that makes saving worthwhile, makes every family in this country more secure and is a much-needed reassurance for the elderly and their children. This is the change we choose – change that will benefit not just the few who can afford to pay but the mainstream majority.

But a fair and responsible Britain must be an accountable Britain – a nation not of powerful institutions but powerful people. And just as I have said that the market needs morals, I also say that politics needs morals too.

Let me say that the vast overwhelming majority of our Labour Members of Parliament are in Parliament not out of self-interest but to serve the public interest. And our new generation of parliamentary candidates want to join them not to make a personal gain but to make a difference. But there are some who let our country down. And never again should any Member of Parliament be more interested in the value of their allowances than the values of their constituents.

Never again should it be said of any Member of Parliament that they are in it for what they can get; all of us should be in Parliament for what we can give. And so where there is proven financial corruption by an MP, and in cases where wrongdoing has been demonstrated but Parliament fails to act, we will give constituents the right to recall their Member of Parliament.

And if we want a politics that is more open, more plural, more local, more democratic, then we will need to make big changes, because the only way to ensure politics serves the people's values is to make all those who wield political power genuinely accountable to the people. There is now a stronger case than ever that MPs should be elected with the support of more than half their voters – as they would be under the alternative voting system. And so I can announce today that in Labour's next manifesto there will be a commitment for a referendum to be held early in the next Parliament – it will be for the people to decide whether they want to move to the alternative vote.

In this next year we will remove the hereditary principle in the House of Lords once and for all. And then, unlike the last election, we will ask for a clear mandate to make the House of Lords an accountable and democratic second chamber for the very first time.

I've been honest with you about where we've got it right and where we've fallen short and have to do more. And I am determined to fight for change to benefit the mainstream majority.

All that we have talked about today would simply not happen if the Conservatives were in power. The Conservative Party want people to believe that the ballot paper has an option marked 'Change without Consequence' – that's it's only a change of the team at the top. They've deliberately held their cards close to their chest. They've done their best to conceal their policies and their instincts. But the financial crisis forced them to show their hand and they showed they had no hearts. And so I say to the British people: the election to come will not be about my future; it's about your future, your job, your home, your children's school, your hospital, your community, your country. And so, when our opponents talk of change, ask yourself, 'Is that change that will benefit my family or only a privileged few?'

Listen to what they say but, more importantly, demand to know what they would do. If you're a family that's feeling the pinch, don't take it from me, just ask them the question: 'If you care about me, why is your first priority to give a £200,000 tax giveaway to each of the 3,000 wealthiest estates?'

And if you're one of the millions of Britons who loves our NHS, don't take it from me, just ask them the question: 'If you care about us, why would you scrap the right to see a cancer specialist within two weeks?'

And if you're worried about crime, don't take it from me, just ask them the question: 'Why would you cut the Home Office budget by the equivalent of 3,500 police officers this year alone and then make it harder for them to catch the most violent criminals using DNA evidence?'

And if you care about a proud Britain, don't take it from me, just ask them the question: 'Why would you put this country's prosperity and power at risk by placing Britain at the fringe of Europe rather than at its heart?' Ask them: 'How can you deliver change when you so clearly haven't even changed your own party?'

Because there is a difference between the parties. It's the difference between Conservatives who embrace pessimism and austerity and progressives like Labour who embrace prosperity and hope. And this is a timeless difference in our approach. It's between those like them whose vision is limited to how things are and those like us who reach for the world that can be.

And isn't this the story of Britain at its best and the Labour Party at its best, that we are people who strive for and achieve great changes even when others say it is impossible?

They said a free National Health Service was impossible, then argued it was unworkable, then said it was unaffordable, but in the last 12 years we have rebuilt it, and it is now, quite simply, for the British people, irreplaceable. They told me debt relief for the poorest was impossible, but we refused to give in, and now, thanks to debt relief and aid, 40 million more children across the world are going to school. And even when they told us last year that a great depression was inevitable and the world could not come together, we did – even when others said it was beyond our grasp.

Maybe you think it's because I'm the guy who doesn't take 'no' for an answer, and you're right – I don't. But it's really because I grew up in a family, a party and a country that believes no obstacle is so great that it can stop the onwards march of fairness and of justice.

And so I urge you, as the poet said: 'Dream not small dreams because they cannot change the world. Dream big dreams and then watch our country soar.'

We can build a new economy which tames the old excesses. We can meet and master the challenge of an ageing society with a national care service. We can, in this generation, be the first to beat cancer. We can transform our politics. We can do all these things and more if we think big and then fight hard.

Since 1997 Labour has given this country back its future. And we are not done yet. We love this country. And we have shown over the years that if you aim high you can lift not just yourself but your country – that there is nothing in life which is inevitable; it's about the change you choose.

And I say to you now: never stop believing in the good sense of the British people. Never stop believing we can move forward to a fairer, more responsible, more prosperous Britain. Never stop believing we can make a Britain equal to its best ideals. Never, never stop believing. And because the task is difficult the triumph will be even greater.

Now is not the time to give in but to reach inside ourselves for the strength of our convictions. Because we are the Labour Party and our abiding duty is to stand. And fight. And win. And serve.